/|\ BOOK TITLE: `-GOD IS `-THE MATHEMATICIAN-'"!!!~' /|\

/|\ BOOK TITLE: `-GOD IS `-THE MATHEMATICIAN-'"!!!~' /|\

Dwayne W. Anderson

/|\ BOOK TITLE: `-GOD IS `-THE MATHEMATICIAN-'"!!!~'/|\

iUniverse books may be ordered through booksellers or by contacting:

iUniverse
1663 Liberty Drive
Bloomington, IN 47403
www.iuniverse.com
1-800-Authors (1-800-288-4677)

ISBN: 978-1-5320-9917-5 (sc)
ISBN: 978-1-5320-9919-9 (hc)
ISBN: 978-1-5320-9918-2 (e)

Library of Congress Control Number: 2020907071

Print information available on the last page.

iUniverse rev. date: 04/21/2020

BULLET POINTS FOR: BOOK TITLE: '-GOD is '-the MATHEMATICIAN-!!!-'

- *THE LIFE AND DEATH OF CELEBRITIES –*
- *THE LIFE AND DEATHS OF PRESIDENTS & FIRST LADIES –*
- *THE LIFE AND DEATHS OF THE FOUNDING FATHERS of the UNITED STATES of AMERICA –*
- *THE LIFE AND DEATH OF COMMON PEOPLE –*
- *THE LIFE AND DEATH OF FAMILY –*
- *THE TIME CLOCK SEQUENCES of WORLD SHATTERING EVENTS –*
- *READING; and, UNDERSTANDING a '-NEW'-SCIENCE in the FOCUS of Reciprocal-Sequencing-Numerology-RSN-'*
- *READING; and, UNDERSTANDING a '-NEW'-SCIENCE in the FOCUS of Reciprocal-Sequenced-Inversed-Realities-RSIR-'*
- *REVELATIONS by & from THE PROPHET DWAYNE W. ANDERSON through & by '-GOD -*
- *DISCOVERER & FOUNDER of RECIPROCAL (TRIGONOMETRY) INVERSE REALITIES – EQUATIONS of '-REALITY in LIFE & DEATH with BOTH AMERICAN & WORLD LEADERS - AUTHOR: DWAYNE W. ANDERSON –*

I've '-CREATED a NEW TYPE of PHILOSOPHY (Reciprocal-Sequencing-Numerology)/ (Reciprocal-Sequenced-Inversed-Realities) that '-PROVES without '-QUESTION the '-PRESENCE of GOD'S EXISTENCE in our DAILY '-LIVES & '-AFFAIRS!!!!!-'

The # `-NUMBER (`-**61**)!!!~'

#14/PRESIDENT FRANKLIN PIERCE `-BIRTHDAY = 11/**23**/1804 = (11 + 23 + 18 + 04) = (`-**56**) = "AGE #**16**/PRESIDENT ABRAHAM LINCOLN `-DIED `-AT"!!!~' #14/PRESIDENT FRANKLIN PIERCE `-DEATH/DAY = 10/08/1869 = (10 + 08 + 18 + 69) = (`-**105**)!!!~' (1869) = (18 + 69) = (`-87) = (8 x 7) = (`-**56**)!!!~'

(105 + 56) = (`-**161**)!!!~'

`-**BIRTHDAY** = (**11/23**) = (11 = ROMAN `-NUMERAL for (`-2) = (2 x 23) = (`-**46**) = RECIPROCAL (MIRROR) = (`-**64**) = "AGE of `-DEATH for #14/PRESIDENT FRANKLIN PIERCE!!!~'

#14/PRESIDENT FRANKLIN PIERCE `-DIED (`-**46**) **DAYS** BEFORE `-HIS `-NEXT `-BIRTHDAY at the `-AGE of (`-**64**)!!!~'

(`-46) = RECIPROCAL (MIRROR) = (`-64)!!!~'

#15/PRESIDENT JAMES BUCHANAN `-DIED on (**6/1**); and, WAS `-BORN on (4/**23**) = (23 + 4) = (`-27) = 2(7's) = (`-**77**) = "AGE of `-DEATH"!!!~' (**423**) = (42 x 3) = (`-**126**) = (`-61) around (`-2)!!!~'

#16/PRESIDENT ABRAHAM LINCOLN was (6' 4") in `-HEIGHT; and, WAS `-BORN on (2/12/1809) = (2 + 12 + 18 + 09) = (`-**41**)!!!~' DIED on (4/15/1865) = (4 + 15 + 18 + 65) = (`-**102**)!!!~'

(102 (-) 41) = (`-**61**)!!!~' PRESIDENTIAL `-TERM STARTED in (`-18**61**)!!!~' #35/PRESIDENT JOHN F. KENNEDY'S PRESIDENTIAL `-TERM STARTED in (`-19**61**)!!!~'

`-**BIRTHDAY** = (`-**212**) = (21 x 2) = (`-**42**) /|\ (21 + 2) = (`-**23**) /|\ (42 + 23) = (`-**65**) = RECIPROCAL (MIRROR) = (`-**56**) = **"AGE of `-DEATH"** for #**16**/PRESIDENT ABRAHAM LINCOLN!!!~'

2

(`-**16**) = RECIPROCAL (MIRROR) = (`-**61**)!!!~'

FIRST LADY MARY TODD LINCOLN'S `-**BIRTHDAY** = (1**2**/1**3**/1818) = (1**2** + 1**3** + 18 + 18) = (`-**61**)!!!~' FIRST LADY MARY TODD LINCOLN'S `-**DEATH/DAY** = (0**7**/1**6**/1882) = (0**7** + 1**6** + 18 + 82) = (`-**123**)!!!~' (82 (-) 18 (-) 16 (-) 7) = (`-**41**)!!!~' (82 (-) 18) = (`-**64**) = RECIPROCAL = (`-**46**) = "MARY TODD LINCOLN'S `-**AGE** at TIME of `-**DEATH** of #**16**/PRESIDENT ABRAHAM LINCOLN"!!!~' (18 + 18) = (`-**36**) = RECIPROCAL = (`-**63**) = "**AGE** of `-**DEATH** of FIRST LADY MARY TODD LINCOLN"!!!~'

#17/PRESIDENT ANDREW JOHNSON was `-BORN on (12/29) = (12 + 29) = (`-**41**)!!!~' (12/29/1808) = (12 + 29 + 18 + 08) = (`-**67**) = "DIED in `-HIS (`-**67**th) YEAR of `-EXISTENCE at the `-AGE of (`-**66**)!!!~' #17/PRESIDENT ANDREW JOHNSON `-**DIED** on (**7**/**31**/1875) = (7 + 31 + 18 + 75) = (`-**131**)!!!~'

(131 (-) 67) = (`-**64**)!!!~' (7 + 31 + 18) = (`-**56**)!!!~'

(`-**31**) = RECIPROCAL (MIRROR) = (`-**13**)!!!~' (**7** x **13**) = (`-**91**) = **"FLIP the (`-9) OVER"** = (`-**61**)!!!~'

#18/PRESIDENT ULYSSES S. GRANT was `-**BORN** on (4/27) = (27 (-) 4) = (`-**23**)!!!~' #18/PRESIDENT ULYSSES S. GRANT `-**DIED** on (7/23) = (7 x 23) = (`-**161**) = **"FULL `-CIRCLE"** (`-**36**0) DEGREES = (`-**36**) = RECIPROCAL (MIRROR) = (`-**63**) = **"AGE of `-DEATH" of #18/PRESIDENT ULYSSES S. GRANT!!!~'**

(`-**427**) = ALMOST `-RECIPROCALS (MIRRORS) = (`-**723**)!!!~'

`-**SEE** the `-MANY `-**PATTERNS** = `-EQUALS = **"The `-HAND of `-GOD"!!!~'**

NOW within MY PUBLISHED `-BOOK = **NEW BOOK /|||\
REAL MESSAGES of `-GOD I, II; & III-!!!~' /|||**

TODAY'S DATE = (1/26/2020) = (1 + 26 + 20 + 20) = (`-**67**) = RECIPROCAL = (`-**76**) = **SIKORSKY S-76B** MANUFACTURED in (`-**1991**) = (`-**19**) = RECIPROCAL = (`-**91**)!!!~'

KOBE BRYANT'S BIRTHDAY = (8/**23**/1978) = (8 + 23 + 19 + 78) = (`-**128**)!!!~'

KOBE BRYANT'S BIRTHDAY in `-REVERSE = (78 (-) 19 (-) 23 (-) 8) = (`-**28**)!!!~'

(128 + 28) = (`-**156**)!!!~'

KOBE BRYANT `-DIED (`-**156**) DAYS **after** `-**HIS** `-**LAST** `-**BIRTHDAY!!!~'**

BIRTHDAY = (8/23) = (8 + 23) = (`-**31**) = RECIPROCAL = (`-**13**) = `-**DAUGHTER** (`-GIANNA) = **"A VERY PIVOTAL #** `-**NUMBER"!!!~'**

BIRTHDAY # `-NUMBER = (`-**128**) & DEATH/DAY # `-NUMBER = (`-**67**)!!!~'

(128 (-) 67) = (`-**61**); WHILE KOBE BRYANT `-**DIED** at the `-**AGE** of (`-**41**)!!!~'

LOS ANGELES LAKERS JERSEY #8 & #24 = (8 + 24) = (`-**32**) = RECIPROCAL = (`-**23**) = -a PROPHETIC # `-NUMBER & `-**HIS** `-**BIRTHDAY** (`-**23**)!!!~' (13 + 23 + 32) = (`-**68**) = **"The** `-**MARK"!!!~'**

The ASSISTANT `-BASKETBALL COACH (CHRISTINA MAUSER) at TIME of `-HER `-DEATH; all, of `-her CHILDREN'S `-AGES; added up TO (`-**32**)!!!~'

KOBE BRYANT'S `-WIFE VANESSA LAINE BRYANT'S `-BIRTHDAY = (5/5 of 19**82**) = (**5**' **5**") in `-HEIGHT!!!~' KOBE BRYANT was (**6**' **6**") = (5' 5")/(6' 6") = (`-**56**)!!!~' (`-**55**) = (**23** + **32**)!!!~'

WIFE'S `-BIRTH/YEAR = (`-**82**) = RECIPROCAL (MIRROR) = (`-**28**) = **KOBE BRYANT'S `-BIRTH #** `-**NUMBERS!!!~'** (82 (-) 19) = (`-**63**)!!!~'

ABE LINCOLN `-**DIED** at (`-**56**) & `-HIS `-WIFE MARY TODD LINCOLN `-**DIED** at (`-**63**)!!!~'

KOBE BRYANT'S WIFE VANESSA LAINE BRYANT'S `-**AGE** at `-**TIME of** `-**HIS** `-**DEATH** = (`-**37**)!!!~' KOBE BRYANT `-**AGE** at `-**TIME of** `-**HIS** `-**DEATH** = (`-**41**)!!!~' (41 + 37) = (`-**78**) = **KOBE BRYANT'S** `-**BIRTH/YEAR** (`-**78**)!!!~' (19 + 78) = (`-**97**) = (9 x 7) = (`-**63**)!!!~'

(WIFE (`-**63**) + (KOBE) `-**63**) = (`-**126**) = **KOBE BRYANT'S** `-**DAY of** `-**DEATH (JANUARY 26**th**)**!!!~' CAREER `-ENDED in (`-**2016**) = (126(0)_)!!!~' The #'S `-NUMBERS are `-THERE; THEY `-ADD `-UP!!!~'

This #**16**/PRESIDENT ABRAHAM LINCOLN `-**PATTERN** was `-**BROUGHT** `-**OUT** in the (`-**5**th) `-BOOK entitled: **"The REAL PROPHET of DOOM (KISMET) – INTRODUCTION – PENDULUM FLOW II"!!!~'**

#16/PRESIDENT ABRAHAM LINCOLN was (6' 4") in `-HEIGHT; and, WAS `-BORN on (2/12/1809) = (2 + 12 + 18 + 09) = (`-**41**)!!!~' DIED on (4/15/1865) = (4 + 15 + 18 + 65) = (`-**102**)!!!~'

(102 (-) 41) = (`-**61**)!!!~' PRESIDENTIAL `-TERM STARTED in (`-18**61**)!!!~' #35/PRESIDENT JOHN F. KENNEDY'S PRESIDENTIAL `-TERM STARTED in (`-19**61**)!!!~'

`-**BIRTHDAY** = (`-**212**) = (21 x 2) = (`-**42**) /|\ (21 + 2) = (`-**23**) /|\ (42 + 23) = (`-**65**) = RECIPROCAL (MIRROR) = (`-**56**) = **"AGE of `-DEATH"** for #**16**/PRESIDENT ABRAHAM LINCOLN!!!~'

(`-**16**) = RECIPROCAL (MIRROR) = (`-**61**)!!!~'

FIRST LADY MARY TODD LINCOLN'S `-**BIRTHDAY** # `-NUMBER = (12/13/1818) = (1**2** + 1**3** + 18 + 18) = (`-**61**) = `-HUSBAND'S ABRAHAM LINCOLN'S `-DEATH/DAY # `-NUMBER `-SUBTRACTED by HIS `-BIRTHDAY # `-NUMBER!!!~' `-**BIRTHDAY** = (1**2**/1**3**) = (23 x 1 x 1) = (`-**23**)!!!~' FIRST LADY MARY TODD LINCOLN'S `-**DEATH/DAY** # `-NUMBER = (0**7**/1**6**/1882) = (0**7** + 1**6** + 18 + 82) = (`-**123**)!!!~' `-**DEATH/DAY** = (7 + 16) = (`-**23**)!!!~' (`-**123**) = (23 x 1) = (`-**23**)!!!~' (23 + 23) = (`-**46**)!!!~' `-**DEATH/DAY** # `-**NUMBER** in `-**REVERSE** = (82 (-) 18 (-) 16 (-) 7) = (`-**41**) = `-HUSBAND'S ABRAHAM LINCOLN'S `-**BIRTHDAY** # `-**NUMBER!!!~'** `-**DEATH/YEAR** = (82 (-) 18) = (`-**64**) = RECIPROCAL = (`-**46**) = "MARY TODD LINCOLN'S `-**AGE** at TIME of `-DEATH of #**16**/PRESIDENT ABRAHAM LINCOLN"!!!~' `-**BIRTH/YEAR** (18 + 18) = (`-**36**) = RECIPROCAL = (`-**63**) = "**AGE** of `-**DEATH** of FIRST LADY MARY TODD LINCOLN"!!!~' **SEE; THE `-NUMBERS!!!~'**

`-**IN** the `-**FAMILY (II)**-!!!~'

PART of `-this **WAS TAKEN** from **MY** `-**PREVIOUS** `-**BOOK:** "The **REAL PROPHET** of **DOOM (KISMET) – INTRODUCTION – PENDULUM FLOW (II)**"!!!~'

THE "PROPHET" HAS TWO `-**UNCLES** that are `-**BURIED** together **IN A -TOMB!!!~'** **THIS ANALYSES** is just *the SAME for ALL of US!!!~'*

UNCLE GERALD `-**BIRTH** = (0**8**/01/19**5**0) & `-**DEATH** = (0**5**/0**8**/2006)!!!~' DIED (`-**85**) DAYS AWAY FROM TURNING (`-**56**)!!!~' (`-**58**) = RECIPROCAL (MIRROR) = (`-**85**) = "IN `-**BIRTH** (0**8**/**50**); AND, IN `-**DEATH** (0**5**/0**8**)!!!~' **DIED** at the `-**AGE** of (`-**55**) = (**23** + **32**)!!!~' `-**BORN** in (`-**8**); and, `-**DIED** in (`-**5**); (`-**85**) DAYS `-**AWAY** from `-HIS `-**NEXT** `-**BIRTHDAY!!!~'**

UNCLE MICHAEL `-**BIRTH** = (0**6**/0**5**/19**56**) & `-**DEATH** = (**09**/1**9**/2003)!!!~' **BIRTHDAY** is the `-**RECIPROCAL (MIRROR)** of `-his **BIRTH/YEAR!!!~'** **DIED** at the `-**AGE** of (`-**47**) ON `-**HIS MOTHER'S** `-**BIRTHDAY!!!~'**

`-**PROPHET'S GRANDMOTHER** (THEIR MOTHER) `-**BIRTH** = (**09/19**/1924) & `-**DEATH** = (0**9**/**30**/2006)!!!~' **DIED** the VERY SAME YEAR as HER SON `-**GERALD!!!~'** AND; HER **DEATH/DAY #** `-**NUMBER** = (09 + 30 + 20 + 06) = (`-**65**) = "THE `-**BIRTHDAY** (0**6**/0**5**) of `-HER SON `-**MICHAEL!!!~'**

THE "PROPHET'S" UNCLE GERALD PASSED AWAY (`-1**45**) DAYS AWAY from HIS `-MOTHER'S `-DEATH/DAY (0**9**/**30**)!!!~' THE "PROPHET'S" UNCLE MICHAEL PASSED AWAY (`-**11**) DAYS or (`-3**54**) DAYS AWAY from HIS MOTHER'S DEATH/DAY (0**9**/**30**)!!!~' (`-**45**) = RECIPROCAL (MIRROR) = (`-**54**)!!!~' (145 + 11) = (`-1**56**)!!!~' THE `-**DIFFERENCE** BETWEEN

DEATH/DAYS of MICHAEL & GERALD is (`-**134**) DAYS = (1 + 3 + 4) = (`-**8**) = **EIGHT** `-KIDS in their `-FAMILY & **DIED** (`-**8**) YEARS APART from EACH OTHER in `-AGE!!!~' THEIR `-**FATHER** **PASSED** **AWAY** at the `-AGE of (`-**88**)!!!~'

THE "PROPHET'S" GRANDMOTHER'S BIRTHDAY # `-**NUMBER** = (09/19/1924) = (09 + 19 + 19 + 24) = (`-**71**) = RECIPROCAL = (`-**17**)!!!~' (71 + 17) = (`-**88**) = "THE `-**AGE** of `-HER HUSBAND'S (THE "PROPHET'S" GRANDFATHER'S) DEATH YEAR of `-**AGE** (`-**88**)!!!~'

(09 + 19 + 19) = (`-**47**) = "AGE of `-DEATH of `-HER SON; the "PROPHET'S" UNCLE MICHAEL"!!!~'

(09 + 19) = (`-**28**) = RECIPROCAL (MIRROR) = (`-**82**) = "AGE of HER OWN `-**DEATH** of the "PROPHET'S" GRANDMOTHER"!!!~'

`-**1924** = (19 + 24) = (`-**43**) = RECIPROCAL (MIRROR) = (`-**34**) = "HER `-BOYS"!!!~'

THE "PROPHET'S" GRANDFATHER'S `-BIRTH = (1**2**/**3**0/1915) & `-DEATH = (10/26/**2**00**4**)!!!~' HIS `-**BIRTHDAY** (`-**30**) = `-EQUALS = "THE `-**DEATH/DAY** (`-**30**) OF `-HIS `-**WIFE!!!~'** HIS `-WIFE was `-**BORN** in (`-**24**); AND, HE `-**DIED** in (`-**24**)!!!~'

(12 + 30 + 19) = (`-**61**)!!!~'

BIRTH = (12 + 30 + 19 + 15) = (`-**76**)!!!~'

(19 + 15) = (`-**34**) = "HIS `-BOYS"!!!~'

(10 + 26 + 20) = (`-**56**) = "HIS `-BOYS"!!!~'

DEATH = (10 + 26 + 20 + 04) = (`-**60**)!!!~'

8

THE "PROPHET'S" GRANDFATHER `-DIED (`-**65**) DAYS AWAY from HIS NEXT BIRTHDAY; WHILE, HIS SON MICHAEL'S BIRTHDAY was on (0**6**/0**5**); AND, HIS `-WIFE'S **DEATH/DAY # `-NUMBER** was (`-**65**)!!!~' IF the `-**PROPHET'S GRANDFATHER** had `-**PASSED** `-**AWAY** at the `-**AGE** of (`-**87**); then, (8 x 7) = (`-**56**) = **RECIPROCAL (MIRROR)** = (`-**65**)!!!~' THE "**PROPHET'S**" **BIRTHDAY # `-NUMBER** = (3 + 20 + 19 + 70) = (`-**112**) (/) **DIVIDED by** (/) **2** = (`-**56**) = RECIPROCAL (MIRROR) = (`-**65**)!!!~'

UNCLE GERALD `-**BIRTH** = (0**8**/01/19**5**0) & `-**DEATH** = (0**5**/0**8**/2006)!!!~'

(08 + 01 + 19) = (`-**28**) = RECIPROCAL (MIRROR) = (`-**82**) = **"MOTHER'S `-AGE of `-DEATH"**!!!~'

`-**BIRTH** = (08 + 01 + 19 + 50) = (`-**78**)!!!~'

`-**DEATH** = (05 + 08 + 20 + 06) = (`-**39**)!!!~' (39 x 2) = (`-**78**) = RECIPROCAL (MIRROR) = (`-**87**)!!!~'

(`-**78**) = (**7** x 8) = (`-**56**) = `-**DIED** LESS (`-**ONE**) `-**YEAR** at (`-**55**)!!!~'

FATHER'S `-BIRTHDAY # `-NUMBER (`-**76**) & `-**DEATH/ DAY # `-NUMBER** (`-**60**)!!!~'

(**76** + **6**0) = (`-**136**) = (13 x 6) = (`-**78**)!!!~'

MOTHER `-**DIED** on (0**9**/**3**0) = (9 + 30) = (`-**39**) = RECIPROCAL (MIRROR) = (`-**93**)!!!~'

UNCLE MICHAEL `-**BIRTH** = (06/05/19**56**) & `-**DEATH** = (**09/19/2**00**3**)!!!~'

9

`-**BIRTH** = (06 + 05 + 19 + 56) = (`-**86**)!!!~'

(`-**86**) = (8 x **6**) = (`-**48**) = `-**DIED** LESS (`-**ONE**) `-**YEAR** at (`-**47**)!!!~'

(**78/86**) = (`-**76**) & (`-**88**) = `-**GRANDFATHER'S** BIRTHDAY # `-**NUMBER**; AND, `-**AGE** of `-**DEATH**!!!~'

`-**IF** the `-**PROPHET'S GRANDFATHER** were (`-**87**) for when `-**HE** `-**DIED**; THEN, HIS `-**BIRTHDAY** # `-**NUMBER** `-PLUS `-**DEATH/DAY** # `-**NUMBER** would be (`-**137**)!!!~'

MICHAEL `-**DIED** (`-**37**) **DAYS** away **FROM HIS FATHER'S** `-**DEATH**; and, GERALD `-**DIED** (`-**171**) **DAYS** away **FROM HIS** `-**FATHER'S** `-**DEATH**!!!~' MICHAEL; AND, HIS `-**MOTHER** (the `-**PROPHET'S** GRANDMOTHER `-**both** `-**DIED** on (**9/19**) = (9 x 19) = (`-**171**)!!!~'

(37 + **171**) = (`-**208**) = (28 + 0) = (`-**28**) = RECIPROCAL (MIRROR) = (`-**82**) = **"THE PROPHET'S GRANDMOTHER (their MOTHER)"**!!!~'

(`-**17**) = RECIPROCAL (MIRROR) = (`-**71**) = **THE "PROPHET'S" GRANDMOTHER'S BIRTHDAY** # `-**NUMBER**!!!~'

(`-**37**) = **3**(**7's**) = (**777**) = (7 x 7 x 7) = (`-**343**) = **"THE** `-**BOYS"**!!!~'

MICHAEL was `-**BORN** in (`-**56**); and, GERALD was `-**BORN** in (`-**50**)!!!~' (56 + 50) = (`-**106**)!!!~'

MICHAEL was `-**BORN** (`-**106**) **DAYS** away **FROM HIS MOTHER'S** `-**BIRTHDAY**; and, GERALD was `-**BORN** (`-**49**) **DAYS** away **FROM HIS** `-**MOTHER'S** `-**BIRTHDAY**!!!~'

(106 + 49) = (`-**155**) = (**55** + 1) = (`-**56**) = **"THE** `-**BOYS"**!!!~'

(106 (-) 49) = (`-**57**)!!!~'

MICHAEL was `-**BORN** (`-**157**) DAYS away **FROM HIS FATHER'S `-BIRTHDAY**; and, GERALD was `-**BORN** (`-**214**) DAYS away **FROM HIS `-FATHER'S `-BIRTHDAY!!!~'**

(157 + 214) = (`-**371**) = (**ALL-IN-ONE-#-NUMBER**) FOR (**37/171**) from `-**ABOVE!!!~'** (**LINKED** in a `-**FULL** `-**CIRCLE** from in the `-**SPAN** of `-**LIFE;** and, from in the `-**SPAN** of `-**DEATH**)!!!~'

MICHAEL'S BIRTH (`-**65**); AND, GERALD'S DEATH (`-**58**)!!!~'

(65 + 58) = (`-**123**) = **"PROPHETIC-LINEAR-PROGRESSION-PLP"!!!~'**

MICHAEL'S DEATH (`-**919**); AND, GERALD'S BIRTH (`-**81**)!!!~'

(919 + 81) = (`-**1000**) = **"A `-FACTOR `-OF"!!!~'**

MICHAEL'S `-**BIRTH/YEAR** (`-**56**) PLUS GERALD'S DEATH/YEAR (`-**26**) = (`-**82**) = **"THEIR `-MOTHER (the `-PROPHET'S GRANDMOTHER)"!!!~'**

GERALD'S BIRTH/YEAR (`-**50**) PLUS MICHAEL'S DEATH/YEAR (`-**23**) = (`-**73**) = **RECIPROCAL (MIRROR)** = (`-**37**) = **3**(**7's**) = (**777**) = (7 x 7 x 7) = (`-**343**) = **"BOTH `-PARENTS (both OF the `-PROPHET'S GRANDPARENTS)"!!!~'**

IN THE `-PROPHET'S TWO PREVIOUS BOOKS IT IS NOTED that ON THE "PROPHET'S" MOTHER'S SIDE of the FAMILY AN UNCLE FRANK that was `-**BORN** in (`-**37**) `-**DIED** in the **YEAR** that **THE "PROPHET'S MOTHER'S TWIN SISTER** was (`-**73**); AND, HER DAUGHTER (MY `-MOTHER'S TWIN SISTER'S) PASSED AWAY (`-**137**) DAYS

BEFORE HER NEXT `-**BIRTHDAY** WHICH WAS ON (`-**731**)
= RECIPROCAL (MIRROR) = (`-**137**)!!!~' (731 + 137) = (`-**868**)
= "The `-**MARK**"!!!~'

FORMER BASKETBALL COMMISSIONER DAVID JOEL
STERN (`-**77**) (BIRTH: SEPTEMBER 22, 19**42**) (DEATH:
JANUARY 1, 2020)!!!~'

WAS `-**BORN** in (`-**42**); and, `-**DIED** in (`-**42**) = DEATH/DAY #
`-NUMBER = (`-**42**)!!!~'

BIRTHDAY # `-NUMBER = (**9** + 2**2** + 1**9** + 42) = **92**

(`-**29**) = RECIPROCAL (MIRROR) = (`-**92**)

DEATH/DAY # `-NUMBER = (1 + 1 + 20 + 20) = **42**

(92 (-) 42) = (`-**50**)!!!~'

(92 + 42) = (`-**134**)!!!~'

HE DIED (`-**101**) DAYS AFTER HIS LAST BIRTHDAY!!!~'

(365 (-) 101) = (`-**264**) = (64 x 2) = (`-**128**) = "KOBE BRYANT"!!!~'

HE DIED AT THE `-AGE of (`-**77**) = (7 x 7) = (`-**49**) =
RECIPROCAL = (`-**94**)!!!~'

SEPTEMBER 22 = (9 x 22) = (`-**198**)!!!~'

JANUARY 1 = (1 x 1) = (`-**1**)!!!~'

(198 (-) 1) = (`-**197**) = "FLIP the (`-7) OVER to a (`-2)" = (`-**192**)!!!~'

SEPTEMBER 22, 1942 = (9 + 2 + 2 + 1 + 9 + 4 + 2) = (`-**29**) = RECIPROCAL = (`-**92**)!!!~'

JANUARY 1, 2020 = (1 + 1 + 2 + 0 + 2 + 0) = (`-**6**)!!!~'

(**29** (-) **6**) = (`-**23**) = -a PROPHETIC # `-NUMBER!!!~'

`-**BIRTHDAY**; and, `-**DEATH/DAY**!!!~':

(**922** + **11**) = (`-**933**) = (9 + 33) = (`-**42**) = "WAS `-BORN in (`-**42**) & `-EQUALS `-DEATH/DAY # `-NUMBER of (`-**42**)!!!~'

(922 + 11) = (`-**933**) = (33 (-) 9) = (`-**24**) = "KOBE BRYANT"!!!~'

(**922** (-) **11**) = (`-**911**) = "EMERGENCY"!!!~'

(911 (-) 42) = (`-**869**) = (86 (-) 9) = (`-**77**) = "AGE of `-DEATH for FORMER BASKETBALL COMMISSIONER DAVID JOEL STERN (`-**77**)"!!!~'

(911 + 42) = (`-**953**) = (95 (-) 3) = (`-**92**) = "REVIEW from `-ABOVE"!!!~'

SEPTEMBER 22 (**BIRTH**) + JANUARY 1 (**DEATH**) = (9 + 22 + 1 + 1) = (`-**33**)!!!~'

`-**DIED** in (`-**1**) & was `-**BORN** in (`-**9**) = (`-**1/9**) = (`-**19**) = RECIPROCAL (MIRROR) (`-**91**)!!!~' (91 (-) 19) = (`-**72**) = RECIPROCAL (MIRROR) = (`-**27**) = **2**(**7's**) = (`-**77**) = "AGE of `-**DEATH for FORMER BASKETBALL COMMISSIONER DAVID JOEL STERN (`-**77**)"!!!~'

GREEN BAY PACKERS HALL of FAME FOOTBALL PLAYER WILLIE WOOD (`-**83**) (BIRTH: DECEMBER **23**, 19**36**) (DEATH: **FEBRUARY 3**, 2020)!!!~'

`-**BORN** on (`-**23**), `-**DIED** on (`-**23**) WITH (`-**323**) DAYS BETWEEN `-**BIRTHDAY** & `-**DEATH/DAY**!!!~'

BIRTHDAY # `-NUMBER = (12 + **23** + 19 + 36) = **90**

(`-**90**) = RECIPROCAL (MIRROR) = (`-**09**)

DEATH/DAY # `-NUMBER = (**2** + **3** + 20 + 20) = **45**

(90 (-) 45) = (`-**45**)!!!~'

(90 + 45) = (`-**135**)!!!~'

HE DIED (`-**42**) DAYS AFTER HIS LAST BIRTHDAY!!!~'

(365 (-) 42) = (`-**323**) = "**R**ECIPROCAL-**S**EQUENCING-**N**UMEROLOGY-**RSN**"!!!~'

HE DIED AT THE `-AGE of (`-**83**) = (8 x 3) = (`-**24**) = RECIPROCAL = (`-**42**) = "**HOW MANY DAYS** `-HE `-**DIED** after `-HIS LAST `-**BIRTHDAY**"!!!~'

DECEMBER 23 = (12 x 23) = (`-**276**)!!!~'

FEBRUARY 3 = (2 x 3) = (`-**6**)!!!~'

(276 + 6) = (`-**282**) = "**R**ECIPROCAL-**S**EQUENCING-**N**UMEROLOGY-**RSN**"!!!~'

(276 (-) 6) = (`-**270**) = (27 + 0) = (`-**27**) = RECIPROCAL (MIRROR) = (`-**72**)!!!~'

DECEMBER 23, 1936 = (1 + 2 + 2 + 3 + 1 + 9 + 3 + 6) = (`-**27**) = RECIPROCAL = (`-**72**)!!!~'

FEBRUARY 3, 2020 = (2 + 3 + 2 + 0 + 2 + 0) = (`-**9**)!!!~'

(**27** + **9**) = (`-**36**) = "YEAR of `-BIRTH (`-**36**)"!!!~'

(36 + 36) = (`-**72**)!!!~'

`-**BIRTHDAY**; and, `-**DEATH/DAY**!!!~':

(**1223** + **23**) = (`-**1246**) = (12 + 46) = (`-**58**)!!!~'

(**1223** (-) **23**) = (`-**1200**) = (12 + 0 + 0) = (`-**12**)!!!~'

(58 (-) 12) = (`-**46**) = (**23 x 2**)!!!~'

DECEMBER 23 (**BIRTH**) + FEBRUARY 3 (**DEATH**) = (12 + 23 + 2 + 3) = (`-**40**)!!!~'

`-DIED in (`-**2**) & was `-BORN in (`-**12**) = (`-**2/12**) = (2 x 12) = (`-**24**) = (8 x 3) = (`-**83**) = "AGE of `-DEATH for GREEN BAY PACKERS HALL of FAME FOOTBALL PLAYER WILLIE WOOD (`-**83**)"!!!~'

`-DIED in (`-**2**) & was `-BORN in (`-**12**) = (`-**2/12**) = "BOILING `-POINT" = "**R**ECIPROCAL-**S**EQUENCING-**N**UMEROLOGY-**RSN**"!!!~'

AMERICAN ACTOR KIRK DOUGLAS (`-**103**) (BIRTH: DECEMBER **9**, 19**16**) (DEATH: FEBRUARY 5, 2020)!!!~'

`-BIRTHDAY & `-DEATH/DAY `-*ADD UP* TO (`-103) = `-HIS `-AGE OF `-DEATH (`-103)!!!~'

BIRTHDAY # `-NUMBER = (12 + 9 + 19 + 16) = **56**

(`-**56**) = RECIPROCAL (MIRROR) = (`-**65**)

DEATH/DAY # `-NUMBER = (2 + 5 + 20 + 20) = **47**

(56 (-) 47) = (`-**9**)!!!~'

(56 + 47) = (`-**103**) = "AGE of `-DEATH (`-**103**)"!!!~'

HE DIED (`-**58**) DAYS AFTER HIS LAST BIRTHDAY!!!~'

(365 (-) 58) = (`-**307**)!!!~'

(`-**47**), (`-**56**), (`-**58**), (`-**37**) = THESE `-NUMBERS #'S are QUITE `-SIMILAR to the `-PROPHET'S GRANDFATHER!!!~'

HE DIED AT THE `-AGE of (`-**103**) = (13 + 0) = (`-**13**) = **"A VERY PIVOTAL # `-NUMBER"!!!~'**

DECEMBER 9 = (12 x 9) = (`-**108**)!!!~'

FEBRUARY 5 = (2 x 5) = (`-**10**)!!!~'

(108 + 10) = (`-**118**)!!!~'

(108 (-) 10) = (`-**98**)!!!~'

(118 + 98) = (`-**216**) = (2 x 16) = (`-**32**) = **-a PROPHETIC # `-NUMBER!!!~'**

DECEMBER 9, 1916 = (1 + **2** + **9** + 1 + 9 + 1 + 6) = (`-**29**) = RECIPROCAL = (`-**92**)!!!~'

FEBRUARY 5, 2020 = (2 + 5 + 2 + 0 + 2 + 0) = (`-**11**)!!!~'

(**29** (-) **11**) = (`-**18**) = (9 x 2)!!!~'

`-**BIRTHDAY**; and, `-**DEATH/DAY**!!!~':

(**129** + **25**) = (`-**154**) = (54 x 1) = (`-**54**)!!!~'

(**129** (-) **25**) = (`-**104**) = "YEAR of `-DEATH"!!!~'

(54 + 104) = (`-**158**) = (58 x 1) = (`-**58**) = "HOW MANY DAYS `-HE -died AFTER `-HIS LAST `-BIRTHDAY"!!!~'

DECEMBER 9 (**BIRTH**) + FEBRUARY 5 (**DEATH**) = (12 + 9 + 2 + 5) = (`-**28**)!!!~'

`-**DIED** in (`-**2**) & was `-**BORN** in (`-**12**) = (`-**2/12**) = "BOILING `-POINT" = "RECIPROCAL-**S**EQUENCING-**N**UMEROLOGY-**RSN**"!!!~'

AMERICAN ACTRESS JEANNETTE DUBOIS "GOOD TIMES" (`-**74**) (BIRTH: AUGUST **5**, 19**45**) (DEATH: FEBRUARY 17, 2020)!!!~'

(8 x 5) = (`-**40**) = `-**BIRTHDAY** / (2 x 17) = (`-**34**) = `-**DEATH/ DAY** / 40 + 34) = (`-**74**) = `-**AGE** of `-**DEATH**!!!~'

BIRTHDAY # `-NUMBER = (8 + 5 + 19 + 45) = **77**

DEATH/DAY # `-NUMBER = (2 + 17 + 20 + 20) = **59**

(77 (-) 59) = (`-**18**)!!!~'

(77 + 59) = (`-**136**)!!!~'

(136 (-) 18) = (`-**118**)!!!~'

SHE DIED (`-**196**) DAYS AFTER HER LAST BIRTHDAY!!!~'
(`-**196**) = (96 x 1) = (`-**96**) = (32 x 3)!!!~'

(365 (-) 196) = (`-**169**) = (69 x 1) = (`-**69**) = (3 x 23)!!!~'

SHE DIED AT THE `-AGE of (`-**74**) = (7 x 4) = (`-**28**)!!!~'

AUGUST 5 = (8 x 5) = (`-**40**)!!!~'

FEBRUARY 17 = (2 x 17) = (`-**34**)!!!~'

(40 + 34) = (`-**74**) = **"AGE of `-DEATH for AMERICAN ACTRESS JEANNETTE DUBOIS "GOOD TIMES" (`-74)"!!!~'**

AUGUST 5, 1945 = (8 + 5 + 1 + 9 + 4 + 5) = (`-**32**) = RECIPROCAL = (`-**23**)!!!~'

FEBRUARY 17, 2020 = (2 + 1 + 7 + 2 + 0 + 2 + 0) = (`-**14**)!!!~'

(**32** + **14**) = (`-**46**) = (**2 x 23**)!!!~'

`-BIRTHDAY; and, `-DEATH/DAY!!!~':

(**85** + **217**) = (`-**302**) = (32 + 0) = (`-**32**) = **-a PROPHETIC # `-NUMBER!!!~'**

(**217** (-) **85**) = (`-**132**) = (32 x 1) = (`-**32**) = **-a PROPHETIC # `-NUMBER!!!~'**

(32 + 32) = (`-**64**) = RECIPROCAL (MIRROR) = (`-**46**)!!!~`

(302 + 132) = (`-**434**) = "**RECIPROCAL-SEQUENCING-NUMEROLOGY-RSN**"!!!~`

AUGUST 5 (**BIRTH**) + FEBRUARY 17 (**DEATH**) = (8 + 5 + 2 + 17) = (`-**32**) = -a PROPHETIC # `-NUMBER!!!~`

`-DIED in (`-**2**) & was `-BORN in (`-**8**) = (`-**2/8**) = (`-**28**) = (7 x 4) = (`-**74**) = "AGE of `-DEATH for AMERICAN ACTRESS JEANNETTE DUBOIS "GOOD TIMES" (`-**74**)"!!!~`

AMERICAN BUSINESS MAN SEYMOUR "SY" SPERLING (`-**78**) (BIRTH: JUNE **25**, 1941) (DEATH: FEBRUARY **19**, 2020)!!!~`

`-**BIRTHDAY** # `-NUMBER = (`-**91**) = RECIPROCAL (MIRROR) = `-DEATH/DAY (`-**19**)!!!~`

BIRTHDAY # `-NUMBER = (6 + 25 + 19 + 41) = **91**

(`-**91**) = RECIPROCAL (MIRROR) = (`-**19**)

DEATH/DAY # `-NUMBER = (2 + 19 + 20 + 20) = **61**

(91 (-) 61) = (`-**30**)!!!~`

(91 + 61) = (`-**152**)!!!~`

(152 (-) 30) = (`-**122**) = (22 + 1) = (`-**23**) = -a PROPHETIC # `-NUMBER!!!~`

HE DIED (`-**127**) DAYS BEFORE HIS NEXT BIRTHDAY!!!~`

(366 (-) 127) = (`-**239**) = (39 x 2) = (`-**78**) = `-**AGE of** `-**DEATH for AMERICAN BUSINESS MAN SEYMOUR "SY" SPERLING** (`-**78**)!!!~'

HE DIED AT THE `-AGE of (`-**78**) = (7 x 8) = (`-**56**) = RECIPROCAL (MIRROR) = (`-**65**)!!!~'

JUNE 25 = (6 x 25) = (`-**150**)!!!~'

FEBRUARY 19 = (2 x 19) = (`-**38**)!!!~'

(150 + 38) = (`-**188**)!!!~'

(150 (-) 38) = (`-**112**)!!!~'

(188 (-) 112) = (`-**76**)!!!~'

JUNE 25, 1941 = (6 + 2 + 5 + 1 + 9 + 4 + 1) = (`-**28**) = RECIPROCAL = (`-**82**)!!!~'

FEBRUARY 19, 2020 = (2 + 1 + 9 + 2 + 0 + 2 + 0) = (`-**16**)!!!~'

(**28** + **16**) = (`-**44**) = (4 x 4) = (`-**16**)!!!~'

`-**BIRTHDAY; and,** `-**DEATH/DAY**!!!~':

(**625** + **219**) = (`-**844**) = (84 + 4) = (`-**88**)!!!~'

(**625** (-) **219**) = (`-**406**) = (46 + 0) = (`-**46**) = (23 x 2)!!!~'

(88 + 46) = (`-**134**) = (13 x 4) = (`-**52**) = RECIPROCAL (MIRROR) = (`-**25**) = **"DAY of** `-**BIRTH** (`-**25**th)"!!!~'

JUNE 25 (**BIRTH**) + FEBRUARY 19 (**DEATH**) = (6 + 25 + 2 + 19) = (`-**52**`) = RECIPROCAL (MIRROR) = (`-**25**`) = "**DAY of `-BIRTH (`-25th`)**"!!!~'

`-DIED in (`-**2**`) & was `-BORN in (`-**6**`) = (`-**2/6**`) = (`-**26**`) = (13 x 2) = (32 x 1) = (`-**32**`) = -a PROPHETIC # `-NUMBER!!!~'

AMERICAN RESTAURATEUR BARBARA ELAINE SMITH (B. SMITH) (`-**70**`) (BIRTH: AUGUST 24, 1**949**) (DEATH: **FEBRUARY 22, 2020**)!!!~'

`-**1949** = (19 + 49) = (`-**68**`) = "The `-**MARK**"!!!~'

`-DEATH/DAY = FEBRUARY 22, 2020 = (02/22/2020) = (2 x 2 x 2 X 2 x 2) = (`-**32**`) = -a **PROPHETIC # `-NUMBER!!!~'** BIRTHDAY = (8/24) = (8 + 24) = (`-**32**`) = -a **PROPHETIC # `-NUMBER!!!~** BIRTHDAY `-**MATCHES** `-DEATH/DAY!!!~'

BIRTHDAY # `-NUMBER = (8 + 24 + 19 + 49) = **100**

DEATH/DAY # `-NUMBER = (2 + 22 + 20 + 20) = **64** = `-**BIRTHDAY/`-DEATH/DAY `-ADDED `-TOGETHER!!!~'**

(100 (-) 64) = (`-**36**`)!!!~'

(100 + 64) = (`-**164**`)!!!~'

(164 (-) 36) = (`-**128**`)!!!~'

SHE DIED (`-**184**`) DAYS BEFORE HER NEXT BIRTHDAY!!!~'

(366 (-) 184) = (`-**182**`) = (82 x 1) = (`-**82**`) = RECIPROCAL (MIRROR) = (`-**28**`)!!!~'

SHE DIED AT THE `-AGE of (`-**70**)!!!~'

AUGUST 24 = (8 x 24) = (`-**192**)!!!~'

FEBRUARY 22 = (2 x 22) = (`-**44**)!!!~'

(192 (-) 44) = (`-**148**) = (48 x 1) = (`-**48**) = RECIPROCAL (MIRROR) = (`-**84**) = `-**DIED** (`-**184**) DAYS **before** HER `-**NEXT** `-**BIRTHDAY!!!~'**

AUGUST 24, 1949 = (8 + 2 + 4 + 1 + 9 + 4 + 9) = (`-**37**) = RECIPROCAL = (`-**73**)!!!~'

FEBRUARY 22, 2020 = (2 + 2 + 2 + 2 + 0 + 2 + 0) = (`-**10**)!!!~'

(**37** + **10**) = (`-**47**)!!!~'

`-**BIRTHDAY; and, `-DEATH/DAY!!!~':**

(**824** + **222**) = (`-**1046**) = (10 + 46) = (`-**56**)!!!~'

(**824** (-) **222**) = (`-**602**) = (6 + 2) = (`-**8**)!!!~'

(56 + 8) = (`-**64**) = "REVIEW `-ABOVE"!!!~'

(32 + 32) = (`-**64**) = RECIPROCAL (MIRROR) = (`-**46**)!!!~'

(56 (-) 8) = (`-**48**) = "**REVIEW `-ABOVE**"!!!~'

AUGUST 24 (**BIRTH**) + FEBRUARY 22 (**DEATH**) = (8 + 24 + 2 + 22) = (`-**56**)!!!~'

DEATH/DAY `-MONTH (`-2) & `-DAY (`-22) = (2 + 22) = (`-**24**) = "**DAY of `-BIRTH (`-24)**"!!!~'

`-DIED in (`-2) & was `-BORN in (`-8) = (`-2/8) = (`-2 + 8) = (`-10) = `-DEATH/DAY of FEBRUARY 22, 2020 = (0 + 2 + 2 + 2 + 0 + 2 + 0) = (`-10)!!!~'

DOCTOR & DIXIE CRUSH LEAD COUNTRY SINGER LINDSEY RENEE LAGESTEE (`-25) (BIRTH: MAY 17, 1994) (DEATH: FEBRUARY 17, 2020)!!!~'

`-1994 = (94 (-) 19) = (`-75) = "FLIP the (`-7) OVER to a (`-2) = (`-25) = "AGE of `-DEATH"!!!~'

(`-94) = RECIPROCAL (MIRROR) = (`-49)!!!~'

`-BORN ON A (`-17th); and, `-DIED on a (`-17th)!!!~' `-DIED in the MONTH of (`-2); AND, WAS `-BORN in the `-MONTH of (`-5) = (`-25) = "AGE of `-DEATH"!!!~'

BIRTHDAY # `-NUMBER = (5 + 17 + 19 + 94) = **135**

(94 (-) 19 (-) 17 (-) 5) = (`-53) = RECIPROCAL (MIRROR) = (`-35)!!!~'

DEATH/DAY # `-NUMBER = (2 + 17 + 20 + 20) = **59**

(135 (-) 59) = (`-76)!!!~'

(135 + 59) = (`-194) = "WAS `-BORN in (`-94)!!!~'

(194 (-) 76) = (`-118)!!!~'

SHE DIED (`-90) DAYS BEFORE HER NEXT BIRTHDAY!!!~'

(366 (-) 90) = (`-276) = (76 x 2) = (`-152) = (52 + 1) = (`-53)!!!~'

SHE DIED AT THE `-AGE of (`-**25**)!!!~'

`-BIRTHDAY = MAY 17 = (5 x 17) = (`-**85**)!!!~'

`-**DEATH/DAY** = FEBRUARY 17 = (2 x 17) = (`-**34**) = `-**DEATH/ DAY** `-EQUALS `-**DAY of** `-**BIRTH** & `-**DAY of** `-**DEATH /** `-**ADDED** `-**UP**!!!~'

(85 (-) 34) = (`-**51**!!!~'

MAY 17, 1994 = (5 + 1 + 7 + 1 + 9 + 9 + 4) = (`-**36**) = RECIPROCAL = (`-**63**)!!!~'

FEBRUARY 17, 2020 = (2 + 1 + 7 + 2 + 0 + 2 + 0) = (`-**14**)!!!~'

(**36** + **14**) = (`-**50**) = DIVIDED by (`-**2**) = (`-**25**) = "**AGE of** `-**DEATH**!!!~'

`-**BIRTHDAY; and,** `-**DEATH/DAY**!!!~':

(**517** + **217**) = (`-**734**)!!!~'

(**517** (-) **217**) = (`-**300**)!!!~'

(734 + 300) = (`-**1034**) = (34 / 10) = (`-**3.4**) = `-BIRTHDAY (`-**17**) (+) `-DEATH/DAY (`-**17**)!!!~'

(734 (-) 300) = (`-**434**) = "**RECIPROCAL-SEQUENCING-NUMEROLOGY-RSN**"!!!~'

MAY 17 (**BIRTH**) + FEBRUARY 17 (**DEATH**) = (5 + 17 + 2 + 17) = (`-**41**)!!!~'

`-**DIED in** (`-**2**) & was `-**BORN in** (`-**5**) = (`-**2/5**) = (`-**25**) = "**AGE** of `-**DEATH** for

DOCTOR & DIXIE CRUSH LEAD COUNTRY SINGER LINDSEY RENEE LAGESTEE (`-25)"!!!~'

DAREDEVIL "MAD" MIKE HUGHES (`-**64**) (BIRTH: FEBRUARY 9, 19**56**) (DEATH: FEBRUARY **22**, **20**20)

`-DEATH/DAY = FEBRUARY 22, 2020 = (02/22/2020) = (2 x 2 x 2 X 2 x 2) = (`-**32**) = -a PROPHETIC # `-NUMBER!!!~' `-**AGE** of `-**DEATH** (`-**64**) = (`-**2** x `-**32**) = -a PROPHETIC # `-NUMBER!!!~'

BIRTHDAY # `-NUMBER = (2 + 9 + 19 + 56) = **86**

(`-**86**) = RECIPROCAL (MIRROR) = (`-**68**) = "The `-**MARK**"!!!~'

DEATH/DAY # `-NUMBER = (2 + 22 + 20 + 20) = **64** = `-**AGE** of `-**DEATH for DAREDEVIL "MAD" MIKE HUGHES** (`-**64**)!!!~'

(86 (-) 64) = (`-**22**)!!!~'

(86 + 64) = (`-**150**)!!!~'

(150 (-) 22) = (`-**128**)!!!~'

HE DIED (`-**13**) DAYS AFTER HIS LAST BIRTHDAY = "**A VERY PIVOTAL # `-NUMBER**"!!!~'

(365 (-) 13) = (`-**352**) = (52 x 3) = (`-**156**) = (56 x 1) = (`-**56**) = "**YEAR** of `-**BIRTH**!!!~'

HE DIED AT THE `-AGE of (`-**64**)!!!~'

FEBRUARY 9 = (2 x 9) = (`-**18**)!!!~'

FEBRUARY 22 = (2 x 22) = (`-**44**)!!!~'

(44 (-) 18) = (`-**26**) = RECIPROCAL (MIRROR) = (`-**62**)!!!~'

BIRTHDAY # `-NUMBER = (2 + 9 + 19 + 56) = **86**

(56 (-) 19 (-) 9 (-) 2) = (`-**26**)!!!~'

FEBRUARY 9, 1956 = (2 + 9 + 1 + 9 + 5 + 6) = (`-**32**) = RECIPROCAL = (`-**23**)!!!~'

FEBRUARY 22, 2020 = (2 + 2 + 2 + 2 + 0 + 2 + 0) = (`-**10**)!!!~'

(**32** (-) **10**) = (`-**22**) = "**DAY** of `-**DEATH**"!!!~'

`-**BIRTHDAY; and, `-DEATH/DAY!!!~**':

(**29** + **222**) = (`-**251**)!!!~'

(**222** (-) **29**) = (`-**193**)!!!~'

(251 + 193) = (`-**444**) = (4 x 4 x 4) = (`-**64**) = `-**AGE of `-DEATH for DAREDEVIL "MAD" MIKE HUGHES** (`-**64**)!!!~'

(32 + 32) = (`-**64**) = RECIPROCAL (MIRROR) = (`-**46**)!!!~'

(251 (-) 193) = (`-**58**) = (5 + 8) = (`-**13**) = "**DIED this `-MANY `-DAYS after `-HIS `-LAST `-BIRTHDAY**" = "**A VERY PIVOTAL # `-NUMBER**"!!!~'

FEBRUARY 9 (**BIRTH**) + FEBRUARY 22 (**DEATH**) = (2 + 9 + 2 + 22) = (`-**35**)!!!~'

26

BIRTHDAY `-MONTH (`-2) & `-DAY (`-9) = (`-29) = `-DIES in a `-LEAP `-YEAR of (`-29) DAYS FOR the `-MONTH of `-FEBRUARY"!!!~'

`-DIED in (`-2) & was `-BORN in (`-2) = (`-2/2) = (`-22nd) of the `-MONTH for a `-DEATH/DAY (`-22)!!!~'

PORTRAYED in the MOVIE *"**HIDDEN FIGURES**"* AMERICAN MATHEMATICIAN KATHERINE COLEMAN GOBLE JOHNSON (`-**101**) (BIRTH: AUGUST **26**, **1918**) (DEATH: FEBRUARY 24, 2020)!!!~'

`-**1918** = (19 (+) 18) = (`-**37**)!!!~'

`-**1956** = (56 (-) 19) = (`-**37**)!!!~'

`-HUSBAND JAMES FRANCIS GOBLE `-DIED in 1956!!!~'

(37 + 37) = (`-**74**) = **"JULY 4th"!!!~'**

`-AUGUST (`-26th) = (8 + 26) = (`-**34**) = RECIPROCAL (MIRROR) = (`-43**) = "AGE of `-DEATH of (1st) HUSBAND JAMES FRANCIS GOBLE!!!~'**

`-AUGUST (`-26th) = (26 (-) 8) = (`-**18**) = "YEAR of `-BIRTH"!!!~'

`-FEBRUARY (`-24th) = (2 + 24) = (`-**26**) = "DAY of `-BIRTH"!!!~'

BIRTHDAY # `-NUMBER = (8 + 26 + 19 + 18) = **71**

DEATH/DAY # `-NUMBER = (2 + 24 + 20 + 20) = **66**

(71 (-) 66) = (`-**5**)!!!~'

(71 + 66) = (`-**137**) = "**SEE** `-**ABOVE**"!!!~'

(137 (-) 5) = (`-**132**) = (32 x 1) = (`-**32**) = -**a PROPHETIC #** `-**NUMBER!!!~**'

SHE DIED (`-**182**) DAYS AFTER HER LAST BIRTHDAY!!!~'

(365 (-) 182) = (`-**183**) = (18 x 3) = (`-**54**)!!!~' **DAUGHTER CONSTANCE GOBLE** `-**DIED** on (`-**5/4**) = **MAY 4**th!!!~'

SHE DIED AT THE `-AGE of (`-**101**)!!!~'

AUGUST 26 = (8 x 26) = (`-**208**)!!!~'

FEBRUARY 24 = (2 x 24) = (`-**48**)!!!~'

(208 + 48) = (`-**256**)!!!~'

(256 (-) 54) = (`-**202**) (/) **DIVIDED by** (/) **2** = (`-**101**) = "**AGE of** `-**DEATH** for **AMERICAN MATHEMATICIAN KATHERINE COLEMAN GOBLE JOHNSON** (`-**101**)"!!!~'

AUGUST 26, 1918 = (8 + 2 + 6 + 1 + 9 + 1 + 8) = (`-**35**) = RECIPROCAL = (`-**53**)!!!~'

FEBRUARY 24, 2020 = (2 + 2 + 4 + 2 + 0 + 2 + 0) = (`-**12**)!!!~'

(**35** (-) **12**) = (`-**23**) = -**a PROPHETIC #** `-**NUMBER!!!~**'

`-**BIRTHDAY; and,** `-**DEATH/DAY!!!~**':

(**826** + **224**) = (`-**1050**)!!!~'

(**826** (-) **224**) = (`-**602**)!!!~'

(1050 + 602) = (`-**1652**) = (16 + 52) = (`-**68**) = "The `-**MARK**"!!!~'

(1050 (-) 602) = (`-**448**) = (48 (-) 4) = (`-**44**) = `-**DAY** of `-**DEATH** (`-**24**) (+) `-**YEAR** of `-**DEATH** (`-**20**) = (24 + 20) = (`-**44**)!!!~'

AUGUST 26 (**BIRTH**) + FEBRUARY 24 (**DEATH**) = (8 + 26 + 2 + 24) = (`-**60**)!!!~'

`-**ADD** `-**DAY** of `-**BIRTH** (`-**26**) to `-**DAY** of `-**DEATH** (`-**24**) = (`-**50**)!!!~'

(60 + 50) = (`-**110**) = "**SWIPE** (`-**1**)" = (`-**101**) = "**AGE** of `-**DEATH** for AMERICAN MATHEMATICIAN KATHERINE COLEMAN GOBLE JOHNSON (`-**101**)"!!!~'

`-**BIRTH** MONTH (`-**8**) (**/**) **DIVIDED by** (**/**) `-**DEATH** MONTH (`-**2**) = (`-**4**) + (19 + 18) = (`-**41**) (+) (`-**60**) = (`-**101**) = "**AGE** of `-**DEATH** for AMERICAN MATHEMATICIAN KATHERINE COLEMAN GOBLE JOHNSON (`-**101**)"!!!~'

`-**DIED** in (`-**2**) & was `-**BORN** in (`-**8**) = (`-**2/8**) = (`-**28**) = RECIPROCAL (MIRROR) = (`-**82**) = (82 + 28) = (`-**110**) = "**SWIPE** (`-**1**)" = (`-**101**) = "**AGE** of `-**DEATH** for AMERICAN MATHEMATICIAN KATHERINE COLEMAN GOBLE JOHNSON (`-**101**)"!!!~'

`-**DIED** in (`-**2**) & was `-**BORN** in (`-**8**) = (`-**2/8**) = (`-**28**) = RECIPROCAL (MIRROR) = (`-**82**) = SHE DIED (`-**182**) DAYS AFTER HER LAST BIRTHDAY!!!~'

KATHERINE COLEMAN GOBLE JOHNSON'S `-**DAUGHTER** CONSTANCE GOBLE'S `-**BIRTHDAY** # `-**NUMBER** = (4/27/1943) = (4 + 27 + 19 + 43) = (`-**93**)!!!~'

KATHERINE COLEMAN GOBLE JOHNSON'S '-**DAUGHTER** CONSTANCE GOBLE'S '-**DEATH/DAY** # '-**NUMBER** = (5/4/2010) = (5 + 4 + 20 + 10) = ('-**39**)!!!~'

('-**39**) = RECIPROCAL (MIRROR) = ('-**93**)!!!~'

KATHERINE COLEMAN GOBLE JOHNSON '-**MARRIED** CONSTANCE GOBLE'S '-**FATHER** (JAMES FRANCIS GOBLE) in ('-1**939**)!!!~'

KATHERINE COLEMAN GOBLE JOHNSON'S '-**DAUGHTER** = '-**RECIPROCAL'S** in '-**LIFE**; and, in '-**DEATH!!!**~'

KATHERINE COLEMAN GOBLE JOHNSON'S '-**DAUGHTER** (CONSTANCE GOBLE) was '-BORN in ('-**43**)!!!~' THE '-**DIFFERENCE** BETWEEN **DEATH/DAY**; and, '-**BIRTHDAY** is ('-**7**) DAYS!!!~' ('-**3**) from '-**APRIL**; and, ('-**4**) from '-**MAY!!!**~'

('-**34**) = RECIPROCAL (MIRROR) = ('-**43**)!!!~'

KATHERINE COLEMAN GOBLE JOHNSON'S '-**DAUGTHER** CONSTANCE GOBLE'S '-**FATHER** (JAMES FRANCIS GOBLE) '-**DIED** at the '-**AGE** of ('-**43**) = '-**DAUGHTER** '-**BORN** in ('-**43**)!!!~' (43 + 43) = ('-**86**) = RECIPROCAL (MIRROR) = ('-**68**) = "The '-**MARK**"!!!~'

KATHERINE COLEMAN GOBLE JOHNSON'S '-**DAUGHTER** (CONSTANCE GOBLE) '-**DIED** in (**MAY**) = ('-**5**); and, WAS '-**BORN** in (**APRIL**) = ('-**4**) = ('-**DEATH/DAY**) = ('-**54**) = **MAY** (**4**[th])!!!~' SHE '-**DIED** at the '-**AGE** of ('-**67**)!!!~' CONSTANCE'S '-**AGE** of '-**DEATH** ('-**67**) '-**PLUS** '-HER '-**FATHER'S** '-**AGE** of '-**DEATH** ('-**43**) = ('-**110**) = "SWIPE ('-**1**)" = ('-**101**) = "**AGE of** '-**DEATH** for AMERICAN MATHEMATICIAN KATHERINE COLEMAN GOBLE JOHNSON ('-**101**)"!!!~'

KATHERINE COLEMAN GOBLE JOHNSON'S `-**DAUGHTER** (CONSTANCE GOBLE) `-**BIRTH** = *APRIL 27th* / *MAY 4th* = `-**DEATH**

(4 (7 (-) 2) /|\ (54)

(**45**) /|\ (**54**)

(`-**45**) = RECIPROCAL (MIRROR) = (`-**54**)!!!~'

`-**RECIPROCALS**-`!!!~'

KATHERINE COLEMAN GOBLE JOHNSON'S (`-**1**st HUSBAND) (JAMES FRANCIS GOBLE'S) `-**BIRTHDAY** # `-**NUMBER** = (3/29/1913) = (3 + 29 + 19 + 13) = (`-**64**)!!!~'

`-**BIRTHDAY** = (3/29) = (3 + 29) = (`-**32**) = -a PROPHETIC # `-**NUMBER**!!!~'

`-**1913** = (19 + 13) = (`-**32**) = -a PROPHETIC # `-**NUMBER**!!!~'

(**2** x **32**) = (`-**64**)!!!~'

KATHERINE COLEMAN GOBLE JOHNSON'S `-**DEATH/ DAY** = (FEBRUARY 24th, 2020) = (24 + 20 + 20) = (`-**64**)!!!~'

KATHERINE COLEMAN GOBLE JOHNSON'S (`-**1**st HUSBAND) (JAMES FRANCIS GOBLE'S) `-**DEATH/DAY** # `-**NUMBER** = (12/20/1956) = (12 + 20 + 19 + 56) = (`-**107**)!!!~'

`-**DEATH/DAY** = (12/20) = (12 + 20) = (`-**32**) = -a PROPHETIC # `-**NUMBER**!!!~'

(107 (-) 64) = (`-**43**) = "**AGE** of `-**DEATH** for **KATHERINE COLEMAN GOBLE JOHNSON'S** (`-**1ˢᵗ HUSBAND**) **(JAMES FRANCIS GOBLE)**"!!!~'

(`-**1956**) = (19 + 56) = (`-**75**) = RECIPROCAL (MIRROR) = (`-**57**)!!!~'

(75 + 57) = (`-**132**) = (32 x 1) = (`-**32**) = -a PROPHETIC # `-NUMBER!!!~'

`-A `-PATTERN in `-DEATHS!!!~'

`-FOUNDING `-FATHER = BENJAMIN FRANKLIN'S `-**BIRTHDAY** = (1/**17**/**17**06); and, `-**DEATH/DAY** = (4/**17**/**17**90)!!!~' (4 x 17) = (`-**68**) = "**The** `-**MARK**"!!!~' `-HE `-**DIED** (`-**90**) **DAYS** after `-**HIS** `-**LAST** `-**BIRTHDAY** = `-**HE** `-**DIED** in (`-**90**)!!!~' (`-**417**) = (47 x 1) = (`-**47**) = RECIPROCAL (MIRROR) = (`-**74**) = **(JULY 4ᵗʰ)**!!!~'

`-FOUNDING `-FATHER = ALEXANDER HAMILTON'S `-**BIRTHDAY** = (**1/11**/`-**55**; or, `-**57**); and, `-**DEATH/DAY** = (7/12/1804)!!!~' "(`-**1804**) was a `-**LEAP** `-**YEAR**"!!!~' `-HE `-**DIED** (`-**184**) **DAYS** before `-**HIS** `-**NEXT** `-**BIRTHDAY** = `-**HE** `-**DIED** in (`-**1804**)!!!~'

#1-PRESIDENT = GEORGE WASHINGTON'S `-**BIRTHDAY** = (2/22/1732); and, `-DEATH/DAY = (**12/14**/1799)!!!~' (12 x 14) = (`-**168**) = "**The** `-**MARK**"!!!~' `-HE `-**DIED** (`-**70**) **DAYS** before `-**HIS** `-**NEXT** `-**BIRTHDAY** = `-**HIS** `-**WIFE** FIRST LADY MARTHA WASHINGTON `-**DIED** at the `-**AGE** of (`-**70**)!!!~'

#2-PRESIDENT = JOHN ADAMS' `-**BIRTHDAY** = (10/30/17**35**); and, `-DEATH/DAY = (7/4/1826)!!!~' `-HE `-**DIED** (`-**118**) **DAYS** before `-HIS `-**NEXT** `-**BIRTHDAY** = `-**DEATH/YEAR** = (`-**1735**) = (35 (-) 17) = (`-**18**)!!!~' (365 (-) 118) = (`-**247**) = RECIPROCAL (MIRROR) = (`-**742**) = `-**DEATH/DAY** & `-**DEATH/TIME** = (`-**2PM/PACIFIC TIME**)!!!~'

#3-PRESIDENT = THOMAS JEFFERSON'S `-**BIRTHDAY** = (**4**/13/17**43**); and, `-DEATH/DAY = (**7**/**4**/18**26**)!!!~' (**43** + **43**) = (`-**86**) = RECIPROCAL (MIRROR) = (`-**68**) = "The `-**MARK**"!!!~' `-HE `-**DIED** (`-**82**) **DAYS** after `-HIS `-**LAST** `-**BIRTHDAY** = `-**BIRTH/YEAR** & `-**DEATH/YEAR** = (`-17**43**) /|\ (`-18**26**)!!!~' FROM `-ABOVE (**NOT in** `-**BOLD**) = (1 + 17 + 16) = (`-**34**) = RECIPROCAL (MIRROR) = (`-**43**)!!!~' FROM `-MIDDLE (**NOT in** `-**BOLD**) = (36 + 11) = (`-**47**) = RECIPROCAL (MIRROR) = (`-**74**) = "**DAY** of `-**DEATH**"!!!~' (365 (-) 82) = (`-**283**) = "(2$^{nd}$) PRESIDENT to `-**DIE** on that `-**DAY** at the `-**AGE** of (`-**83**)"; while, **DYING** before #2-PRESIDENT JOHN ADAMS at the `-**AGE** of (`-**90**)!!!~' (90 + 83) = (`-**173**) = (73 x 1) = (`-**73**) = "**AGE** of `-**DEATH** of `-**NEXT** `-**PRESIDENT** to `-**DIE** on (`-JULY 4th) = #5-PRESIDENT JAMES MONROE!!!~'

#4-PRESIDENT = JAMES MADISON'S `-**BIRTHDAY** = (3/**16**/1751); and, `-**DEATH/DAY** = (**6**/28/1836)!!!~' `-**BIRTH/ YEAR** (`-**1751**) = (17 + 51) = (`-**68**) = "The `-**MARK**"!!!~' `-**DEATH/ DAY** = (6 x 28) = (`-**168**) = "The `-**MARK**"!!!~' `-HE `-**DIED** (`-**104**) **DAYS** after `-HIS `-**LAST** `-**BIRTHDAY**!!!~' (365 (-) 104) = (`-**261**)!!!~' `-**BIRTHDAY** = (3 x 16) = (`-**48**)!!!~' `-**BIRTHDAY** (`-**48**) **PLUS** (**+**) **DEATH/DAY** (`-**168**) = (`-**216**) = "SWIPE (`-**1**)" = (`-**261**)!!!~'

#5-PRESIDENT = JAMES MONROE `-**BIRTHDAY** = (4/28/1758); and, `-**DEATH/DAY** = (**7**/**4**/1831)!!!~' `-HE `-**DIED** (`-**67**) **DAYS** after `-HIS `-**LAST** `-**BIRTHDAY**!!!~' (`-**67**) = RECIPROCAL

(MIRROR) = (`-<u>76</u>) = (`-17<u>76</u>) = `-INDEPENDENCE `-DAY!!!~'
`-<u>BIRTHDAY</u> = (4/28) = (4 + 28) = (`-<u>32</u>) = -a PROPHETIC #
`-NUMBER!!!~' `-BIRTHDAY # `-NUMBER = (4 + 28 + 17 +
58) = (`-<u>107</u>)!!!~' `-DEATH/DAY # `-NUMBER = (7 + 4 + 18 +
31) = (`-<u>60</u>)!!!~' (107 (-) 60) = (`-<u>47</u>) = RECIPROCAL (MIRROR)
= (`-<u>74</u>) = "<u>JULY 4</u><sup>th</sup>" = `-<u>DAY</u> of `-<u>DEATH</u>!!!~'

<u>#6</u>-PRESIDENT = JOHN QUINCY ADAMS' `-<u>BIRTHDAY</u> =
(7/11/1<u>767</u>); and, `-DEATH/DAY = (2/<u>23</u>/1<u>848</u>)!!!~' "(`-<u>1848</u>) was
a `-<u>LEAP</u> `-<u>YEAR</u>"!!!~' `-HE `-<u>DIED</u> (`-<u>139</u>) DAYS before `-HIS
`-<u>NEXT</u> `-<u>BIRTHDAY</u>!!!~' `-<u>BIRTHDAY</u> # `-NUMBER = (7 + 11
+ 17 + 67) = (`-<u>102</u>) /|\ `-<u>DEATH/DAY</u> # `-NUMBER = (2 + 23 +
18 + 48) = (`-<u>91</u>) /|\ (102 + 91) = `-<u>193</u>!~' (`-<u>93</u>) = RECIPROCAL
(MIRROR) = (`-<u>39</u>)!!!~'

<u>#7</u>-PRESIDENT = ANDREW JACKSON'S `-<u>BIRTHDAY</u> =
(3/15/1<u>767</u>); and, `-<u>DEATH/DAY</u> = (<u>6/8</u>/1<u>845</u>)!!!~' (`-<u>68</u>) = "The
`-<u>MARK</u>"!!!~' `-HE `-<u>DIED</u> (`-<u>85</u>) <u>DAYS</u> after `-HIS `-<u>LAST</u>
`-<u>BIRTHDAY</u>!!!~' RACHEL JACKSON (ANDREW JACKSON'S
WIFE) that `-<u>DIED</u> at the `-<u>AGE</u> of (`-<u>61</u>) = `-<u>BIRTHDAY</u> #
`-NUMBER = (6 + 15 + 17 + 67) = (`-<u>105</u>) /|\ `-<u>DEATH/DAY</u> #
`-NUMBER = (12 + 22 + 18 + 28) = (`-<u>80</u>) /|\ (105 + 80) = `-<u>185</u>!~'
(`-<u>185</u>) = (85 x 1) = (`-<u>85</u>) = "<u>DAYS</u> PAST `-<u>BIRTHDAY</u> until
`-<u>HIS</u> `-<u>DEATH</u>"!!!~'

<u>#8</u>-PRESIDENT = MARTIN VAN BUREN'S `-<u>BIRTHDAY</u>
= (12/5/1782); and, `-<u>DEATH/DAY</u> = (<u>7/24</u>/1862)!!!~' (7 x 24)
= (`-<u>168</u>) = "The `-<u>MARK</u>"!!!~' `-HE `-<u>DIED</u> (`-<u>134</u>) <u>DAYS</u>
before `-HIS `-<u>NEXT</u> `-<u>BIRTHDAY</u>!!!~' `-<u>BIRTHDAY</u> (`-<u>12</u>/`-
<u>5</u>) & `-<u>BIRTH/CENTURY</u> (`-<u>17</u>) = (12 + 5 + 17) = (`-<u>34</u>)!!!~'
(365 (-) <u>134</u>) = (`-<u>231</u>) = (23 x 1) = (`-<u>23</u>) = -a PROPHETIC #
`-NUMBER!!!~'

#9-PRESIDENT = WILLIAM HENRY HARRISON'S `-**BIRTHDAY** = (2/9/1773); and, `-**DEATH/DAY** = (4/4/1841)!!!~' `-**DIED** at the `-**AGE** of (`-**68**) = "The `-**MARK**"!!!~' `-HE `-**DIED** (`-**54**) **DAYS** after `-HIS `-last `-**BIRTHDAY**!!!~' (5 + 4) = (`-**9**ᵗʰ) **PRESIDENT of the UNITED STATES of AMERICA;** although, **IT** was **ONLY** for (`-**31**) **DAYS** being THE (**1**ˢᵗ) **PRESIDENT** to `-**DIE** in `-**OFFICE**!!!~' (`-**31**) = RECIPROCAL (MIRROR) = (`-**13**) = **"A VERY PIVOTAL #** `-**NUMBER**"!!!~' (365 (-) **54**) = (`-**311**) = (31 x 1) = (`-**31**) = `-**DAYS** in `-**OFFICE**!!!~' `-BORN FEBRUARY 9ᵗʰ, 1773 /|\ `-DIED **APRIL 4**ᵗʰ, 1841 /|\ `-BIRTHDAY # `-NUMBER = (2 + 9 + 17 + 73) = `-**101** /|\ (**4** + **4** + 18 + **41**) = `-**67** /|\ (101 + 67) = `-**168** = "The `-**MARK**"!!!~' (101 (-) 67) = (`-**34**) = **"The `-PRESIDENTIAL #** `-**NUMBERS**"!!!~'

#10-PRESIDENT = JOHN TYLER'S `-**BIRTHDAY** = (3/29/1790); and, `-**DEATH/DAY** = (1/18/1862)!!!~' `-HE `-**DIED** (`-**70**) **DAYS** before `-HIS `-**NEXT** `-**BIRTHDAY**!!!~' `-HIS `-**AGE** of `-**DEATH** was (`-**71**) = **"WOULD** `-**EQUAL;** if `-**IT** were a `-**LEAP** `-**YEAR** (`-**70**)"!!!~'

#11-PRESIDENT = JAMES K. POLK'S `-**BIRTHDAY** = (11/2/1795); and, `-**DEATH/DAY** = (6/15/1849)!!!~' `-HE `-**DIED** (`-**140**) **DAYS** before `-HIS `-**NEXT** `-**BIRTHDAY**!!!~' #11-PRESIDENT JAMES K. POLK `-**DIED** at the `-**AGE** of (`-**53**); and, `-HIS `-WIFE FIRST LADY SARAH CHILDRESS POLK `-**DIED** at the `-**AGE** of (`-**87**)!!!~' (87 + 53) = (`-**140**)!!!~' **SHE** `-**DIED** on (`-**AUGUST 14**ᵗʰ)!!!~'

#12-PRESIDENT = ZACHARY TAYLOR'S `-**BIRTHDAY** = (11/24/1784); and, `-**DEATH/DAY** = (7/9/**1850**)!!!~' `-**DEATH/ YEAR** = (`-**1850**) = (18 + 50) = (`-**68**) = "The `-**MARK**"!!!~' `-HE `-**DIED** (`-**138**) **DAYS** before `-HIS `-**NEXT** `-**BIRTHDAY**!!!~' `-HIS `-WIFE FIRST LADY MARGARET TAYLOR POLK

`-**DIED** (`-**38**) **DAYS** before `-**HER** `-**NEXT** `-**BIRTHDAY**!!!~'
SHE `-**DIED** on (`-**AUGUST 14**th); `-**TOO**!!!~'

#13-PRESIDENT = MILLARD FILLMORE'S `-**BIRTHDAY** =
(1/7/1800); and, `-**DEATH/DAY** = (**3/8**/1874)!!!~' `-**DEATH/DAY** =
(`-**3/8**) = "**SEE** `-**PRESIDENT** (`-**#12**) **ABOVE**"!!!~' `-HE `-**DIED**
(`-**60**) **DAYS** after `-**HIS** `-**LAST** `-**BIRTHDAY**!!!~' (365 (-) 60) =
(`-**305**) = (35 + 0) = (`-**35**) = RECIPROCAL (MIRROR) = (`-**53**) =
FIRST LADY ABIGAIL FILLMORE `-**DIED** in the `-**MONTH**
`-**SHE** was `-**BORN** & `-**DIED** within; which was (`-**1953**)!!!~'
THEY `-**both** `-**DIED** in the `-**MONTH** of `-**MARCH**!!!~' **SHE** on
the (`-**13**<sup>th</sup>) was `-**BORN**!!!~' HE `-**DIED** on the (`-**8**th); and, `-**SHE**
`-**DIED** on the (`-**30**th)!!!~' (`-**38**) = RECIPROCAL (MIRROR) =
(`-**83**)!!!~'

#14-PRESIDENT = FRANKLIN PIERCE `-**BIRTHDAY** =
(11/23/1804); and, `-**DEATH/DAY** = (10/8/1869)!!!~' `-HE `-**DIED**
(`-**46**) **DAYS** before `-**HIS** `-**NEXT** `-**BIRTHDAY** at the `-AGE
of (`-**64**)!!!~' (`-**64**) = RECIPROCAL (MIRROR) = (`-**46**)!!!~'
`-BIRTHDAY # `-NUMBER = (11 + 23 + 18 + 04) = (`-**56**)!!!~'
FIRST LADY JANE PIERCE **BIRTHDAY #** `-**NUMBER** = (3
+ 12 + 18 + 06) = (`-**39**)!!!~' `-**DEATH/DAY #** `-**NUMBER** = (12
+ 2 + 18 + 63) = (`-**95**)!!!~' (95 (-) 39) = (`-**56**)!!!~' **HUSBAND**;
and, **WIFE** `-*LINKED* `-*TOGETHER* in `-**TIME** (`-**56**)!!!~' (`-
56) = RECIPROCAL (MIRROR) = (`-**65**)!!!~' #14-PRESIDENT
FRANKLIN PIERCE `-**DIED** within `-HIS (`-**65**th) YEAR of
`-EXISTENCE; while, `-HIS `-**WIFE** `-**DIED** (`-2**65**) **DAYS AWAY**
from `-**HER** `-**BIRTHDAY**!!!~'

#15-PRESIDENT = JAMES BUCHANAN'S `-**BIRTHDAY** =
(4/23/1791); and, `-**DEATH/DAY** = (6/1/1**868**)!!!~' `-**BIRTH/
YEAR** (`-1**868**) = "The `-**MARK**"!!!~' `-HE `-**DIED** (`-**39**) **DAYS**
after `-**HIS** `-**LAST** `-**BIRTHDAY**!!!~' (`-**39**) = RECIPROCAL
(MIRROR) = (`-**93**)!!!~' FORMER FIRST LADY HARRIET

LANE (**NIECE**) of the `-BACHELOR #15-PRESIDENT JAMES BUCHANAN `-**DIED** in (`-19**03**) = (93 x 1 + 0) = (`-**93**)!!!~'

#**16**-PRESIDENT = ABRAHAM LINCOLN'S `-**BIRTHDAY** = (2/12/1809); and, `-**DEATH/DAY** = (4/15/18**65**)!!!~' `-**DIED in** (`-**65**) **at the** `-**AGE of** (`-**56**)!!!~' (`-**65**) = RECIPROCAL (MIRROR) = (`-**56**)!!!~' `-HE `-**DIED** (`-**62**) **DAYS** after `-HIS `-**LAST** `-**BIRTHDAY**!!!~' (`-**61**) DAYS (LIE-IN-BETWEEN)!!!~' `-BORN FEBRUARY 12th, 1809 /|\ `-DIED APRIL 15th, 18**65** /|\ (2 + 12 + 18 + 09) = `-**41** /|\ (4 + 15 + 18 + **65**) = `-**102** /|\ (102 (-) 41) = (`-**61**) = **JUNE 1st** = #**15**-PRESIDENT = JAMES BUCHANAN'S `-**DEATH/DAY** # `-**NUMBER**!!!~'

#**17**-PRESIDENT = ANDREW JOHNSON'S `-**BIRTHDAY** = (12/29/1808); and, `-**DEATH/DAY** = (7/31/1875)!!!~' `-HE `-**DIED** (`-**151**) **DAYS** before `-HIS `-**NEXT** `-**BIRTHDAY**!!!~' *14th, 15th, `-16th & 18th* `-PRESIDENTS (`-**161**)!!!~' (365 (-) 151) = (`-**214**) = (24 (-) 1) = (`-**23**) = -a PROPHETIC # `-**NUMBER**!!!~' FIRST LADY ELIZA McCARDLE JOHNSON `-**DIED** (`-**103**) **DAYS** after `-HER `-**LAST** `-**BIRTHDAY**!!!~' (`-**103**) = (13 + 0) = (`-**13**) = "A VERY PIVOTAL # NUMBER"!!!~' SHE `-**DIED** at the `-**AGE** of (`-**65**) = #**16** PRESIDENT /|\ & /|\ #**14** PRESIDENT!!!~'

#**18**-PRESIDENT = ULYSSES S. GRANT'S `-**BIRTHDAY** = (4/27/1822); and, `-**DEATH/DAY** = (7/**23**/1885)!!!~' `-HE `-**DIED** (`-**87**) **DAYS** after `-HIS `-**LAST** `-**BIRTHDAY**!!!~' (8 x 7) = (`-**56**) = #**16** PRESIDENT /|\ & /|\ #**14** PRESIDENT!!!~' `-BORN APRIL 27th, 1822 /|\ `-DIED JULY **23**rd, 1885 /|\ (4 + 27 + 18 + 22) = `-**71** /|\ (7 + **23** + 18 + 85) = `-**133** /|\ (133 + 71) = `-**204** = (24 + 0) = (`-**24**) = #*17th* PRESIDENT in `-DAYS after `-DEATH (`-**214**) = (24 x 1) = (`-**24**)!!!~'

#**19**-PRESIDENT = RUTHERFORD B. HAYES' `-**BIRTHDAY** = (10/4/1822); and, `-**DEATH/DAY** = (1/17/1893)!!!~' `-HE

`-**DIED** (`-**105**) **DAYS** after `-**HIS** `-**LAST** `-**BIRTHDAY**!!!~' (`-**105**) = (**10/5**) = OCTOBER 5th = "**DAY** after `-**BIRTHDAY**"!!!~' `-`-**BIRTHDAY** = (10/4) + `-**DEATH/DAY** (1/17) = (10 + 4 + 1 + 17) = (`-**32**) = -a PROPHETIC # `-**NUMBER**!!!~' BORN OCTOBER 4th, 1822 /|\ `-DIED JANUARY 17$^{th}$, 18**93** /|\ 10 + 4 + 18 + 22) = `-**54** /|\ (1 + 17 + 18 + **93**) = `-**129** /|\ (129 + 54 = (`-**183**) = RECIPROCAL (MIRROR) = `-**DEATH/DAY** # `-**NUMBER** of **FIRST LADY LUCY WEBB HAYES** = (6 + 25 + 18 + 89) = (`-**138**)!!!~'

#20-PRESIDENT = JAMES A. GARFIELD'S `-**BIRTHDAY** = (11/19/1831); and, `-**DEATH/DAY** = (**9/19**/1881)!!!~' `-HE `-**DIED** (`-**61**) **DAYS** before `-**HIS** `-**NEXT** `-**BIRTHDAY**!!!~' (365 (-) 61) = (`-**304**) = (34 + 0) = (`-**34**)!!!~' FORMER FIRST LADY LUCRETIA GARFIELD `-**DIED** ON (`-**314**) = (34 x 1) = (`-**34**)!!!~' `-BORN on a (`-**19$^{th}$**); AND, `-DIED on a (`-**19$^{th}$**) JUST LIKE BENJAMIN FRANKLIN was `-BORN on a (`-**17$^{th}$**); AND, `-DIED on a (`-**17$^{th}$**)!!!~' (`-**19**) = RECIPROCAL (MIRROR) = (`-**91**)!!!~' (`-**91**) = "FLIP the (`-**9**) OVER to a (`-**6**) = (`-**61**)!!!~' `-BORN NOVEMBER 19th, 1831 /|\ `-DIED SEPTEMBER 19$^{th}$, 1881 /|\ (11 + 19 + 18 + 31) = `-**79** /|\ (9 + 19 + 18 + 81) = `-**127** /|\ (**127** (-) **79**) = `-**48** = (4 x 8) = (`-**32**) = -a PROPHETIC # NUMBER!!!~' FIRST LADY LUCRETIA GARFIELD was `-BORN in (`-**1832**)!!!~' **LUCRETIA GARFIELD** (WIFE of JAMES A. GARFIELD) that `-**DIED** at the `-**AGE** of (`-**85**) = `-**BIRTHDAY** # `-**NUMBER** = (4 + 19 + 18 + 32) = (`-**73**) /|\ `-**DEATH/DAY** # `-**NUMBER** = (3 + 14 + 19 + 18) = (`-**54**) /|\ (73 + 54) = `-**127** = `-**DEATH/DAY** # `-**NUMBER** of #20-PRESIDENT JAMES A. GARFIELD (`-**127**)!!!~' **HUSBAND**; and, **WIFE** `-*LINKED* `-*TOGETHER* in `-**TIME** by (`-**127**)!!!~' PRESIDENT `-**AGE** of `-**DEATH** (`-**49**); and, FIRST LADY (`-**85**) `-**ADDED** `-**UP** = (`-**134**) = (34 x 1) = (`-**34**) = "The `-**PRESIDENTIAL** # `-**NUMBERS**"!!!~' (85 (-) **49**) = (`-**36**) = (4 x 9) = "The PATTERN of # `-**NUMBERS**"!!!~'

FIRST LADY LUCRETIA GARFIELD '-**DIED** ('-**36**) **DAYS** before '-**HER** '-**NEXT** '-**BIRTHDAY!!!~'**

#21-PRESIDENT = CHESTER A. ARTHUR'S '-**BIRTHDAY** = (10/5/1829); and, '-**DEATH/DAY** = (11/18/18**86**)!!!~' '-**BIRTH/ YEAR** ('-**86**) = RECIPROCAL (MIRROR) = ('-**68**) = "The '-**MARK**"!!!~' '-HE '-**DIED** ('-**44**) **DAYS** after '-HIS '-**LAST** '-**BIRTHDAY!!!~'** (365 (-) **44**) = ('-**321**) = (32 x 1) = ('-**32**) = -a PROPHETIC # '-**NUMBER!!!~'** '-BORN OCTOBER 5th, 1829 /|\ '-DIED NOVEMBER 18th, 18**86** /|\ (10 + 5 + 18 + 29) = '-**62** /|\ (11 + 18 + 18 + **86**) = '-**133** /|\ (133 (-) 62) = '-**71** = **#18**-PRESIDENT = ULYSSES S. GRANT'S **BIRTHDAY** # '-**NUMBER** ('-**71**)!!!~' #21-PRESIDENT CHESTER A. ARTHUR'S WIFE (NELL ARTHUR) '-**DIED** ('-**230**) DAYS before '-**HER** '-**NEXT** '-**BIRTHDAY!!!~'** ('-230) = (23 + 0) = ('-**23**) = RECIPROCAL (MIRROR) = ('-**32**)!!!~' **HUSBAND**; and, **WIFE** '-*LINKED* '-*TOGETHER* in '-**TIME** by ('-**23/32**) **DYING** from '-**BIRTHDAYS!!!~'**

#22/#24-PRESIDENT = GROVER CLEVELAND'S '-**BIRTHDAY** = (3/18/18**37**); and, '-**DEATH/DAY** = (6/24/19**08**)!!!~' '-HE '-**DIED** ('-**98**) **DAYS** after '-HIS '-**LAST** '-**BIRTHDAY!!!~'** **DIED** in ('-19**08**) = (98 x 1 + 0) = ('-**98**)!!!~' FIRST LADY FRANCES CLEVELAND '-**DIED** at the '-**AGE** of ('-**83**) = RECIPROCAL (MIRROR) = ('-**38**)!!!~' '-BORN MARCH 18th, 18**37** /|\ '-DIED JUNE 24th, **1908** /|\ '-BORN in ('-**37**) with **#36**-PRESIDENT LYNDON B. JOHNSON BEING '-BORN in ('-**1908**); AND, '-DYING in ('-19**73**)!!!~' '-As #22/#24-PRESIDENT GROVER CLEVELAND '-DIED in ('-**1908**)!!!~' (**RECIPROCAL-INVERSED-REALITIES**)!!!~' ('-**37**) = RECIPROCAL (MIRROR) = ('-**73**)!!!~' BIRTHDAY # '-**NUMBER** = (3 + 18 + 18 + **37**) = '-**76** /|\ DEATH/DAY # '-**NUMBER** = (6 + 24 + 19 + 08) = '-**57**!!!~' **DEATH/DAY** # '-**NUMBER**; and, **BIRTHDAY** # '-**NUMBER** are '-ALMOST

`-**RECIPROCALS** of `-**EACH** `-**OTHER**!!!~' (**57/76**) = FIRST LADY FRANCES CLEVELAND was `-**MARRIED** to GROVER CLEVELAND for (`-**22**) YEARS; and, then `-HER (**2**nd) `-**HUSBAND** for (`-**34**) `-**YEARS** = (22 + 34) = (`-**56**)!!!~' #18; and, **#21 PRESIDENTS** (`-**71**) with **#22/#24**-PRESIDENT GROVER CLEVELAND `-**DYING** at the `-**AGE** of (`-**71**)!!!~'

#23-PRESIDENT = BENJAMIN HARRISON'S `-**BIRTHDAY** = (8/20/18**33**); and, `-**DEATH/DAY** = (**3**/**13**/1901)!!!~' `-HE `-**DIED** (`-**160**) **DAYS** before `-**HIS** `-**NEXT** `-**BIRTHDAY**!!!~' `-HIS `-**BIRTHDAY** was on (**8/20**) = (8 x 20) = (`-**160**)!!!~' FIRST LADY CAROLINE HARRISON `-**DIED** at the `-**AGE** of (`-**60**)!!!~' `-BORN AUGUST 20th, 18**33** /|\ `-DIED **MARCH** 13th, 1901 /|\ (8 + 20 + 18 + **33**) = `-**79** /|\ (**3** + **13** + 19 + 01) = `-**36** /|\ (79 (-) 36) = `-**43** = RECIPROCAL (MIRROR) = (`-**34**) = FIRST LADY CAROLINE HARRISON `-**DIED** (`-**341**) = (34 x 1) = (`-**34**) DAYS AWAY from `-**HER** `-**BIRTHDAY**!!!~' (`-**341**) = (41 x 3) = (`-**123**) = (23 x 1) = (`-**23**) = -a PROPHETIC # `-**NUMBER**"!!!~' "The `-**PRESIDENTIAL** # `-**NUMBERS**"!!!~' (`-**16**) = RECIPROCAL (MIRROR) = (`-**61**)!!!~' FIRST LADY CAROLINE HARRISON'S `-**BIRTHDAY** # `-**NUMBER** = (10 + 1 + 18 + 32) = (`-**61**) = "The # `-**NUMBER** of `-**PRESIDENTS**"!!!~'

#25-PRESIDENT = WILLIAM MCKINLEY `-**BIRTHDAY** = (1/29/18**43**); and, `-**DEATH/DAY** = (**9**/**14**/1901)!!!~' (9 + 14) = (`-**23**) = -a PROPHETIC # `-**NUMBER**"!!!~' `-HE `-**DIED** (`-**137**) **DAYS** before `-**HIS** `-**NEXT** `-**BIRTHDAY**!!!~' (`-**137**) = (13 x 7) = (`-**91**) = **DIED** in (`-**1901**) = (19 x 1 + 0) = (`-**91**) = #25-PRESIDENT WILLIAM MCKINLEY'S `-**BIRTHDAY** # `-**NUMBER** (`-**91**)!!!~' `-BORN JANUARY 29th, 18**43** /|\ `-DIED SEPTEMBER 14th, 1901 /|\ (1 + 29 + 18 + **43**) = `-**91** /|\ (9 + 14 + 19 + 01) = `-**43** /|\ (91 + **43**) = (`-**134**) = (34 x 1) = (`-**34**) = "The `-**PRESIDENTIAL** # `-**NUMBERS**"!!!~' `-**DEATH/DAY** # `-**NUMBER** was (`-**43**); AND, `-**HE** was `-**BORN** in (`-**43**)!!!~'

#25-PRESIDENT WILLIAM MCKINLEY `-**DIED** at the `-**AGE** of (`-**58**)!!!~' FIRST LADY IDA SAXTON MCKINLEY had `-**DIED** (`-**5**) DAYS in `-**MAY**; and, (`-**8**) DAYS in `-**JUNE** in-between HER `-**BIRTHDAY**; and, `-**DEATH/DAY**!!!~' FIRST LADY IDA SAXTON MCKINLEY was `-born ON (**6/8**) = "**The** `-**MARK**"!!!~' FIRST LADY IDA SAXTON MCKINLEY `-DIED at the `-AGE of (`-**59**)!!!~'

#**26**-PRESIDENT = THEODORE ROOSEVELT'S `-**BIRTHDAY** = (10/27/1**858**); and, `-**DEATH/DAY** = (1/6/1**919**)!!!~' `-HE `-**DIED** (`-**71**) **DAYS** after `-HIS `-**LAST** `-**BIRTHDAY**!!!~' LOOK at THE `-**PREVIOUS** `-**PRESIDENTS** with the # `-**NUMBER** (`-**71**)!!!~' `-BORN OCTOBER 27th, 1**858** /|\ `-DIED JANUARY 6th, 1**919** /|\ (10 + 27 + 18 + 58) = `-**113** /|\ (1 + 6 + 19 + 19) = `-**45** /|\ (113 (-) 45) = (`-**68**) = "The `-**MARK**"!!!~' #**20**-PRESIDENT = JAMES A. GARFIELD `-**DAY** of `-**DEATH** (`-**919**) with #**26**-PRESIDENT = THEODORE ROOSEVELT `-**DYING** within (`-1**919**)!!!~' FIRST LADY EDITH ROOSEVELT `-**DIED** at the `-**AGE** of (`-**87**)!!!~' "The `-**MARK**" = (`-**68**) = RECIPROCAL (MIRROR) = (`-**86**)!!!~' HER `-**BIRTHDAY** # `-**NUMBER** = (**8** + **6** + 1**8** + **61**) = (`-**93**) /|\ `-**DEATH/DAY** # `-**NUMBER** = (**9** + **3**0 + 19 + 48) = (`-1**06**) /|\ (106 (-) 93) = `-**13** = "A VERY PIVOTAL # `-**NUMBER**"!!!~' `-**DEATH/DAY** # `-**NUMBER** of EDITH ROOSEVELT (`-1**06**) = (16 + 0) = (`-**16**) = `-**DEATH/DAY** of THEODORE ROOSEVELT (**1/6**)!!!~' HUSBAND; and, **WIFE** `-*LINKED* `-*TOGETHER* in `-**TIME** by (`-**16/61**)!!!~' EDITH also was `-**BORN** in (`-**61**); while **THEODORE** `-**DIED** on (`-**1/6**)!!!~' **SEE** the `-**PROPHET'S** `-**PREVIOUS** `-**BOOK** `-**ENTITLED**: ""`-/|\ **REAL MESSAGES** of `-**GOD I**, **II**; & **III**-!!!~ /|\`'

#**27**-PRESIDENT = WILLIAM HOWARD TAFT'S `-**BIRTHDAY** = (9/15/1857); and, `-**DEATH/DAY** = (3/8/1**930**)!!!~' `-HE `-**DIED** (`-**174**) **DAYS** after `-HIS `-**LAST** `-**BIRTHDAY**!!!~' DEATH/ YEAR (`-1930) (**-**) BIRTH/YEAR (`-1857) = (`-**73**) = (74 (-) 1)

= (`-**73**)!!!-' #**27**-PRESIDENT = WILLIAM HOWARD TAFT had `-**DIED** at the `-**AGE** of (`-**72**)!!!-' (`-**72**) = RECIPROCAL (MIRROR) = (`-**27**)!!!-' `-BORN SEPTEMBER 15th, **1857** /|\ `-DIED MARCH 8th, 1**930** /|\ (9 + 15 + 18 + 57) = `-**99** /|\ (3 + 8 + 19 + 30) = `-**60** /|\ (99 (-) 60) = `-**39**!!!-' BIRTH/YEAR (`-**1857**) = (57 (-) 18) = (`-**39**) = RECIPROCAL (MIRROR) = (`-**93**)!!!-' FIRST LADY HELEN HERRON TAFT was `-**BORN** in (`-**61**); and, `-**DIED** in (`-**43**)!!!-' **SEE** the `-**PROPHET'S** `-**PREVIOUS** `-**BOOK** `-**ENTITLED**: ""`-/|\ **REAL MESSAGES** of `-**GOD I, II; & III**-!!!-' /||'

#**28**-PRESIDENT = WOODROW WILSON'S `-**BIRTHDAY** = (12/28/18**56**); and, `-**DEATH/DAY** = (2/**3**/1924)!!!-' `-HE `-**DIED** (`-**37**) **DAYS** after `-**HIS** `-**LAST** `-**BIRTHDAY**!!!-' SEE the `-other `-PRESIDENTS for the # (`-**37**)!!!-' (`-**37**) = RECIPROCAL (MIRROR) = (`-**73**)!!!-' FIRST LADY EDITH WILSON `-**DIED** (`-**74**) DAYS AFTER `-**HER** `-**BIRTHDAY** with (`-**73**) **DAYS** `-LYING (**in-between**) **THESE** `-**DAYS**!!!-' `-BORN DECEMBER **28**th, 18**56** /|\ `-DIED **FEBRUARY 3**rd, 19**24** /|\ (12 + 28 + 18 + 56) = `-**114** /|\ (2 + 3 + 19 + 24) = `-**48** /|\ (114 + 48) = (`-**162**) = (16 x 2) = (`-**32**) = -a **PROPHETIC # `-NUMBER**"!!!-' *DEATH/YEAR* = (1924 (-) 1856) = *BIRTH/YEAR* = (`-**68**!) = "The `-**MARK**"!!!-' FIRST LADY EDITH WILSON `-**DIED** in (`-**61**); WHILE, FIRST LADY ELLEN AXSON WILSON `-**DIED** on (**8**/**6**) while BEING `-**BORN** in (1**860**)!!!-' **SEE** the `-**PROPHET'S** `-**PREVIOUS** `-**BOOK** `-**ENTITLED**: ""`-/|\ **REAL MESSAGES** of `-**GOD I, II; & III**-!!!-' /||'

WARREN G. HARDING'S **BIRTH/YEAR** = (`-**65**) = RECIPROCAL (MIRROR) = (`-**56**) = WOODROW WILSON'S `-**BIRTH/YEAR**!!!-'

#**29**-PRESIDENT = WARREN G. HARDING'S `-**BIRTHDAY** = (11/**2**/18**65**); and, `-**DEATH/DAY** = (8/**2**/19**23**)!!!-' `-HE `-**DIED**

(`-92) **DAYS** before `-HIS `-<u>**NEXT**</u> `-<u>**BIRTHDAY**</u>!!!~' (`-92) = RECIPROCAL (MIRROR) = (`-29) = (`-29<sup>th</sup> **PRESIDENT**)!!!~' `-BORN NOVEMBER 2nd, 18<u>65</u> /|\ `-DIED AUGUST 2<sup>nd</sup>, 19<u>23</u> /|\ (11 + 2 + 18 + **65**) = `-<u>**96**</u> /|\ (8 + 2 + 19 + **23**) = `-<u>52</u> /|\ (96 + 52) = `-<u>**148**</u> = (48 x 1) = `-<u>48</u> = (4 x 8) = (`-<u>32</u>) = -a PROPHETIC # `-<u>**NUMBER**</u>!!!~' `-BORN on a (<u>2nd</u>); and, `-DIED on a (<u>2<sup>nd</sup></u>)!!!~' SAME `-BIRTHDAY as <u>#11</u>-PRESIDENT = JAMES K. POLK (<u>**11/2**</u>) = (11 x 2) = (`-<u>22</u>) = <u>**2**</u>(<u>**2's**</u>)!!!~' 29<sup>th</sup> PRESIDENT x **2** = (<u>29</u> x **2**) = `-<u>**58**</u>!!!~' (1923 (-) 1865) = `-<u>58</u>!!!~' `-<u>**DEATH/DAY**</u> (8/2); and, `-**DEATH/CENTURY** (19) `-ADDED `-UP = (8 + 2 + 19) = (`-<u>29</u>) = (`-29<sup>th</sup> **PRESIDENT**)!!!~' WITH a `-<u>**DEATH/YEAR**</u> of (`-<u>23</u>) = -a PROPHETIC # `-<u>**NUMBER**</u>!!!~' FIRST LADY FLORENCE HARDING'S `-<u>**BIRTHDAY**</u> = (<u>**8/15**</u>) = (8 + 15) = (`-<u>23</u>)!!!~'

<u>#30</u>-PRESIDENT = CALVIN COOLIDGE `-<u>**BIRTHDAY**</u> = (7/4/1872); and, `-<u>**DEATH/DAY**</u> = (1/5/1933)!!!~' `-HE `-<u>**DIED**</u> (`-<u>185</u>) **DAYS** before `-HIS `-<u>**NEXT**</u> `-<u>**BIRTHDAY**</u>!!!~' (`-<u>85</u>) = RECIPROCAL (MIRROR) = (`-<u>58</u>) = `-<u>**DEATH/DAY**</u> # `-**NUMBER** (`-<u>58</u>)!!!~' `-BORN <u>**JULY**</u> 4th, 1872 /|\ `-DIED JANUARY 5<sup>th</sup>, 19<u>33</u> /|\ (<u>7</u> + **4** + 18 + 72) = `-<u>101</u> /|\ (1 + 5 + 19 + 33) = `-<u>58</u> /|\ (101 (-) 58) = `-<u>43</u> = "The `-<u>**PRESIDENTIAL**</u> # `-**NUMBERS**"!!!~' (<u>43</u> x 2) = `-<u>86</u> = <u>**RECIPROCAL**</u> (<u>**MIRROR**</u>) = `-<u>68</u>! = "The `-<u>**MARK**</u>"!!!~' (1933 (-) 1872) = (`-<u>61</u>)!!!~'

<u>#31</u>-PRESIDENT = HERBERT HOOVER `-<u>**BIRTHDAY**</u> = (8/10/18<u>74</u>); and, `-<u>**DEATH/DAY**</u> = (10/20/19<u>64</u>)!!!~' `-HE `-<u>**DIED**</u> (`-<u>71</u>) **DAYS** before `-HIS `-<u>**NEXT**</u> `-<u>**BIRTHDAY**</u>!!!~' LOOK at THE `-<u>**PREVIOUS**</u> `-<u>**PRESIDENTS**</u> with the # `-<u>**NUMBER**</u> (`-71)!!!~' (`-<u>71</u>) = RECIPROCAL (MIRROR) = (`-<u>17</u>) = FIRST LADY LOU HENRY HOOVER had a `-DEATH/DAY that `-EQUALED = (<u>**1/7**</u>)!!!~' `-BORN AUGUST 10<sup>th</sup>, 18<u>74</u> /|\ `-DIED OCTOBER 20th, 19<u>64</u> /|\ (8 + <u>10</u> + 18 + <u>74</u>) = `-<u>110</u> /|\ (<u>10</u> + 20 + 19 + 64) = `-<u>113</u> /|\ (110 + 113) = `-2<u>23</u>!!!~' (2 x 23) = (`-<u>46</u>) = RECIPROCAL (MIRROR) = (`-<u>64</u>) = "<u>**YEAR of**</u> `-<u>**DEATH**</u> (`-<u>64</u>)"!!!~' `-(18<u>74</u>) =

(74 (-) 18) = (`-**56**)!!!~' `-(19**64**) = (64 + 19) = `-**83** = RECIPROCAL = `-**38**!!!~'

#**32**-PRESIDENT = FRANKLIN D. ROOSEVELT'S `-**BIRTHDAY** = (1/30/1882); and, `-**DEATH/DAY** = (4/12/1945)!!!~' `-HE `-**DIED** (`-**72**) **DAYS** after `-**HIS** `-**LAST** `-**BIRTHDAY**!!!~' (`-**72**) = RECIPROCAL (MIRROR) = (`-**27**) = FIRST LADY ELEANOR ROOSEVELT `-**DIED** (`-**27**) **DAYS AFTER** `-**HER** `-**LAST** `-**BIRTHDAY**!!!~'

#**33**-PRESIDENT = HARRY S. TRUMAN'S `-**BIRTHDAY** = (5/8/1884); and, `-**DEATH/DAY** = (12/26/1972)!!!~' `-HE `-**DIED** (`-**232**) **DAYS** after `-**HIS** `-**LAST** `-**BIRTHDAY**!!!~' FIRST LADY BESS TRUMAN'S `-**BIRTHDAY** = (**2**/1**3**) = (23 x 1) = (`-**23**) = -a PROPHETIC # `-**NUMBER**!!!~' (`-**23**) = RECIPROCAL (MIRROR) = (`-**32**)!!!~'

#**34**-PRESIDENT = DWIGHT D. EISENHOWER'S `-**BIRTHDAY** = (10/14/1890); and, `-**DEATH/DAY** = (3/28/1969)!!!~' `-HE `-**DIED** (`-**165**) **DAYS** after `-**HIS** `-**LAST** `-**BIRTHDAY**!!!~' FIRST LADY MAMIE EISENHOWER `-**DIED** (`-**352**) **DAYS** from `-**HER** `-**BIRTHDAY**!!!~' (`-**352**) = (52 x 3) = (`-**156**) = (56 x 1) = (`-**56**) = RECIPROCAL (MIRROR) = (`-**65**) = (1 x 65) = (`-**165**) = **DAYS from** `-**DEATH in** `-**BIRTHDAY**!!!~' `-BORN OCTOBER 14th, 1890 /|\ (10 + 14 + 18 + 90) = (`-**132**) /|\ (`-1**32**) = (32 x 1) = (`-**32**) = -a PROPHETIC # `-**NUMBER**!!!~'

#**35**-PRESIDENT = JOHN F. KENNEDY `-**BIRTHDAY** = (5/29/1917); and, `-**DEATH/DAY** = (11/22/1963)!!!~' `-HE `-**DIED** (`-**188**) **DAYS** before `-**HIS** `-**NEXT** `-**BIRTHDAY**!!!~' (`-**188**) = (88 x 1) = (`-**88**) = **2**(**8's**) = (`-**28**) = RECIPROCAL MIRROR = (`-**82**) = (19 + 63) = "**YEAR of** `-**ASSASSINATION**" = (`-**82**)!!!~' `-**BIRTH/YEAR** = (`-**1917**) = (19 + 17) = (`-**36**) = RECIPROCAL (MIRROR) = (`-**63**) = "**YEAR of** `-**DEATH**"!!!~'

#36-PRESIDENT = LYNDON B. JOHNSON'S `-**BIRTHDAY** = (8/27/1908); and, `-**DEATH/DAY** = (1/22/1973)!!!~' `-HE `-**DIED** (`-**148**) **DAYS** before `-**HIS** `-**NEXT** `-**BIRTHDAY**!!!~' `-BORN AUGUST 27th, 1908 /|\ `-DIED JANUARY **22**nd, 19**73** /|\ (8 + 27 + 19 + 08) = `-**62** /|\ (1 + **22** + 19 + 73) = `-**115** /|\ (115 (-) 62) = (`-**53**) = **RECIPROCAL MIRROR** = (**#35**-)**PRESIDENT = JOHN F. KENNEDY**!!!~' *(115 (+) 62)* = (`-**177**) = (**#35**-)**PRESIDENT** JOHN F. KENNEDY'S DIRECTION from THE OTHER WAY; ALSO, with that; HE HAD `-**DIED** (`-**177**) **DAYS** **AWAY** from `-**HIS** `-**LAST** `-**BIRTHDAY**!!!~' (188 + 177) = (`-**365**) = **DAYS** for **NON-LEAP-YEAR**!!!~'

#37-PRESIDENT = RICHARD NIXON `-**BIRTHDAY** = (1/9/**1913**); and, `-**DEATH/DAY** = (4/22/1994)!!!~' `-HE `-**DIED** (`-**103**) **DAYS** after `-**HIS** `-**LAST** `-**BIRTHDAY**!!!~' (`-**103**) = (13 + 0) = (`-**13**) = **RICHARD NIXON'S** `-**BIRTH/YEAR** = (`-**13**) = "A VERY PIVOTAL # `-NUMBER"**!!!~' BIRTH/YEAR = (`-**1913**) = (19 + 13) = (`-**32**) = **-a PROPHETIC # `-NUMBER**!!!~' (`-**32**) = RECIPROCAL (MIRROR) = (`-**23**)!!!~' FIRST LADY PAT NIXON `-**DEATH/DAY** = (**6**/**22**) = (6 x 22) = (`-**132**) = (32 x 1) = (`-**32**) = **-a PROPHETIC # `-NUMBER**!!!~'

#38-PRESIDENT = GERALD FORD'S `-**BIRTHDAY** = (7/14/19**13**); and, `-**DEATH/DAY** = (12/**26**/**2006**)!!!~' `-HE `-**DIED** (`-**165**) **DAYS** after `-**HIS** `-**LAST** `-**BIRTHDAY**!!!~' `-19**13** = (1**9** + 1**3**) = `-**32** = **-a PROPHETIC NUMBER**!!!~' HE; and, **FIRST LADY BETTY FORD** `-**DIED** at the `-**AGE** of (`-**93**)!!!~' `-**DIED** on a (`-**26**) in (`-**2006**)!!!~' **#38**-PRESIDENT GERALD FORD'S `-**DEATH/DAY** = (**12**/**26**) = (12 x 26) = (`-**312**)!!!~' (`-**312**) (*/*) **DIVIDED** by (*/*) `-**2** = (`-**156**)!!!~' (`-**56**) = RECIPROCAL MIRROR = (`-**65**)!!!~'

`-**JIMMY CARTER** is the **#39**th-**PRESIDENT** of the `-**UNITED** `-**STATES** of `-**AMERICA**!!!~'

#40-PRESIDENT = RONALD REAGAN `-**BIRTHDAY** = (2/6/19**11**); and, `-**DEATH/DAY** = (6/5/2004)!!!-᾿ `-HE `-**DIED** (`-**119**) **DAYS** after `-**HIS** `-**LAST** `-**BIRTHDAY**!!!-᾿ BIRTH/ CENTURY; and, **BIRTH/YEAR** (`-**911**) = RECIPROCAL MIRROR = (`-**119**)!!!-᾿ `-**DAY** of `-**DEATH** = **JUNE** 5th = (**6/5**) = (**65**) = (`-**65**) = RECIPROCAL MIRROR = `-(**56**)!!!-᾿ `-**BIRTHDAY** = (2/6); WHILE, **#38**-PRESIDENT = GERALD FORD `-**DIED** on a (`-**26**) in (`-**2006**)!!!-᾿ **#38**-GERALD FORD; AND, **#40**-RONALD REAGAN `-**BOTH** `-**DIED** at the `-**AGE** of (`-**93**)!!!-᾿ (**93** x **2**) = `-1**86** = (86 x 1) = (`-**86**) = **RECIPROCAL** = (`-**68**) = "The `-**MARK**"!!!-᾿

#41-PRESIDENT = GEORGE H. W. BUSH `-**BIRTHDAY** = (6/1**2**/1924); and, `-**DEATH/DAY** = (11/30/2018)!!!-᾿ `-HE `-**DIED** (`-**171**) **DAYS** after `-**HIS** `-**LAST** `-**BIRTHDAY**!!!-᾿ (`-**171**) = (11 + 7) = (`-**18**) = `-**DEATH/RESULT**!!!-᾿ LOOK at THE `-**PREVIOUS** `-**PRESIDENTS** with the # `-**NUMBER** (`-**71**)!!!-᾿ `-BORN **JUNE** 12th, 19**24** /|\ `-DIED NOVEMBER 30th, **2**018 /|\ BIRTHDAY # `-NUMBER = (**6** + 1**2** + 19 + **24**) = (`-**61**) /|\ DEATH/DAY # `-NUMBER = (11 + 30 + **20** + **18**) = (`-**79**) /|\ (79 (-) 61) = (`-**18**)!!!-᾿ (**2**018 (-) 19**24**) = `-**94**!!!-᾿ **DIED** at the `-**AGE** of (`-**94**)!!!-᾿ (**#41**-) PRESIDENT GEORGE H. W. BUSH'S OPPOSITE DIRECTION from THE OTHER WAY; with that, HE HAD `-**DIED** at (`-**194**) **DAYS AWAY** from `-**HIS** `-**LAST** `-**BIRTHDAY**!!!-᾿ (194 + 171) = (`-**365**) = **DAYS** for **NON-LEAP-YEAR**!!!-᾿

`-**BORN** on (**6/12**) = (**62** x 1) = (`-**62**) = **RECIPROCAL MIRROR** = (`-**26**) with **#40**-PRESIDENT = RONALD REAGAN `-**BIRTHDAY** = (2/6); WHILE, **#38**-PRESIDENT = GERALD FORD `-**DIED** on a (`-**26**) in (`-**2006**)!!!-᾿ FIRST LADY BARBARA BUSH was `-**BORN** on (6/8); and, `-**DIED** on (4/1**7**) = (**4** x 1**7**) = (`-**68**) = "The `-**MARKS**"!!!-᾿

`-<u>BILL</u> <u>CLINTON</u> is the #<u>42</u><u>nd</u>-PRESIDENT of the `-UNITED `-STATES of `-AMERICA!!!~'

`-<u>GEORGE</u> <u>W.</u> <u>BUSH</u> is the #<u>43</u><u>rd</u>-PRESIDENT of the `-UNITED `-STATES of `-AMERICA!!!~'

`-<u>BARACK OBAMA</u> is the #<u>44</u><u>th</u>-PRESIDENT of the `-UNITED `-STATES of `-AMERICA!!!~'

`-<u>DONALD TRUMP</u> is the #<u>45</u><u>th</u>-PRESIDENT of the `-UNITED `-STATES of `-AMERICA; while, `-<u>CURRENTLY</u> `-<u>BEING</u>; (`-<u>74</u>), `-<u>YEARS</u> `-<u>OF</u> `-<u>AGE</u> in the `-

CALENDAR `-YEAR of (`-<u>20</u>20) = (<u>20</u> + <u>20</u>) = (`-<u>40</u>)!!!~' (7 x 4) = (`-<u>28</u>) + (`-<u>40</u>) = (`-<u>68</u>) = "The `-<u>MARK</u>"!!!~'

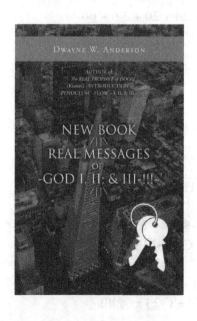

AMERICAN NOVELIST CLIVE CUSSLER (`-**88**) (BIRTH: JULY 15, 1931) (DEATH: FEBRUARY 24, 2020)!!!~'

(**LEAP YEAR**) = `-**DIED** (`-**224**) DAYS AWAY from `-**HIS** `-**BIRTHDAY** = (2/24) = "**DAY** of `-**DEATH** (**FEBRUARY 24**th)!!!~'

`-**BIRTHDAY** # `-NUMBER = (`-**72**) = RECIPROCAL (MIRROR) = `-FRAGMENTED `-BIRTHDAY # `-NUMBER (`-**27**)!!!~' (**LEAP YEAR**) = `-**DIED** (`-**224**) DAYS AWAY from `-**HIS** `-**BIRTHDAY** = (22 x 4) = (`-**88**) = `-**AGE of `-DEATH for AMERICAN NOVELIST CLIVE CUSSLER (`-88**)!!!~'

BIRTHDAY # `-NUMBER = (7 + 15 + 19 + 31 = **72**

(`-**72**) = RECIPROCAL (MIRROR) = (`-**27**)

DEATH/DAY # `-NUMBER = (2 + 24 + 20 + 20) = **66**

(72 (-) 66) = (`-**6**)!!!~'

(72 + 66) = (`-**138**)!!!~'

(138 (-) 6) = (`-**132**) = (32 x 1) = (`-**32**) = -**a PROPHETIC # `-NUMBER**!!!~'

HE DIED (`-**142**) DAYS BEFORE HIS NEXT BIRTHDAY!!!~'

(366 (-) 142) = (`-**224**) = (22 x 4) = (`-**88**) = `-**AGE of `-DEATH for AMERICAN NOVELIST CLIVE CUSSLER (`-88**)!!!~'

HE DIED AT THE `-AGE of (`-**88**) = (8 x 8) = (`-**64**) = RECIPROCAL (MIRROR) = (`-**46**) = (`-**23** x `-**2**)!!!~'

JULY 15 = (7 x 15) = (`-**105**)!!!~'

FEBRUARY 24 = (2 x 24) = (`-**48**)!!!~'

(105 + 48) = (`-**153**)!!!~'

(105 (-) 48) = (`-**57**)!!!~'

(153 (-) 57) = (`-**96**) = (`-**32** x `-**3**)!!!~'

JULY 15, 1931 = (7 + 1 + 5 + 1 + 9 + 3 + 1) = (`-**27**) = RECIPROCAL (MIRROR) = (`-**72**) = **BIRTHDAY # `-NUMBER!!!~'**

FEBRUARY 24, 2020 = (2 + 2 + 4 + 2 + 0 + 2 + 0) = (`-**12**)!!!~'

(**27** + **12**) = (`-**39**) = (3 x 9) = (`-**27**)!!!~'

`-BIRTHDAY; and, `-DEATH/DAY!!!~':

(**715** + **224**) = (`-**939**) = (93 (-) 9) = (`-**84**)!!!~'

(**715** (-) **224**) = (`-**491**) = (91 x 4) = (`-**364**)!!!~'

(364 (-) 84) = (`-**280**) = (28 + 0) = (`-**28**) = **2**(**8**'s) = (`-**88**) = **`-AGE of `-DEATH for AMERICAN NOVELIST CLIVE CUSSLER (`-88**)!!!~'**

JULY 15 (**BIRTH**) + FEBRUARY 24 (**DEATH**) = (7 + 15 + 2 + 24) = (`-**48**) = (4 x 8) = (`-**32**) = **-a PROPHETIC # `-NUMBER!!!~'**

`-DIED in (`-2) **& was `-BORN in (`-7**) = (`-**2/7**) = (`-**27**) = **RECIPROCAL (MIRROR) = (`-72**) = **`-BIRTHDAY # `-NUMBER!!!~'**

AMERICAN TELEVISION HOST LEE PHILLIP BELL (`-**91**)
(BIRTH: JUNE 10, 1928) (DEATH: FEBRUARY 25, 2020)

`-**BIRTHDAY** = (**6**/**1**0) = (61 + 0) = (`-**61**) = "FLIP the (`-**6**) OVER
to a (`-**9**) = "**AGE of `-DEATH for AMERICAN TELEVISION
HOST LEE PHILLIP BELL (`-91)**"!!!-'

BIRTHDAY # `-NUMBER = (6 + 10 + 19 + 28) = **63**

(`-**63**) = RECIPROCAL (MIRROR) = (`-**36**)

DEATH/DAY # `-NUMBER = (2 + 25 + 20 + 20) = **67**

(67 (-) 63) = (`-**4**)!!!-'

(67 + 63) = (`-**130**)!!!-'

(130 (-) 4) = (`-**126**)!!!-'

SHE DIED (`-**106**) DAYS BEFORE HER NEXT BIRTHDAY!!!-'

(`-**106**) = RECIPROCAL (MIRROR) = (`-**610**) = "**BIRTHDAY for
AMERICAN TELEVISION HOST LEE PHILLIP BELL**"!!!-'

(366 (-) 106) = (`-**260**) = (26 + 0) = (`-**26**) = RECIPROCAL
(MIRROR) = (`-**62**)!!!-'

SHE DIED AT THE `-AGE of (`-**91**)!!!-'

JUNE 10 = (6 x 10) = (`-**60**)!!!-'

FEBRUARY 25 = (2 x 25) = (`-**50**)!!!-'

(60 + 50) = (`-**110**) = (11 + 0) = (`-**11**)!!!-'

JUNE 10, 1928 = (6 + 1 + 0 + 1 + 9 + 2 + 8) = (`-**27**) = RECIPROCAL (MIRROR) = (`-**72**)!!!~'

`-FRAGMENTED `-BIRTHDAY # `-NUMBER = (`-**27**) = (2 + 25) = (**2/25**) = "**DAY** of `-**DEATH** for AMERICAN TELEVISION HOST LEE PHILLIP BELL"!!!~'

FEBRUARY 25, 2020 = (2 + 2 + 5 + 2 + 0 + 2 + 0) = (`-**13**)!!!~'

(**27** + **13**) = (`-**40**)!!!~'

`-**BIRTHDAY;** and, `-**DEATH/DAY!!!~':**

(**610** + **225**) = (`-**835**)!!!~'

(**610** (-) **225**) = (`-**385**) = "SWIPE (`-**1**) from `-ABOVE (`-**835**)!!!~'

(835 + 385) = (`-**1220**) = (12 + 20) = (`-**32**) = -a PROPHETIC # `-NUMBER!!!~'

JUNE 10 (**BIRTH**) + FEBRUARY 25 (**DEATH**) = (6 + 10 + 2 + 25) = (`-**43**)!!!~'

`-**DIED** in (`-**2**) & was `-**BORN** in (`-**6**) = (`-**2/6**) = (`-**26**) = `-**DIED** (`-**260**) DAYS AWAY from `-BIRTHDAY!!!~'

AMERICAN ENTREPRENEUR JOSEPH HARDIN COULOMBE "FOUNDER of GROCERY STORE CHAIN (TRADER JOE'S)" (`-**89**) (BIRTH: JUNE 3, 1930) (DEATH: FEBRUARY 28, 2020)

`-**BORN** in the `-**YEAR** of (`-**30**) = **MONTH;** and, **DAY** `-**HE** `-**DIED** = (**2/28**) = (2 + 28) = (`-**30**)!!!~'

`-**1930** = (30 + 19) = (`-**49**) = (4 x 9) = (`-**36**) = RECIPROCAL (MIRROR) = (`-**63**) = `-**BIRTHDAY** for **AMERICAN ENTREPRENEUR JOSEPH HARDIN COULOMBE (JUNE 3rd)!!!**-'

FOUNDED "TRADER JOE'S" in (`-19**67**); AND, was `-MARRIED for (`-**67**) YEARS to `-HIS `-WIFE ALICE COULOMBE!!!-' THEY were `-MARRIED in (`-**1953**)!!!-'

`-**1953** = (19 + 53) = (`-**72**) = (8 x 9) = (`-**89**) = `-**AGE of** `-**DEATH for AMERICAN ENTREPRENEUR JOSEPH HARDIN COULOMBE "FOUNDER of GROCERY STORE CHAIN (TRADER JOE'S)"** (`-**89**)!!!-'

BIRTHDAY # `-NUMBER = (6 + 3 + 19 + 30) = **58**

(`-**58**) = RECIPROCAL (MIRROR) = (`-**85**)

DEATH/DAY # `-NUMBER = (2 + 28 + 20 + 20) = **70**

(70 (-) 58) = (`-**12**)!!!-'

(70 + 58) = (`-**128**)!!!-'

(128 (-) 12) = (`-**116**)!!!-'

HE DIED (`-**96**) DAYS BEFORE HIS NEXT BIRTHDAY!!!-'

(366 (-) 96) = (`-**270**) = (27 + 0) = (`-**27**) = RECIPROCAL (MIRROR) = (`-**72**)!!!-'

HE DIED AT THE `-AGE of (`-**89**) = (8 x 9) = (`-**72**) = RECIPROCAL (MIRROR) = (`-**27**) = `-**DIED** (`-**270**) **DAYS AWAY from** `-**BIRTHDAY!!!**-'

JUNE 3 = (6 x 3) = (`-**18**)!!!~'

FEBRUARY 28 = (2 x 28) = (`-**56**)!!!~'

(56 + 18) = (`-**74**)!!!~'

(56 (-) 18) = (`-**38**)!!!~'

(74 (-) 38) = (`-**36**) = RECIPROCAL (MIRROR) = (`-**63**) = `-<u>BIRTHDAY</u> for **AMERICAN ENTREPRENEUR JOSEPH HARDIN COULOMBE (JUNE 3**rd**)!!!~'**

JUNE 3, 1930 = (6 + 3 + 1 + 9 + 3 + 0) = (`-**22**)!!!~'

FEBRUARY 28, 2020 = (2 + 2 + 8 + 2 + 0 + 2 + 0) = (`-**16**)!!!~'

(**22** + **16**) = (`-**38**)!!!~'

`-<u>BIRTHDAY</u>; and, `-<u>DEATH/DAY</u>!!!~':

(**228** + **63**) = (`-**291**) = (91 x 2) = (`-**182**)!!!~'

(**228** (-) **63**) = (`-**165**) = (16 x 5) = (`-**80**)!!!~'

(182 + 80) = (`-**262**) = "**RECIPROCAL-<u>S</u>EQUENCING-NUMEROLOGY-<u>RSN</u>**"!!!~'

JUNE 3 (**<u>BIRTH</u>**) + FEBRUARY 28 (**<u>DEATH</u>**) = (6 + 3 + 2 + 28) = (`-**39**)!!!~'

`-<u>DIED</u> in (`-**2**) & was `-<u>BORN</u> in (`-**6**) = (`-**2/6**) = (`-**26**) = **RECIPROCAL (MIRROR) = (`-62)!!!~'**

(62 + 26) = (`-**88**) = `-<u>**DIED**</u> the `-<u>**YEAR AFTER**</u> /|\ at the `-<u>**AGE**</u> of (`-**89**)!!!~'

AMERICAN EXECUTIVE (GE) GENERAL ELECTRIC JACK WELCH (`-**84**) (BIRTH: NOVEMBER 19, 1935) (DEATH: MARCH 1, 2020)!!!~'

`-<u>**BIRTHDAY**</u> = NOVEMBER 19 = (**11**/**19**) = (11 + 19) = (`-**30**) = (3 + 0) = (`-**3**) = `-<u>**MARCH**</u> = "<u>**MONTH**</u> of `-<u>**DEATH**</u>"!!!~'

`-<u>**BIRTHDAY**</u> # `-<u>**NUMBER**</u> = (`-**84**) = `-<u>**EQUALS**</u> = "<u>**AGE**</u> of `-<u>**DEATH**</u> for AMERICAN EXECUTIVE (GE) GENERAL ELECTRIC JACK WELCH (`-**84**)"!!!~'

(84 + 84) = (`-**168**) = "The `-<u>**MARK**</u>"!!!~'

BIRTHDAY # `-NUMBER = (11 + 19 + 19 + 35) = **84**

(`-**84**) = RECIPROCAL (MIRROR) = (`-**48**)

DEATH/DAY # `-NUMBER = (3 + 1 + 20 + 20) = **44**

(84 (-) 44) = (`-**40**)!!!~'

(84 + 44) = (`-**128**)!!!~'

(128 + 40) = (`-**168**) = "The `-<u>**MARK**</u>"!!!~'

HE DIED (`-**103**) DAYS AFTER HIS LAST BIRTHDAY!!!~'

(366 (-) 103) = (`-**263**) = (63 x 2) = (`-**126**)!!!~'

HE DIED AT THE `-AGE of (`-**84**) = (8 x 4) = (`-**32**) = **-a PROPHETIC # `-NUMBER!!!~'**

NOVEMBER 19 = (11 x 19) = (`-**209**)!!!~'

MARCH 1 = (3 x 1) = (`-**3**)!!!~'

(209 + 3) = (`-**212**) = **"BOILING POINT"!!!~'**

(209 (-) 3) = (`-**206**)!!!~'

(212 + 206) = (`-**418**) = (48 x 1) = (`-**48**) = RECIPROCAL (MIRROR) = (`-**84**) = **"AGE of `-DEATH for AMERICAN EXECUTIVE (GE) GENERAL ELECTRIC JACK WELCH (`-84)"!!!~'**

NOVEMBER 19, 1935 = (1 + 1 + 1 + 9 + 1 + 9 + 3 + 5) = (`-**30**)!!!~'

MARCH 1, 2020 = (3 + 1 + 2 + 0 + 2 + 0) = (`-**8**)!!!~'

(**30** + **8**) = (`-**38**)!!!~'

`-BIRTHDAY; and, `-DEATH/DAY!!!~':

(**1119** + **31**) = (`-**1150**) = (11 + 50) = (`-**61**)!!!~'

(**1119** (-) **31**) = (`-**1088**) = (10 + 88) = (`-**98**)!!!~'

(98 (-) 61) = (`-**37**) = **3**(**7**'**s**) = (7 x 7 x 7) = (`-**343**) = **"RECIPROCAL-SEQUENCING-NUMEROLOGY-RSN"!!!~'**

NOVEMBER 19 (**BIRTH**) + MARCH 1 (**DEATH**) = (11 + 19 + 3 + 1) = (`-**34**)!!!~'

`-DIED in (`-3) & was `-BORN in (`-11) = (`-3/11) = (`-3/1) x 1 = (`-3/1) = "DAY of `-DEATH for AMERICAN EXECUTIVE (GE) GENERAL ELECTRIC JACK WELCH (MARCH 1ˢᵗ)"!!!~'

AMERICAN WRITER JAMES LIPTON (`-93) (BIRTH: SEPTEMBER 19, 1926) (DEATH: MARCH 2, 2020)!!!~'

(9 + 1 + 9 + 1 + 9) = "RECIPROCAL-SEQUENCING-NUMEROLOGY-RSN"!!!~'

(9 + 1 + 9 + 1 + 9) = 3(9's) = (`-39) = RECIPROCAL (MIRROR) = (`-93) = "AGE of `-DEATH for AMERICAN WRITER JAMES LIPTON (`-93)"!!!~'

`-BIRTH/YEAR = `-1926 = (19 + 26) = (`-45) = `-DEATH/DAY # `-NUMBER (`-45) = "The `-DAY, `-MONTH; and, `-YEAR; `-HE was `-GOING to `-DIE `-ON"!!!~'

BIRTHDAY # `-NUMBER = (9 + 19 + 19 + 26) = 73

(`-73) = RECIPROCAL (MIRROR) = (`-37)

DEATH/DAY # `-NUMBER = (3 + 2 + 20 + 20) = 45

(73 (-) 45) = (`-28)!!!~'

(73 + 45) = (`-118)!!!~'

(118 + 28) = (`-146) = (46 x 1) = (`-46) = (`-23 x `-2)!!!~'

HE DIED (`-165) DAYS AFTER HIS LAST BIRTHDAY!!!~'

(366 (-) 165) = (`-**201**) = (21 + 0) = (`-**21**) = (3 x 7) = (`-**37**) = RECIPROCAL (MIRROR) = (`-**73**) = `-**BIRTHDAY #** `-**NUMBER!!!~'**

HE DIED AT THE `-AGE of (`-**93**) = (9 x 3) = (`-**27**) = RECIPROCAL (MIRROR) = (`-**72**)!!!~'

SEPTEMBER 19 = (9 x 19) = (`-**171**)!!!~'

MARCH 2 = (3 x 2) = (`-**6**)!!!~'

(171 + 6) = (`-**177**)!!!~'

(171 (-) 6) = (`-**165**) = "**DIED** this `-**MANY** `-**DAYS** after `-**HIS** `-**BIRTHDAY**"!!!~'

(177 + 165) = (`-**342**) = (34 x 2) = (`-**68**) = "The `-**MARK**"!!!~'

SEPTEMBER 19, 1926 = (9 + 1 + 9 + 1 + 9 + 2 + 6) = (`-**37**)!!!~'

MARCH 2, 2020 = (3 + 2 + 2 + 0 + 2 + 0) = (`-**9**)!!!~'

(**37** + **9**) = (`-**46**) = (`-**23** x `-**2**)!!!~'

`-**BIRTHDAY; and, `-DEATH/DAY!!!~'**:

(**919** + **32**) = (`-**951**)!!!~'

(**919** (-) **32**) = (`-**887**)!!!~'

(951 (-) 887) = (`-**64**) = RECIPROCAL (MIRROR) = (`-**46**) = (`-**23** x `-**2**)!!!~'

SEPTEMBER 19 (**BIRTH**) + MARCH 2 (**DEATH**) = (9 + 19 + 3 + 2) = (`-**33**)!!!~'

'-DIED in (`-**3**) & was '-BORN in (`-**9**) = (`-**3/9**) = (`-**39**) = RECIPROCAL (MIRROR) = (`-**93**) = "**AGE** of '-**DEATH** for AMERICAN WRITER JAMES LIPTON (`-**93**)"!!!~'

The "**PROPHET'S**" '-**MESSAGE**:

'-GOD Indeed created '-LIFE for '-OTHER '-LIFE '-itself!!!~' FROM the '-VEGETATION on the '-GROUND, to the '-FRUITS of the '-TREES, they; '-ALL serve AS '-FOOD for '-GOD'S other '-CREATIONS!!!~' These '-FRUITS & '-VEGETATION have '-DNA; and, indeed are a '-**MARVELOUS '-CREATION in '-ITSELF**; but yet, THEY still '-SERVE as '-FOOD for '-OTHER '-CREATIONS of '-GOD'S!!!~' '-GOD has '-CREATED '-ANIMALS to '-LIKEWISE '-DOMINATE the '-TERRAIN; but, as yet; **THEY STILL '-SERVE as '-FOOD for '-OTHER '-CREATIONS of '-GOD'S!!!~'** LOOK at '-HUMANS and '-OUR LOVE for '-EATING '-CHICKEN, '-TURKEY, '-STEAK & '-EGGS; and, the '-OTHERS!!!~' WE '-HUMANS '-too; CAN '-SERVE as '-FOOD for '-OTHER '-CREATIONS, just as '-WELL; ESPECIALLY, in '-DECOMPOSITION!!!~' The '-IMPORTANCE in '-GOD'S '-CREATIONS '-LIVING; and, '-STAYING '-ALIVE; is '-**RELATIVE**, *to* '-***GOD***; and, to '-**GOD'S '-UNDERSTANDING of** '-LIFE '-**ITSELF!!!~'** Have '-**YOU** ever '-**SEEN** a '-**SPIDER** eat a '-**GRASSHOPPER!!!~'** SOME '-**MIGHT** '-**SAY** that '-**GOD** wants '-**US** to '-**LIVE** '-**FOREVER!!!~'** Does '-**HE**???~' **IT'S** been '-**BILLIONS** of '-**YEARS** of '-**CREATIONS** to at '-**LEAST** '-**NOW**; WHY '-**CHANGE** '-**ANYTHING** '-**NOW**; and, even '-going '-**FORWARD!!!~'** (Perhaps), '-**GOD** likes '-**it**; JUST the '-**WAY**, it '-**IS!!!~'**

'-**GOD** also, '-**CREATED** a '-**VIRUS, BACTERIUM, MOLD,** etc., etc., etc....** They have a '-**PURPOSE**; too, even as to

(**BACTERIUM**) **COMPOSING** LARGE QUANTITIES of '-**OUR** very '-**OWN** '-**BODIES**; and, having '-**THEM** WORK '-**PROPERLY**; and, as with '-**FUNGUS** to the '-**ROOTS** of '-**TREES!!!~' THEY have a '-RIGHT to '-LIVE, '-TOO!!!~'** DO '-YOU want '-**THEM** to '-**LIVE** '-**FOREVER!!!~' IF;** '-YOU '-**DO**, they'll '-**LIVE** '-**FOREVER** with; and, within; '-**YOU**, '-**too!!!~'**

The '-PROPHET being an '-**ENGINEER** in '-**ELECTRICITY**; and, '-**ELECTROMAGNETISM** knows these '-**LAWS of** '-**PHYSICS!!!~'** What; '-KEEPS these '-LAWS '-CONSTANT; and, in their '-ORDER of '-CONSTRUCTION; and, in '-COMPLETION???~' **GOD**, marvelously; does this '-**ULTIMATELY**-', '-too!!!~' GOD has set these '-LAWS in '-ORDER of '-CONSTRUCT to '-WORK on '-their '-OWN; but yet, '-HE even still '-CONTROLS '-THEM; '-SIMULTANEOUSLY, just as well!!!~' The '-SAME goes for the '-SPERM; and, the '-EGG; at the '-BEGINNING; to the '-NEW '-CELL '-CONSTRUCT, to the '-GROWTH of '-MATURITY; '-**ALL** '-**CREATED in the** '-**LAWS by the** '-**ORDER of** '-**CONSTRUCT; but yet,** '-**still** '-**CONTROLLED by** '-**GOD;** '-**SIMULTANEOUSLY!!!~'**

'-**IMAGINE**, rubbing your '-**HEAD**; and, rubbing your '-**TUMMY**; SIMULTANEOUSLY as an '-**INDIVIDUAL!!!~'** This, is '-WHAT '-**GOD** does with '-**US** and all of '-**HIS** '-**CREATION**; SIMULTANEOUSLY, with a '-**PAST**, '-**PRESENT**; and, '-**FUTURE "POINT of** '-**VIEW"!!!~'** FROM '-**YOU**, to '-**EVERY INSECT, to** '-**EVERY** '-**STAR & **'-**GALAXY & **'-**BEYOND; and, even to** EVERY '-**ATOM** '-**just as well; throughout** THE '-**ENTIRE** '-**UNIVERSE; this is** '-**DONE!!!~'** HOW '-**POWERFUL is** '-**GOD!!!~'**

AMERICAN JOURNALIST (CNN) BOBBIE BATTISTA (`-**67**) (BIRTH: JULY 23, **1952**) (DEATH: **MARCH 3**, 2020)

`-**1952** = (52 (-) 19) = (`-**33**) = "DAY of `-DEATH (`-**33**)" = "MARCH 3ʳᵈ"!!!~'

JULY 23ʳᵈ = (`-**723**) = "FLIP the (`-**7**) OVER to a (`-**2**); AND, `-YOU have HOW MANY DAYS SHE DIED FROM `-**HER** `-**BIRTHDAY** (`-**223**)!!!~'

SHE `-DIED (`-**142**) DAYS AWAY FROM BEFORE HER `-BIRTHDAY = (`-**142**) = (42 x 1) = (`-**42**) = (6 x 7) = (`-**42**) = "SHE `-**DIED** at the `-**AGE** of (`-**67**)"!!!~'

BIRTHDAY # `-NUMBER = (7 + 23 + 19 + 52) = **101**

DEATH/DAY # `-NUMBER = (3 + 3 + 20 + 20) = **46** = (`-**23** x `-**2**)!!!~'

(101 (-) 46) = (`-**55**) = (`-**23** + `-**32**)!!!~'

(101 + 46) = (`-**147**)!!!~'

(147 (-) 55) = (`-**92**) = `-FRAGMENTED `-BIRTHDAY # `-**NUMBER** (RECIPROCAL MIRROR) = (`-**29**)!!!~'

SHE DIED (`-**142**) DAYS BEFORE HER NEXT BIRTHDAY!!!~'

(365 (-) 142) = (`-**223**) = (23 x 2) = (`-**46**) = `-**DEATH/DAY #** `-**NUMBER** for AMERICAN JOURNALIST (CNN) BOBBIE BATTISTA (`-**46**)!!!~'

SHE DIED AT THE `-AGE of (`-**67**) = (6 x 7) = (`-**42**) = "SHE `-DIED (`-**142**) DAYS **AWAY** from `-**HER** `-**BIRTHDAY**!!!~'

JULY 23 = (7 x 23) = (`-**161**)!!!~'

MARCH 3 = (3 x 3) = (`-**9**)!!!~'

(161 (-) 9) = (`-**152**) = (52 x 1) = (`-**52**) = AMERICAN JOURNALIST (CNN) BOBBIE BATTISTA was `-**BORN in** (`-19**52**)!!!~'

JULY 23, 1952 = (7 + 2 + 3 + 1 + 9 + 5 + 2) = (`-**29**) = RECIPROCAL (MIRROR) = (`-**92**)!!!~'

MARCH 3, 2020 = (3 + 3 + 2 + 0 + 2 + 0) = (`-**10**)!!!~'

(**29** + **10**) = (`-**39**)!!!~'

`-**BIRTHDAY; and, `-DEATH/DAY!!!~'**:

(**723** + **33**) = (`-**756**)!!!~'

(**723** (-) **33**) = (`-**690**) = (69 + 0) = (`-**69**) = (`-**3** x `-**23**)!!!~'

(756 + 690) = (`-**1446**) = (46 (-) 14) = (`-**32**) = -a PROPHETIC # `-**NUMBER!!!~'**

JULY 23 (**BIRTH**) + MARCH 3 (**DEATH**) = (7 + 23 + 3 + 3) = (`-**36**)!!!~'

`-**DIED in** (`-**3**) & was `-**BORN in** (`-**7**) = (`-**3/7**) = (`-**37**) = RECIPROCAL (MIRROR) = (`-**73**)!!!~'

(73 (-) 37) = (`-**36**)!!!~'

AMERICAN ACTOR NICHOLAS TUCCI (`-**38**) (BIRTH: **APRIL 3**, 1981) (DEATH: **MARCH 3**, 2020)

`-**DIED** (`-**334**) DAYS AWAY from HIS `-BIRTHDAY!!!~' `-BOTH `-**DEATH** & `-**BIRTH** are `-**INSCRIBED** `-HERE:

`-**334** (**ALL-IN-ONE-#-NUMBER**) = (`-**33**) = `-DAY of `-**DEATH!!!~**' (`-**34**) = RECIPROCAL (MIRROR) = (`-**43**) = `-DAY of `-**BIRTH!!!~**'

`-**DEATH/DAY** = (`-**33**) + `-**BIRTHDAY** (`-**43**) = (`-**76**) / `-**2** = (`-**38**) = `-**AGE** of `-**DEATH** for AMERICAN ACTOR NICHOLAS TUCCI (`-**38**)!!!~'

BIRTHDAY # `-NUMBER = (4 + 3 + 19 + 81) = **107**

DEATH/DAY # `-NUMBER = (3 + 3 + 20 + 20) = **46** = (`-**23** x `-**2**)!!!~'

(107 (-) 46) = (`-**61**)!!!~'

(107 + 46) = (`-**153**)!!!~'

(153 + 61) = (`-**214**) = (24 x 1) = (`-**24**) = (**3** x **8**) = "**AGE** of `-**DEATH** (`-**38**)"!!!~'

HE DIED (`-**31**) DAYS BEFORE HIS NEXT BIRTHDAY!!!~'

(365 (-) 31) = (`-**334**) = (33 x 4) = (`-**132**) = (32 x 1) = (`-**32**) = -a PROPHETIC # `-NUMBER!!!~'

HE DIED AT THE `-AGE of (`-**38**) = (3 x 8) = (`-**24**) = RECIPROCAL (MIRROR) = (`-**42**)!!!~'

APRIL 3 = (4 x 3) = (`-**12**)!!!~'

MARCH 3 = (3 x 3) = (`-**9**)!!!~'

$(12 + 9) = (`-\underline{21})!!!~'$

APRIL 3, 1981 = $(4 + 3 + 1 + 9 + 8 + 1) = (`-\underline{26}) =$ RECIPROCAL (MIRROR) = $(`-\underline{62})!!!~'$

MARCH 3, 2020 = $(3 + 3 + 2 + 0 + 2 + 0) = (`-\underline{10})!!!~'$

$(\underline{26} + \underline{10}) = (`-\underline{36})!!!~'$

`-BIRTHDAY; and, `-DEATH/DAY!!!~':

$(\underline{43} + \underline{33}) = (`-\underline{76})!!!~'$

$(\underline{43} (-) \underline{33}) = (`-\underline{10})!!!~'$

$(76 (-) 10) = (`-\underline{66}) = (`-66 / `-2) = (`-\underline{33}) =$ **"<u>DAY</u> of `-DEATH (<u>MARCH</u> 3rd)"!!!~'**

$(76 + 10) = (`-\underline{86}) = (`-86 / `-2) = (`-\underline{43}) =$ **"<u>DAY</u> of `-BIRTH (<u>APRIL</u> 3rd)"!!!~'**

APRIL 3 (**<u>BIRTH</u>**) + MARCH 3 (**<u>DEATH</u>**) = $(4 + 3 + 3 + 3) = (`-\underline{13}) =$ **"A VERY PIVOTAL # `-NUMBER"!!!~'**

`-DIED in (`-\underline{3}) & was `-BORN in (`-\underline{4}) = (`-\underline{3/4}) = (`-\underline{34}) = RECIPROCAL (MIRROR) = (`-\underline{43}) = "<u>DAY</u> of `-BIRTH for AMERICAN ACTOR NICHOLAS TUCCI (<u>APRIL</u> 3rd)"!!!~'

FRENCH-SWEDISH ACTOR MAX VON SYDOW (`-**\underline{90}**) (BIRTH: **APRIL 10**, 1929) (DEATH: **MARCH 8**, 2020)!!!~' HEIGHT 6' 4"!!!~'

`-**1929** = (19 + 29) = (`-**48**) = RECIPROCAL (MIRROR) = (20 + 20 + 8) = (`-**48**)**!!!**~'

BIRTHDAY # `-NUMBER = (4 + 10 + 19 + 29) = **62**

DEATH/DAY # `-NUMBER = (3 + 8 + 20 + 20) = **51**

(62 (-) 51) = (`-**11**)**!!!**~'

(62 + 51) = (`-**113**) = (13 x 1) = (`-**13**) = **"A VERY PIVOTAL # `-NUMBER"!!!**~'

(113 + 11) = (`-**124**) = (24 x 1) = (`-**24**) = (**3** x **8**) = **"DAY of `-DEATH (`-38) = (MARCH 8th)"!!!**~'

HE DIED (`-**33**) DAYS BEFORE HIS NEXT BIRTHDAY**!!!**~'

(365 (-) 33) = (`-**332**) = (32 x 3) = (`-**96**)**!!!**~'

HE DIED AT THE `-AGE of (`-**90**)**!!!**~'

APRIL 10 = (4 x 10) = (`-**40**)**!!!**~'

MARCH 8 = (3 x 8) = (`-**24**)**!!!**~'

(40 + 24) = (`-**64**) = (`-**2** x `-**32**)**!!!**~'

APRIL 10, 1929 = (4 + 1 + 0 + 1 + 9 + 2 + 9) = (`-**26**) = RECIPROCAL (MIRROR) = (`-**62**) = `-**BIRTHDAY # `-NUMBER** (`-**62**)**!!!**~'

MARCH 8, 2020 = (3 + 8 + 2 + 0 + 2 + 0) = (`-**15**)**!!!**~'

(**26** + **15**) = (`-**41**) = **"ADD a (`-0)"** = `-**BIRTHDAY** of FRENCH-SWEDISH ACTOR MAX VON SYDOW = (`-**410**) = **"APRIL 10th"!!!**~'

`-BIRTHDAY; and, `-DEATH/DAY!!!~':

$(\underline{410} + \underline{38}) = (`-\underline{448}) = (44 + 8) = (`-\underline{52})$!!!~'

$(\underline{410} (-) \underline{38}) = (`-\underline{372}) = (37 + 2) = (`-\underline{39})$!!!~'

$(52 + 39) = (`-\underline{91}) = $ `-**DIED** in `-HIS (`-**91**[st]) **YEAR** of `-**EXISTENCE**!!!~'

APRIL 10 (**BIRTH**) + MARCH 8 (**DEATH**) = $(4 + 10 + 3 + 8) = $ (`-**25**)!!!~'

`-**DIED** in (`-**3**) & was `-**BORN** in (`-**4**) = (`-**3/4**) = (`-**34**) = RECIPROCAL (MIRROR) = (`-**43**)!!!~'

$(34 + 43) = (`-\underline{77})$!!!~' `-**DIED** (`-**13**) **YEARS AWAY** from this `-**NUMBER** at the `-**AGE of** (`-**90**)!!!~'

$(43 (-) 34) = (`-\underline{9})$!!!~' **"ADD a (`-0)"** = `-**AGE** of `-**DEATH** for FRENCH-SWEDISH ACTOR MAX VON SYDOW = (`-**90**)!!!~'

AUSTRALIAN NOVELIST STEPH BOWE (`-**25**) (BIRTH: **FEBRUARY 1**, 1994) (DEATH: **JANUARY 20**, 2020)

`-**1994** = $(94 (-) 19) = (`-\underline{75}) = $ "FLIP the (`-**7**) OVER to a (`-**2**) = (`-**25**) = **"AGE of `-DEATH**!!!~'

`-**BIRTHDAY** = (`-**21**) = RECIPROCAL (MIRROR) = (`-**12**) = `-**DEATH/DAY**!!!~' JANUARY 20[th] = $(\underline{120}) = (12 + 0) = (`-\underline{12})$!!!~'

BIRTHDAY # `-**NUMBER** = $(2 + 1 + 19 + 94) = \underline{116}$

`-**116** = $(16 \times 1) = (`-\underline{16}) = $ RECIPROCAL (MIRROR) = (`-**61**)!!!~'

DEATH/DAY # `-NUMBER = (1 + 20 + 20 + 20) = (**61**)!!!~'

(116 (-) 61) = (`-**55**) = (`-**23** + `-**32**)!!!~'

(116 + 61) = (`-**177**)!!!~'

(177 + 55) = (`-**232**) = "**RECIPROCAL-SEQUENCING-NUMEROLOGY-RSN**"!!!~'

SHE DIED (`-**12**) DAYS BEFORE HER NEXT BIRTHDAY!!!~'

(`-**12**) = RECIPROCAL (MIRROR) = (`-**21**)

(365 (-) 12) = (`-**353**) = "**RECIPROCAL-SEQUENCING-NUMEROLOGY-RSN**"!!!~'

SHE DIED AT THE `-AGE of (`-**25**)!!!~'

FEBRUARY 1 = (2 x 1) = (`-**2**)!!!~'

JANUARY 20 = (1 x 20) = (`-**20**)!!!~'

(2 + 20) = (`-**22**)!!!~'

FEBRUARY 1, 1994 = (2 + 1 + 1 + 9 + 9 + 4) = (`-**26**) = RECIPROCAL (MIRROR) = (`-**62**)!!!~'

JANUARY 20, 2020 = (1 + 2 + 0 + 2 + 0 + 2 + 0) = (`-**7**)!!!~'

(**26** + **7**) = (`-**33**)!!!~'

`-**BIRTHDAY; and, `-DEATH/DAY**!!!~':

(**120** + **21**) = (`-**141**) = "**RECIPROCAL-SEQUENCING-NUMEROLOGY-RSN**"!!!~'

(**120** (-) **21**) = (`-**99**)!!!~'

(141 + 99) = (`-**240**) = (24 + 0) = (`-**24**)!!!~'

FEBRUARY 1 (**BIRTH**) + JANUARY 20 (**DEATH**) = (2 + 1 + 1 + 20) = (`-**24**)!!!~'

`-DIED in (`-**1**) & was `-BORN in (`-**2**) = (`-**1/2**) = (`-**12**) = RECIPROCAL (MIRROR) = (`-**21**) = `-**BIRTHDAY** of AUSTRALIAN NOVELIST STEPH BOWE (**FEBRUARY 1**st)!!!~'

SCREENWRITER for "MARY TYLER MORE & CHEERS" WRITER EARL POMERANTZ (`-**75**) (BIRTH: **FEBRUARY 4, 1945**) (DEATH: **MARCH 7, 2020**)!!!~'

FEBRUARY 4 = (`-**24**) = "**FLIP** the (`-**2**) **OVER** to a (`-**7**) = (`-**74**) = **RECIPROCAL (MIRROR)** = (20 + 20 + 7) = (`-**47**)!!!~'

`-**1945** = (19 + 45) = (`-**64**) = (`-**2** x `-**32**)!!!~'

(`-**BIRTHDAY** = **24** + **37** = `-**DEATH/DAY**) = (`-**61**)!!!~'

`-**AGE** of `-**DEATH** = `-**EQUALS** = (`-**75**)!!!~' BIRTHDAY # `-**NUMBER** = (2 + 4 + 19 + 45) = (`-**70**)!!!~' DEATH/DAY # `-**NUMBER** = (3 + 7 + 20 + 20) = (`-**50**)!!!~' (**70/50**) = (75 + 0 + 0) = (`-**75**) = "**AGE** of `-**DEATH**"!!!~'

`-**DIED** (`-**32**) **DAYS** after `-**HIS** `-**LAST** `-**BIRTHDAY**!!!~' (366 (-) 32) = (`-**334**)!!!~' (33 x 4) = (`-**132**) = (32 x 1) = (`-**32**) = -a PROPHETIC # `-**NUMBER**!!!~'

`-**DIED** (`-**334**) **DAYS AWAY** from **HIS** `-**BIRTHDAY**!!!~' `-**SAME** as for **AMERICAN ACTOR NICHOLAS TUCCI** who

`-DIED at (`-**38**)!!!~' (75 (-) 38) = (`-**37**) = "**DAY** of `-**DEATH** = (**MARCH** 7ᵗʰ)" = (33 + 4) = (`-**334**)!!!~'

BIRTHDAY # `-NUMBER = (2 + 4 + 19 + 45) = **70**

DEATH/DAY # `-NUMBER = (3 + 7 + 20 + 20) = **50**

(70 (-) 50) = (`-**20**)!!!~'

(70 + 50) = (`-**120**)!!!~'

(120 (-) 20) = (`-**100%**)!!!~'

HE DIED (`-**32**) DAYS AFTER HIS LAST BIRTHDAY!!!~'

(366 (-) 32) = (`-**334**) = (33 x 4) = (`-**132**) = (32 x 1) = (`-**32**) = -a PROPHETIC # `-NUMBER!!!~'

HE DIED AT THE `-AGE of (`-**75**) = (7 x 5) = (`-**35**) = RECIPROCAL (MIRROR) = (`-**53**)!!!~'

FEBRUARY 4 = (2 x 4) = (`-**8**)!!!~'

MARCH 7 = (3 x 7) = (`-**21**)!!!~'

(21 (-) 8) = (`-**13**) = "**A VERY PIVOTAL # `-NUMBER**"!!!~'

FEBRUARY 4, 1945 = (2 + 4 + 1 + 9 + 4 + 5) = (`-**25**) = RECIPROCAL (MIRROR) = (`-**52**)!!!~' **FLIP** the (`-**2**) **OVER** to a (`-**7**) = (`-**75**) = "**AGE** of `-**DEATH** for SCREENWRITER for "MARY TYLER MORE & CHEERS" WRITER EARL POMERANTZ (`-**75**)"**!!!~'

MARCH 7, 2020 = (3 + 7 + 2 + 0 + 2 + 0) = (`-**14**)!!!~'

68

(**25** + **14**) = (`-**39**)!!!~'

`-**BIRTHDAY**; and, `-**DEATH/DAY**!!!~':

(**37** + **24**) = (`-**61**)!!!~'

(**37** (-) **24**) = (`-**13**)!!!~'

(61 + 13) = (`-**74**) = "**DIED** (`-**32**) DAYS LATER from `-**BEING** (`-**74**) YEARS of `-**AGE**"!!!~'

FEBRUARY 4 (**BIRTH**) + MARCH 7 (**DEATH**) = (2 + 4 + 3 + 7) = (`-**16**)!!!~'

`-**DIED** in (`-**3**) & was `-**BORN** in (`-**2**) = (`-**3/2**) = (`-**32**) = -a PROPHETIC # `-**NUMBER**!!!~'

(16 x 2) = (`-**32**) = -a PROPHETIC # `-**NUMBER**!!!~'

`-**GOD** can `-**LET US** `-**DESTROY OURSELVES** by a **NUCLEAR ANNIHILATION**!!!~' `-**GOD** with `-**HIS** `-**PERFECT MEMORY** can `-**RESURRECT** `-**ALL** that have ever `-**DIED** before **US**; and, have `-**THEM LIVE** on a `-**PARADISE** `-**EARTH**!!!~' OR; `-**GOD** can just `-**LEAVE** `-**THINGS**, just the `-**WAY**; `-**THEY ARE**!!!~'

AMERICAN MYSTERY WRITER BARBARA ANN NEELY (`-**78**) (BORN: NOVEMBER 30, 1941) (DEATH: **MARCH 2**, 2020)!!!~'

`-**BORN** NOVEMBER 30 = (11 + 30) = (`-**41**) = "**YEAR** of `-**BIRTH** (`-**41**)"!!!~'

MARCH 2 = 3(2's) = (03/0**2**/**2**0**2**0) = **3(2's)**!!!~'

BIRTHDAY # `-NUMBER = (11 + 30 + 19 + 41) = **101**

SAME `-BIRTHDAY # `-NUMBER (`-**101**) as AMERICAN JOURNALIST (CNN) BOBBIE BATTISTA (`-**67**) (BIRTH: JULY **23**, **1952**) (DEATH: **MARCH 3**, 2020)

DEATH/DAY # `-NUMBER = (3 + 2 + 20 + 20) = **45**!!!~'

(101 (-) 45) = (`-**56**)!!!~'

(101 + 45) = (`-**146**)!!!~'

(146 + 56) = (`-**202**) = 2(20's) = (`-**2020**) `-DIES `-WITHIN!!!~'

(101 + 101) = (`-**202**)!!!~'

SHE DIED (`-**93**) DAYS AFTER HER LAST BIRTHDAY!!!~'

(366 (-) 93) = (`-**273**) = (73 x 2) = (`-**146**) = `-**DEATH/DAY #** `-**NUMBER** for AMERICAN JOURNALIST (CNN) BOBBIE BATTISTA (`-**46**)!!!~'

SHE DIED AT THE `-AGE of (`-**78**) = (7 x 8) = (`-**56**)!!!~'

NOVEMBER 30 = (11 x 30) = (`-**330**)!!!~'

MARCH 2 = (3 x 2) = (`-**6**)!!!~'

(330 + 6) = (`-**336**) = (33 + 6) = (`-**39**) x `-2) = (`-**78**) = "AGE of `-**DEATH for AMERICAN MYSTERY WRITER BARBARA ANN NEELY (`-78)**"!!!~'

NOVEMBER 30, 1941 = (1 + 1 + 3 + 0 + 1 + 9 + 4 + 1) = (`-**20**) = RECIPROCAL (MIRROR) = (`-**02**)!!!~'

MARCH 2, 2020 = (3 + 2 + 2 + 0 + 2 + 0) = (`-**9**)!!!~'

(**20** + **9**) = (`-**29**)!!!~'

`-**BIRTHDAY**; and, `-**DEATH/DAY**!!!~':

(**730** + **32**) = (`-**762**)!!!~'

(**730** (-) **32**) = (`-**698**)!!!~'

(762 (-) 698) = (`-**64**) = (2 x 32) = (`-**32**) = -a **PROPHETIC #** `-**NUMBER**!!!~'

`-**DIED** on (`-**3/2**) = **MARCH 2**[nd]!!!~'

NOVEMBER 30 (**BIRTH**) + MARCH 2 (**DEATH**) = (11 + 30 + 3 + 2) = (`-**46**) = RECIPROCAL (MIRROR) = (`-**64**)!!!~'

(`-**46**) = (23 x 2)!!!~'

`-**DIED** in (`-**3**) & was `-**BORN** in (`-**11**) = (`-**3/11**) = 3(1 + 1) = (`-**32**) = "**DAY** of `-**DEATH** (**MARCH 2**[nd]) for AMERICAN MYSTERY WRITER BARBARA ANN NEELY (`-**78**)"!!!~'

(`-**32**) = RECIPROCAL (MIRROR) = (`-**23**)!!!~'

AMERICAN ACTOR "7th `-HEAVEN" LORENZO BRINO (`-**21**) (BIRTH: SEPTEMBER **21**, 1998) (DEATH: **MARCH 9**, 2020)!!!~'

WAS `-**BORN** on the (`-**21**st); and, `-**DIED** at the `-**AGE** of (`-**21**)!!!~'

`-FRAGMENTED `-**BIRTHDAY** # `-**NUMBER** (`-**39**) = EQUALS = `-**HIS** `-**DAY OF** `-**DEATH** (**MARCH 9**th)!!!~'

`-**1998** = (19 + 98) = (`-**117**) = (1 x 17) = (`-**17**) = RECIPROCAL (MIRROR) = (`-**71**) = "FLIP the (`-**7**) OVER to a (`-**2**) = (`-**21**) = "**AGE** of `-**DEATH** for AMERICAN ACTOR "7th `-**HEAVEN**" LORENZO BRINO (`-**21**)"!!!~'

`-**BIRTHDAY** (**9/21**) = 9 (2 + 1) = (`-**93**) = RECIPROCAL (MIRROR) = (`-**39**) = "**DAY of `-DEATH for AMERICAN ACTOR "7**th **`-HEAVEN" LORENZO BRINO!!!~'**

BIRTHDAY # `-NUMBER = (9 + 21 + 19 + 98) = **147**

DEATH/DAY # `-NUMBER = (3 + 9 + 20 + 20) = **52**

(147 (-) 52) = (`-**95**)!!!~'

(147 + 52) = (`-**199**)!!!~'

(199 (-) 95) = (`-**104**) / `-**2**) = (`-**52**) = `-**DEATH/DAY** # `-**NUMBER** (`-**52**)!!!~'

HE DIED (`-**196**) DAYS BEFORE HIS NEXT BIRTHDAY!!!~'

(365 (-) 196) = (`-**169**) = (69 x 1) = (`-**69**) = (3 x 23)!!!~'

HE DIED AT THE `-**AGE** of (`-**21**)!!!~'

SEPTEMBER 21 = (9 x 21) = (`-**189**) = (18 + 9) = (`-**27**) = (3 x 9) = "**DAY of `-DEATH for AMERICAN ACTOR "7**$^{th}$ **`-HEAVEN" LORENZO BRINO (MARCH(3) 9**th)"!!!~'

MARCH 9 = (3 x 9) = (`-**27**)!!!~'

(189 + 27) = (`-**216**) = (2 x 16) = (`-**32**) = -a PROPHETIC # `-NUMBER!!!~'

FRAGMENTED `-BIRTHDAY # `-NUMBER = SEPTEMBER 21, 1998 = (9 + 2 + 1 + 1 + 9 + 9 + 8) = (`-**39**) = "DAY of `-DEATH (MARCH(3) 9ᵗʰ)"!!!~'

MARCH 9, 2020 = (3 + 9 + 2 + 0 + 2 + 0) = (`-**16**)!!!~'

(**39** (-) **16**) = (`-**23**) = -a PROPHETIC # `-NUMBER!!!~'

(39 + 16) = (`-**55**) = (23 + 32)!!!~'

`-**BIRTHDAY**; and, `-**DEATH/DAY!!!~**':

(**921** + **39**) = (`-**960**)!!!~'

(**921** (-) **39**) = (`-**882**)!!!~'

(960 (-) 882) = (`-**78**)!!!~'

(960 + 882) = (`-1842) = (42 (-) 18) = (`-**24**)!!!~'

SEPTEMBER 21 (**BIRTH**) + MARCH 9 (**DEATH**) = (9 + 21 + 3 + 9) = (`-**42**) = RECIPROCAL (MIRROR) = (`-**24**)!!!~'

`-**DIED** in (`-**3**) & was `-**BORN** in (`-**9**) = (`-**3/9**) = (`-**39**) = "**DAY of `-DEATH for** AMERICAN ACTOR "7ᵗʰ `-**HEAVEN**" LORENZO BRINO (**MARCH 9**ᵗʰ)"!!!~'

AMERICAN COMPOSER CHARLES WUORINEN (`-**81**) (BIRTH: JUNE 9, 1938) (DEATH: MARCH 11, 2020)!!!~'

`-**BIRTHDAY** = **JUNE 9$^{th}$** = (`-**69**) = (3 x 23)!!!~'

BIRTHDAY # `-NUMBER = (6 + 9 + 19 + 38) = **72**

DEATH/DAY # `-NUMBER** = (3 + 11 + 20 + 20) = **54** = `-BIRTHDAY (6 x 9)!!!~'**

(72 (-) 54) = (`-**18**) = RECIPROCAL (MIRROR) = (`-**81**) = "**AGE of `-DEATH**"!!!~'

(72 + 54) = (`-**126**) = (12 x 6) = (`-**72**) = BIRTHDAY # `-NUMBER!!!~'

(126 (-) 18) = (`-**108**) = (18 + 0) = (`-**18**) = RECIPROCAL (MIRROR) = (`-**81**) = "**AGE of `-DEATH for AMERICAN COMPOSER CHARLES WUORINEN (`-81)**"!!!~'

HE DIED (`-**90**) DAYS BEFORE HIS NEXT BIRTHDAY!!!~'

(365 (-) 90) = (`-**275**) = (75 x 2) = (`-**150**)!!!~'

HE DIED AT THE `-AGE of (`-**81**) = (9 x 9)!!!~'

JUNE 9 = (6 x 9) = (`-**54**) = `-**DEATH/DAY # `-NUMBER** (`-**54**) = RECIPROCAL (MIRROR) = (`-**45**)!!!~'

MARCH 11 = (3 x 11) = (`-**33**)!!!~'

(54 + 33) = (`-**87**)!!!~'

(54 (-) 33) = (`-**21**)!!!~'

74

(87 + 21) = (`-**108**) = (18 + 0) = (`-**18**) = RECIPROCAL (MIRROR) = (`-**81**) = "AGE of `-DEATH for AMERICAN COMPOSER CHARLES WUORINEN (`-**81**)"!!!~'

JUNE 9, 1938 = (6 + 9 + 1 + 9 + 3 + 8) = (`-**36**) = (3 x 6) = (`-**18**) = RECIPROCAL (MIRROR) = (`-**81**) = "AGE of `-DEATH for AMERICAN COMPOSER CHARLES WUORINEN (`-**81**)"!!!~'

MARCH 11, 2020 = (3 + 1 + 1 + 2 + 0 + 2 + 0) = (`-**9**)!!!~'

(**36** (-) **9**) = (`-**27**)!!!~'

(36 + 9) = (`-**45**) = RECIPROCAL (MIRROR) = (`-**54**) = `-DEATH/ DAY # `-NUMBER (`-**54**)!!!~'

`-**BIRTHDAY**; and, `-**DEATH/DAY**!!!~':

(**311** + **69**) = (`-**380**) = (38 + 0) = (`-**38**) = `-**BORN** in (`-**38**)!!!~'

(**311** (-) **69**) = (`-**242**) = "**R**ECIPROCAL-**S**EQUENCING-**N**UMEROLOGY-**RSN**"!!!~'

(380 (-) 242) = (`-**138**) = (38 x 1) = (`-**38**) = "The `-DEATH # `-**NUMBERS**"!!!~'

(380 + 242) = (`-**622**) = (22 x 6) = (`-**132**) = (32 x 1) = (`-**32**) = -a PROPHETIC # `-NUMBER!!!~'

JUNE 9 (**BIRTH**) + MARCH 11 (**DEATH**) = (6 + 9 + 3 + 11) = (`-**29**) = **2**(**9**'s) = (9 x 9) = (`-**81**) = "AGE of `-DEATH for AMERICAN COMPOSER CHARLES WUORINEN (`-**81**)"!!!~'

`-DIED in (`-**3**) & was `-BORN in (`-**6**) = (`-**3/6**) = (`-**36**) = (3 x 6) = (`-**18**) = RECIPROCAL (MIRROR) = (`-**81**) = "AGE of `-DEATH for **AMERICAN COMPOSER CHARLES WUORINEN** (`-**81**)"!!!~'

AMERICAN FILM ACTOR STUART MAXWELL WHITMAN (`-**92**) (BIRTH: FEBRUARY 1, 19**2**8) (DEATH: MARCH 16, 2020)!!!~'

`-**AGE** of `-**DEATH** = (`-**92**) = (9 x 2) = (`-**18**) = "SEE `-ABOVE at (`-19**2**8)"!!!~'

FEBRUARY 1 = (2 x 1) = (`-**2**)!!!~'

MARCH 16 = (3 + 16) = (`-**19**) = (1 x 9) = (`-**9**)!!!~'

(`-**29**) = RECIPROCAL (MIRROR) = (`-**92**) = "**AGE** of `-**DEATH**"!!!~'

BIRTHDAY # `-NUMBER = (2 + 1 + 19 + 28) = **50**

DEATH/DAY # `-NUMBER = (3 + 16 + 20 + 20) = **59**

(59 (-) 50) = (`-**9**)!!!~'

(59 + 50) = (`-**109**)!!!~'

(109 + 9) = (`-**118**) = (18 x 1) = (`-**18**) = (9 x 2) = (`-**92**) = "**AGE** of `-**DEATH** for **AMERICAN FILM ACTOR STUART MAXWELL WHITMAN** (`-**92**)!!!~'

HE DIED (`-**44**) DAYS AFTER HIS LAST BIRTHDAY!!!~'

(366 (-) 44) = (`-**322**) = (32 x 2) = (`-**64**)!!!~'

HE DIED AT THE `-AGE of (`-**92**)!!!~'

FEBRUARY 1 = (2 x 1) = (`-**2**)!!!~'

MARCH 16 = (3 x 16) = (`-**48**)!!!~'

(48 + 2) = (`-**50**) = `-BIRTHDAY # `-NUMBER (`-**50**)!!!~'

(48 (-) 2) = (`-**46**) = (`-**23** x `-2)!!!~'

(50 + 46) = (`-**96**) = (`-3 x `-**32**)!!!~'

FEBRUARY 1, 1928 = (2 + 1 + 1 + 9 + 2 + 8) = (`-**23**) = RECIPROCAL (MIRROR) = (`-**32**) = -**PROPHETIC** # `-**NUMBERS**!!!~'

MARCH 16, 2020 = (3 + 1 + 6 + 2 + 0 + 2 + 0) = (`-**14**)!!!~'

(**23** (-) **14**) = (`-**9**)!!!~'

(23 + 14) = (`-**37**)!!!~'

(37 (-) 9) = (`-**28**) = "WAS `-**BORN** in (`-**28**)"!!!~'

`-**BIRTHDAY; and, `-DEATH/DAY**!!!~':

(**316** + **21**) = (`-**337**)!!!~'

(**316** (-) **21**) = (`-**295**)!!!~'

(337 (-) 295) = (`-**42**) = **"The `-MARK"**!!!~'

FEBRUARY 1 (**BIRTH**) + MARCH 16 (**DEATH**) = (**2** + 1 + **3** + 16) = (`-**22**)!!!~'

`-DIED in (`-**3**) & was `-BORN in (`-**2**) = (`-**3/2**) = (`-**32**) = -a PROPHETIC # `-NUMBER!!!~'

AMERICAN ACTOR LYLE WAGGONER (`-**84**) (BIRTH: **APRIL** 1**3**, 1935) (DEATH: **MARCH** 1**7**, 2020)!!!~'

(`-**MARCH**) (31 (-) 17) = (`-**14**) + (`-**APRIL**) (`-**13**) = (`-**43** x 1) = `-**BIRTHDAY** (`-**413**)!!!~'

`-AGE of `-DEATH = (`-**84**) = (8 x 4) = (`-**32**) = -a PROPHETIC # `-NUMBER!!!~'

`-**BIRTHDAY** = (**4/13**) = (4 + 13) = (`-**17**) = "**DAY** of `-**DEATH**"!!!~'

BIRTHDAY # `-NUMBER = (4 + 13 + 19 + 35) = **71** = RECIPROCAL (MIRROR) = (`-**17**) = (`-**DEATH/DAY** (`-**17**))!!!~'

DEATH/DAY # `-NUMBER = (3 + **17** + 20 + 20) = **60**

(71 (-) 60) = (`-**11**)!!!~'

(71 + 60) = (`-**131**) = "**RECIPROCAL-SEQUENCING-NUMEROLOGY-RSN**"!!!~'

(131 + 11) = (`-**142**) = (42 x 1) = (`-**42**) = "The `-**MARK**"!!!~'

HE DIED (`-**27**) DAYS BEFORE HIS NEXT BIRTHDAY!!!~'

(365 (-) 27) = (`-**338**) = (33 x 8) = (`-**264**) = (64 / 2) = (`-**32**) = -a PROPHETIC # `-NUMBER!!!~'

HE DIED AT THE `-AGE of (`-**84**) = (`-**42** x `-**2**)!!!~'

APRIL 13 = (4 x 13) = (`-**52**)!!!~'

MARCH 17 = (3 x 17) = (`-**51**)!!!~'

(52 + 51) = (`-**103**)!!!~'

(52 (-) 51) = (`-**1**)!!!~'

(103 + 1) = (`-**104**)!!!~'

APRIL 13, 1935 = (4 + 1 + 3 + 1 + 9 + 3 + 5) = (`-**26**) = RECIPROCAL (MIRROR) = (`-**62**)!!!~'

MARCH 17, 2020 = (3 + 1 + 7 + 2 + 0 + 2 + 0) = (`-**15**)!!!~'

(**26** (-) **15**) = (`-**11**)!!!~'

(26 + 15) = (`-**41**)!!!~'

(41 + 11) = (`-**52**) = `-**BIRTHDAY** (**4**/**13**) = (4 x 13) = (`-**52**)!!!~'

`-**BIRTHDAY**; and, `-**DEATH/DAY**!!!~':

(**413** + **317**) = (`-**730**) = (73 + 0) = (`-**73**) = RECIPROCAL (MIRROR) = (`-**37**) = "DAY of `-DEATH = (`-**317**) = (37 x 1) = (`-**37**)!!!~'

(**413** (-) **317**) = (`-**96**) = (`-32 X `-3)!!!~'

(730 (-) 96) = (`-**634**) = (63 x 4) = (`-**252**) = "**RECIPROCAL-SEQUENCING-NUMEROLOGY-RSN**"!!!~'

APRIL 13 (**BIRTH**) + MARCH 17 (**DEATH**) = (4 + 13 + 3 + 17) = (`-**37**)!!!~'

'-DIED in ('-3) & was '-BORN in ('-4) = ('-3/4) = ('-34) = RECIPROCAL (MIRROR) = ('-43) = **'-BIRTHDAY (413)** = (43 x 1) = ('-43)!!!-'

CZECHOSLOVAK ICE HOCKEY PLAYER VLADIMIR ZABRODSKY ('-97) (BIRTH: **MARCH 7**, 19**23**) (DEATH: **MARCH 20, 2020**)!!!-'

MARCH 20th = **"THE '-PROPHET'S '-BIRTHDAY"**!!!-' (3 + 20 + 20 + 20) = ('-63) = **"AGE of '-DEATH of '-the "PROPHET'S" MOTHER ('-63)**!!!-' 3(20's)!!!-'

'-**1923** = (19 + 23) = ('-42) = **"The '-MARK"**!!!-'

BIRTHDAY # '-NUMBER = (3 + 7 + 19 + 23) = **52**

DEATH/DAY # '-NUMBER = (**3** + **2**0 + 20 + 20) = **63**

(63 (-) 52) = ('-11)!!!-'

(63 + 52) = ('-115)!!!-'

(115 + 11) = ('-126) = ('-2 x '-63)!!!-'

HE DIED ('-13) DAYS AFTER HIS LAST BIRTHDAY!!!-'

('-13) = **"A VERY PIVOTAL # '-NUMBER"**!!!-'

(365 (-) 13) = ('-352) = (35 x 2) = ('-70) = **"THE '-YEAR THE "PROPHET"** was '-**BORN** ('-70)"!!!-'

HE DIED AT THE `-AGE of (`-**97**) = (9 x 7) = (`-**63**) = **"AGE of `-DEATH of THE "PROPHET'S" MOTHER (`-63); AND, `-HIS `-DEATH/DAY # `-NUMBER (`-63)"!!!~'**

MARCH 7 = (3 x 7) = (`-**21**)!!!~'

MARCH 20 = (3 x 20) = (`-**60**)!!!~'

(60 + 21) = (`-**81**)!!!~'

(60 (-) 21) = (`-**39**)!!!~'

(81 + 39) = (`-**120**) = (20 x 1) = (`-**20**th) = **"DAY Of `-DEATH"!!!~'**

(81 (-) 39) = (`-**42**) = **"The `-MARK"!!!~'**

MARCH 7, 1923 = (3 + 7 + 1 + 9 + 2 + 3) = (`-**25**) = RECIPROCAL (MIRROR) = (`-**52**) = **`-BIRTHDAY # `-NUMBER (`-52)!!!~'**

MARCH 20, 2020 = (3 + 2 + 0 + 2 + 0 + 2 + 0) = (`-**9**)!!!~'

(**25** (-) **9**) = (`-**16**)!!!~'

(25 + 9) = (`-**34**)!!!~'

(34 + 16) = (`-**50**) = **`-AT this `-BIRTHDAY/DEATH/DAY = The "PROPHET'S" `-AGE = (`-50)!!!~'**

`-BIRTHDAY; and, `-DEATH/DAY!!!~':

(**320** + **37**) = (`-**357**) = (57 x 3) = (`-**171**) = **"RECIPROCAL-SEQUENCING-NUMEROLOGY-RSN"!!!~'**

(**320** (-) **37**) = (`-**283**) = (28 x 3) = (`-**84**) = (8 x 4) = (`-**32**) = -a **PROPHETIC # `-NUMBER"!!!~'**

(357 (-) 283) = (`-**74**) = JULY 4<sup>th</sup> = "**INDEPENDENCE `-DAY**"!!!~'

(357 + 283) = (`-**640**) = (64 + 0) = (`-**64**) = (`-**2** x `-**32**)!!!~'

MARCH 7 (**BIRTH**) + MARCH 20 (**DEATH**) = (3 + 7 + 3 + 20) = (`-**33**)!!!~'

`-**DIED** in (`-**3**) & was `-**BORN** in (`-**3**) = (`-**3/3**) = (`-**33**) = DEATH/DAY + BIRTHDAY `-ADDED `-UP `-TOGETHER = (`-**33**)!!!~'

(33 + 33) = (`-**66**) = "**AGE** of `-**DEATH** of **THE** "**PROPHET'S**" **FATHER** (`-**66**)!!!~'

AMERICAN SINGER/SONGWRITER KENNY ROGERS (`-**81**) (BIRTH: **AUGUST 21, 1938**) (DEATH: **MARCH 20, 2020**)!!!~'

MARRIED to `-WIFE WANDA MILLER for (`-**23**) YEARS from (19**97**-TO-2020)!!!~'

AUGUST 21 = (8/21) = (81 x 2) = (`-**162**) = (62 + 1) = (`-**63**) = "DEATH/DAY # `-NUMBER (`-63)"!!!~'**

MARCH 20th = "THE `-PROPHET'S `-BIRTHDAY"!!!~' (3 + 20 + 20 + 20) = (`-**63**) = "**AGE** of `-**DEATH** of `-the "**PROPHET'S**" **MOTHER** (`-**63**)!!!~' **3**(20's)!!!~'

BIRTHDAY # `-NUMBER = (8 + 21 + 19 + 38) = **86** = "**AGE** of `-**DEATH** for THE "**PROPHET'S**" MOTHER'S FATHER (`-**86**)"!!!~'

DEATH/DAY # `-NUMBER = (**3** + **2**0 + 20 + 20) = **63**

(86 (-) 63) = (`-**23**) = -a PROPHETIC # `-NUMBER!!!~'

(86 + 63) = (`-**149**) = (49 + 1) = (`-**50**) = "AGE of the "PROPHET" on this `-PARTICULAR `-BIRTHDAY / `-DEATH/DAY (`-**50**)"!!!~'

(149 (-) 23) = (`-**126**) = (`-2 x `-**63**)!!!~'

HE DIED (`-**154**) DAYS BEFORE HIS NEXT BIRTHDAY!!!~'

(365 (-) 154) = (`-**211**) = (21 x 1) = (`-**21**) = "**DAY of `-BIRTH**"!!!~'

HE DIED AT THE `-AGE of (`-**81**) = (9 x 9)!!!~'

AUGUST 21 = (8 x 21) = (`-**168**) = (68 x 1) = (`-**68**) = "The `-**MARK**"!!!~'

MARCH 20 = (3 x 20) = (`-**60**)!!!~'

(168 + 60) = (`-**228**)!!!~'

(168 (-) 60) = (`-**108**) = (18 + 0) = (`-**18**) = RECIPROCAL (MIRROR) = (`-**81**) = "**AGE of `-DEATH for AMERICAN SINGER/ SONGWRITER KENNY ROGERS (`-81)**"!!!~'

(228 + 108) = (`-**336**) = (36 x 3) = (`-**108**) = (18 + 0) = (`-**18**) = RECIPROCAL (MIRROR) = (`-**81**) = "**AGE of `-DEATH for AMERICAN SINGER/SONGWRITER KENNY ROGERS (`-81)**"!!!~

(228 (-) 108) = (`-**120**) = (20 x 1) = (`-**20**th) = "**DAY Of `-DEATH**"!!!~'

FRAGMENTED `-BIRTHDAY # `-NUMBER = AUGUST 21, 1938 = (8 + 2 + 1 + 1 + 9 + 3 + 8) = (`-**32**) = RECIPROCAL (MIRROR) = (`-**23**)!!!~'

FRAGMENTED `-BIRTHDAY # `-NUMBER = (`-**32**) = **3**(**20**'s) for `-**DEATH/DAY** & `-**DEATH/YEAR!!!~'**

MARCH (3) 20, 2020 = (**3** + **2** + 0 + 2 + 0 + 2 + 0) = (`-**9**)!!!~'

(**32** (-) **9**) = (`-**23**) = -a PROPHETIC # `-NUMBER!!!~'

(32 + 9) = (`-**41**)!!!~'

(41 + 23) = (`-**64**) = (`-**2** x `-**32**)!!!~'

(41 (-) 23) = (`-**18**) = RECIPROCAL (MIRROR) = (`-**81**) = "AGE of `-DEATH for AMERICAN SINGER/SONGWRITER KENNY ROGERS (`-**81**)"!!!~

`-**BIRTHDAY**; and, `-**DEATH/DAY!!!~**':

(**821** + **320**) = (`-**1141**) = (11 + 41) = (`-**52**) = `-**BIRTHDAY** & `-**DEATH/DAY** `-**ADDED** `-**UP** `-**TOGETHER** (`-**52**)!!!~'

(**821** (-) **320**) = (`-**501**) = (50 x 1) = (`-**50**) = "**NOW** `-**CURRENT** `-**AGE** of the `-**PROPHET** (`-**50**)"!!!~'

(1141 (-) 501) = (`-**640**) = (64 + 0) = (`-**64**) = (`-**2** x `-**32**)!!!~'

(1141 + 501) = (`-**1642**) = (16 + 42) = (`-**58**) = (5 + 8) = (`-**13**) = "**A VERY PIVOTAL # `-NUMBER**"!!!~'

AUGUST 21 (**BIRTH**) + MARCH 20 (**DEATH**) = (8 + 21 + 3 + 20) = (`-**52**)!!!~'

`-**DIED** in (`-**3**) & was `-**BORN** in (`-**8**) = (`-**3/8**) = (`-**38**) = WAS `-**BORN** in (`-**38**)!!!~'

`-NOW; GO `-**BACK** and `-**NOTICE**, `-**ALL** of the `-**CORRELATIONS**; between, `-**ALL; of the** `-**CELEBRITIES!!!~'**

`-**GOD is a** `-**MATHEMATICIAN!!!~'** The `-**PATTERNS** may `-**VARY**; but, `-**THEY** are `-**ALWAYS** `-**TRUE!!!~'** `-**GOD**; likes, `-**VARIETY!!!~'** `-**GOD;** `-**loves,** `-**ALL** of `-**US!!!~'**

CAMEROONIAN MUSICIAN MANU DIBANGO (`-**86**) (BIRTH: **DECEMBER 12**, 19**33**) (DEATH: MARCH **24**, 2020)!!!~'

`-BIRTHDAY = (**12/12**) = (12 + 12) = (`-**24**) = `-**DAY of** `-**DEATH** (`-**24**th)!!!~'

`-BIRTHDAY # `-NUMBER = (12 + 12 + 19 + 33) = (`-**76**)!!!~'

`-DEATH/DAY # `-NUMBER = (3 + 24 + 20 + 20) = (`-**67**)!!!~'

(`-**67**) = RECIPROCAL (MIRROR) = (`-**76**)

(67 + 76) = (`-**143**) = (14 x 3) = (`-**42**) = "The `-**MARK**"!!!~'

(`-**86** / `-**2**) = (`-**43**)!!!~' MARCH(**3**) **2**0/**2**0 = (3 + 20 + 20) = (`-**43**)!!!~'

PART of `-BIRTHDAY # `-NUMBER = (12 + 12 + 19) = (`-**43**)!!!~'

`-**DIED** (`-**103**) DAYS AFTER `-**HIS** `-**LAST** `-**BIRTHDAY!!!~'** (366 (-) 103) = (`-**263**)!!!~'

`-**263** = (2 x 63) = (`-**126**)!!!~'

AMERICAN PLAYWRIGHT TERRENCE MCNALLY (-**81**) (BIRTH: **NOVEMBER(11) 3, 1938**) (DEATH: MARCH 24, 2020)!!!~'

`-BIRTHDAY # `-NUMBER = (11 + 3 + 19 + 38) = (`-**71**)!!!~'

`-DEATH/DAY # `-NUMBER = (3 + 24 + 20 + 20) = (`-**67**)!!!~'

(71 + 67) = (`-**138**) = (38 x 1) = (`-**38**) = "WAS `-BORN in (`-**38**)"!!!~' (38 + 38) = (`-**76**) = RECIPROCAL (MIRROR) = (`-**67**) = `-DEATH/DAY # `-NUMBER (`-**67**)!!!~'

`-**DIED** (`-**142**) DAYS AFTER `-HIS `-LAST `-BIRTHDAY!!!~' (366 (-) 142) = (`-**224**)!!!~'

(2 x 24) = (`-**48**) = (8 x 6) = (`-**86**) = "AGE of `-DEATH for MANU DIBANGO"!!!~'

(`-**224**) = **TWO** to `-**DIE** on the (`-**24**th) of `-MARCH!!!~'

`-**AGES of `-DEATH** = (81 + 86) = (`-**167**) = (67 x 1) = (`-**67**) = **`-DEATH/DAY # `-NUMBER for `-BOTH MANU DIBANGO & TERRENCE MCNALLEY!!!~'**

`-**1933** = (19 + 33) = (`-**52**) = "FLIP the (`-**2**) OVER to a (`-**7**) = (`-**57**) = TERRENCE MCNALLY = `-**1938** = (19 + 38) = (`-**57**)!!!~' (38 (-) 19) = (`-**19**) = **"BOTH `-MEN `-DIED from the `-CORONAVIRUS DISEASE (COVID-19)"!!!~'**

(1933 + 1938) = (`-**3871**) = "SEE the # `-NUMBERS `-ABOVE"!!!~' (71 (-) 38) = (`-**33**) = BIRTH/YEAR of MANU DIBANGO!!!~'

CAMEROONIAN MUSICIAN MANU DIBANGO (`-**86**) (BIRTH: **DECEMBER 12**, 19**33**) (DEATH: MARCH **24**, 2020)!!!~'

BIRTHDAY # `-NUMBER = (12 + 12 + 19 + 33) = **76** = RECIPROCAL (MIRROR) = (`-**67**) = (`-**DEATH/DAY** # (`-**67**))!!!~'

DEATH/DAY # `-NUMBER = (3 + 24 + 20 + 20) = **67**

(76 (-) 67) = (`-**9**)!!!~'

(76 + 67) = (`-**143**)!!!~'

(143 + 9) = (`-**152**) = (52 x 1) = (`-**52**) = (19 + 33) = **"YEAR of `-BIRTH"**!!!~'

HE DIED (`-**103**) DAYS AFTER HIS LAST BIRTHDAY!!!~'

(366 (-) 103) = (`-**263**) = (63 x 2) = (`-**126**)!!!~'

HE DIED AT THE `-AGE of (`-**86**) = (`-**43** x `-**2**)!!!~'

DECEMBER 12 = (12 x 12) = (`-**144**)!!!~'

MARCH 24 = (3 x 24) = (`-**72**)!!!~'

(144 + 72) = (`-**216**) = (2 x 16) = (`-**32**) = -a PROPHETIC # `-NUMBER!!!~'

(144 (-) 72) = (`-**72**)!!!~'

(216 + 72) = (`-**288**) = (88 (-) 2) = (`-**86**) = **"AGE of `-DEATH for CAMEROONIAN MUSICIAN MANU DIBANGO (`-86)"**!!!~'

DECEMBER 12, 1933 = (1 + 2 + 1 + 2 + 1 + 9 + 3 + 3) = (`-**22**)!!!~'

MARCH 24, 2020 = (3 + 2 + 4 + 2 + 0 + 2 + 0) = (`-**13**)!!!~'

(**22** (-) **13**) = (`-**9**)!!!~'

(22 + 13) = (`-**35**)!!!~'

(35 (-) 9) = (`-**26**)!!!~'

`-**BIRTHDAY**; and, `-**DEATH/DAY**!!!~':

(**1212** + **324**) = (`-**1536**) = (15 + 36) = (`-**51**)!!!~'

(**1212** (-) **324**) = (`-**888**) = 3(8's) = (`-**38**)!!!~'

(1536 (-) 888) = (`-**648**) = (48 x 6) = (`-**288**) = "SEE `-ABOVE & `-BELOW"!!!~'

(1536 + 888) = (`-**2424**) = 2(24's) = (24 + 24) = (`-**48**) = (8 x 6) = (`-**86**) = "AGE of `-DEATH for CAMEROONIAN MUSICIAN MANU DIBANGO (`-**86**)"!!!~'

(1536 + 888) = (`-**2424**) = 2(24's) = "THE `-AMOUNT of `-DAYS AMERICAN PLAYWRIGHT TERRENCE MCNALLY `-**DIED** from `-**HIS** `-**BIRTHDAY** (`-**224**)!!!~'

DECEMBER 12 (**BIRTH**) + MARCH 24 (**DEATH**) = (12 + 12 + 3 + 24) = (`-**51**) = "SEE `-ABOVE"!!!~'

`-**DIED** in (`-**3**) & was `-**BORN** in (`-**12**) = (`-**3/12**) = (32 x 1) = (`-**32**) = -a PROPHETIC # `-NUMBER!!!~'

AMERICAN PLAYWRIGHT TERRENCE MCNALLY (-**81**) (BIRTH: **NOVEMBER (11) 3**, **1938**) (DEATH: MARCH 24, 2020)!!!~'

WAS `-**BORN** in (`-**38**) = (3 x 8) = (`-**24**) = `-**DAY** of `-**DEATH** (`-**24**ᵗʰ)!!!~'

PART of `-BIRTHDAY # `-NUMBER = (11 + 3 + 19) = (`-**33**) = "**YEAR of `-BIRTH for CAMEROONIAN MUSICIAN MANU DIBANGO (`-19**33**)**"!!!~'

BIRTHDAY # `-NUMBER = (11 + 3 + 19 + 38) = **71** = RECIPROCAL (MIRROR) = (`-**17**)!!!~' **YEAR** of `-**BIRTH** (`-**38**) + **MANU DIBANGO'S YEAR of `-BIRTH** (`-**33**) = (`-**71**)!!!~'

DEATH/DAY # `-NUMBER = (3 + 24 + 20 + 20) = **67**

(71 (-) 67) = (`-**4**)!!!~'

(71 + 67) = (`-**138**) = (38 x 1) = (`-**38**) = WAS `-**BORN** in (`-**38**)!!!~'

(138 + 4) = (`-**142**) = "**DIED this `-MANY `-DAYS after `-HIS `-BIRTHDAY**"!!!~'

HE DIED (`-**142**) DAYS AFTER HIS LAST BIRTHDAY!!!~'

(366 (-) 142) = (`-**224**) = "**SEE `-ABOVE**"!!!~'

HE DIED AT THE `-AGE of (`-**81**) = (`-**9** x `-**9**)!!!~'

NOVEMBER 3 = (11 x 3) = (`-**33**) = **MANU DIBANGO'S `-YEAR** of `-**BIRTH**!!!~'

MARCH 24 = (3 x 24) = (`-**72**)!!!~'

(72 + 33) = (`-**105**)!!!~'

(72 (-) 33) = (`-**39**)!!!~'

(105 + 39) = (`-**144**) = (`-1 `-HALF) the # `-NUMBER of CAMEROONIAN MUSICIAN MANU DIBANGO (`-**288**)"!!!~'

FRAGMENTED BIRTHDAY # `-NUMBER = NOVEMBER 3, 1938 = (1 + 1 + 3 + 1 + 9 + 3 + 8) = (`-**26**)!!!~'

MANU DIBANGO FRAGMENTED BIRTHDAY # `-NUMBER = (`-**22**)!!!~'

(26 + 22) = (`-**48**) = "**SEE ABOVE**"!!!~'

FRAGMENTED DEATH/DAY # `-NUMBER = MARCH 24, 2020 = (3 + 2 + 4 + 2 + 0 + 2 + 0) = (`-**13**)!!!~'

(**26** (-) **13**) = (`-**13**)!!!~'

(26 + 13) = (`-**39**)!!!~'

(39 (-) 13) = (`-**26**)!!!~'

MANU DIBANGO & TERRENCE MCNALLY `-BOTH = `-EQUAL = (`-**26**)!!!~'

FRAGMENTED **DEATH/DAY** # `-**NUMBERS** (`-TIMES (`-2)) = (`-1**3** x `-**2**)!!!~'

`-**BIRTHDAY**; and, `-**DEATH/DAY**!!!~':

(**324** + **113**) = (`-**437**) = (43 x 7) = (`-**301**) = RECIPROCAL (MIRROR) = (`-**103**) = THE `-AMOUNT of `-DAYS that

CAMEROONIAN MUSICIAN MANU DIBANGO `-DIED after `-HIS `-LAST `-BIRTHDAY!!!~`

$(\underline{324}$ (-) $\underline{113})$ = (`-$\underline{211}$) = (11 x 2) = (`-$\underline{22}$) = FRAGMENTED `-BIRTHDAY # `-NUMBER of MANU DIBANGO = (DECEMBER 12, 1933) = (1 + 2 + 1 + 2 + 1 + 9 + 3 + 3) = (`-$\underline{22}$)!!!~`

(437 (-) 211) = (`-$\underline{226}$) = (22 x 6) = (`-$\underline{132}$) = (32 x 1) = (`-$\underline{32}$) = -a PROPHETIC # `-NUMBER!!!~`

(437 (-) 211) = (`-$\underline{226}$) = (113 x 2) = `-**BIRTHDAY** `-**TWICE** $(\underline{11}/\underline{3})$!!!~`

NOVEMBER 3 (**BIRTH**) + MARCH 24 (**DEATH**) = (11 + 3 + 3 + 24) = (`-$\underline{41}$)!!!~`

(11 + 33 + 24) = (`-$\underline{68}$) = RECIPROCAL (MIRROR) = (`-$\underline{86}$) = "AGE of `-DEATH for CAMEROONIAN MUSICIAN MANU DIBANGO (`-$\underline{86}$)"!!!~`

`-DIED in (`-$\underline{3}$) & was `-BORN in (`-$\underline{11}$) = (`-$\underline{3/11}$) = (31 x 1) = (`-$\underline{31}$) = RECIPROCAL (MIRROR) = (`-$\underline{13}$) = "A VERY PIVOTAL # NUMBER" & FRAGMENTED DEATH/DAY # `-NUMBER (`-$\underline{13}$)!!!~`

`-**BIRTHDAY** = $(1\underline{1}/\underline{3})$ = (13 x 1) = (`-$\underline{13}$)!!!~`

`-DIED in (`-$\underline{3}$) & was `-BORN in (`-$\underline{11}$) = (`-$\underline{3/11}$) = (3 x 11) = (`-$\underline{33}$) = MANU DIBANGO was `-BORN in (`-$\underline{33}$)!!!~`

`-DIED in (`-$\underline{3}$) & was `-BORN in (`-$\underline{11}$) = (`-$\underline{3/11}$) = RECIPROCAL (MIRROR) = (11/3) = `-BIRTHDAY of AMERICAN

PLAYWRIGHT TERRENCE MCNALLY (<u>NOVEMBER</u> (11) 3rd)!!!~'

---

*IF `-<u>**WE**</u> choose **TO** `-**JUMP** `-**OFF** a `-**CLIFF**; then, `-**<u>GOD</u>** will `-**ALLOW** `-**US** to do `-SO; but <u>**AND**</u> yet, `-IT will be `-PERFECTLY `-**<u>SCRIPTED</u>**; by `-**<u>HIM</u>**, in `-**<u>TIME</u>**; and, `-**<u>ESSENCE</u>**!!!~'*

`-<u>NEXT</u> `-<u>LAYER</u>-!!!~'

CHEF FLOYD CARDOZ (`-<u>**59**</u>) (BIRTH: OCTOBER 2, 1960) (DEATH: MARCH 25, 2020)!!!~'

BIRTHDAY # `-NUMBER = (10 + 2 + 19 + 60) = <u>**91**</u> = RECIPROCAL (MIRROR) = (`-<u>**19**</u>)!!!~'

DEATH/DAY # `-NUMBER = (3 + 25 + 20 + 20) = <u>**68**</u> = "The `-<u>**MARK**</u>"!!!~'

(91 (-) 68) = (`-<u>**23**</u>) = -a PROPHETIC # `-NUMBER!!!~'

(91 + 68) = (`-<u>**159**</u>) = (59 x 1) = (`-<u>**59**</u>) = "AGE of `-DEATH"!!!~'

(159 + 23) = (`-<u>**182**</u>) = (82 x 1) = (`-<u>**82**</u>) = RECIPROCAL (MIRROR) = (`-<u>**28**</u>) = <u>**2**</u>(<u>**8's**</u>) = (`-<u>**88**</u>)!!!~'

HE DIED (`-<u>**175**</u>) DAYS AFTER HIS LAST BIRTHDAY!!!~'

(`-<u>**175**</u>) = (17 x 5) = (`-<u>**85**</u>) = `-**BIRTHDAY # `-NUMBER for FREDERICK "CURLY" NEAL**!!!~'

(366 (-) 175) = (`-**191**) = (91 x 1) = (`-**91**) = `-BIRTHDAY # `-NUMBER of CHEF FLOYD CARDOZ (`-**91**)!!!~'

HE DIED AT THE `-AGE of (`-**59**) = (`-**5** x `-**9**) = (`-**45**) = RECIPROCAL (MIRROR) = (`-**54**) = "The `-**NEXT** `-**TWO** to `-**DIE** in this `-**LAYER** (FRED NEAL & MARK BLUM)"!!!~'

OCTOBER 2 = (10 x 2) = (`-**20**)!!!~'

MARCH 25 = (3 x 25) = (`-**75**)!!!~'

(75 + 20) = (` -**95**) = RECIPROCAL (MIRROR) = (`-**59**) = "AGE of `-DEATH for CHEF FLOYD CARDOZ (`-**59**)"!!!~'

(75 (-) 20) = (`-**55**) = (**23** + **32**)!!!~'

(95 + 55) = (`-**150**)!!!~'

FRAGMENTED BIRTHDAY # `-NUMBER = OCTOBER 2, 1960 = (1 + 0 + 2 + 1 + 9 + 6 + 0) = (`-**19**) = RECIPROCAL (MIRROR) = (`-**91**) = `-BIRTHDAY # `-NUMBER!!!~'

FRAGMENTED DEATH/DAY # `-NUMBER = MARCH 25, 2020 = (3 + 2 + 5 + 2 + 0 + 2 + 0) = (`-**14**)!!!~'

(**19** (-) **14**) = (`-**5**)!!!~'

(19 + 14) = (`-**33**)!!!~'

(33 (-) 5) = (`-**28**) = **2**(**8's**) = (`-**88**)!!!~'

`-**BIRTHDAY**; and, `-**DEATH/DAY**!!!~':

(**325** + **102**) = (`-**427**)!!!~'

(<u>325</u> (-) <u>102</u>) = (`-<u>223</u>)!!!~'

(427 (-) 223) = (`-<u>204</u>)!!!~'

(427 + 223) = (`-<u>650</u>)!!!~'

(427 + 223 + 204 + 650) = (`-<u>1504</u>) = (54 x 1 + 0) = "The `-<u>NEXT</u> `-<u>TWO</u> to `-<u>DIE</u> in this `-<u>LAYER</u> (FRED NEAL & MARK BLUM)"!!!~'

OCTOBER 2 (<u>BIRTH</u>) + MARCH 25 (<u>DEATH</u>) = (10 + <u>2</u> + <u>3</u> + 25) = (`-<u>40</u>) = "<u>DIED</u> in (`-<u>20/20</u>)"!!!~'

(10 + 23 + 25) = (`-<u>58</u>) = RECIPROCAL (MIRROR) = (`-<u>85</u>) = `-BIRTHDAY # `-NUMBER of FREDERICK "CURLY" NEAL (`-<u>85</u>)!!!~'

`-DIED in (`-<u>3</u>) & was `-BORN in (`-<u>10</u>) = (`-<u>3/10</u>) = RECIPROCAL (MIRROR) = (<u>10/3</u>) = "<u>DAY</u> `-AFTER `-<u>BIRTHDAY</u>"!!!~'

AMERICAN BASKETBALL PLAYER "**THE HARLEM GLOBETROTTERS**" FREDERICK "CURLY" NEAL (`-<u>77</u>) (BIRTH: <u>MAY</u> 19, 1942) (DEATH: MARCH 26, 2020)!!!~'

<u>MAY</u> 19[th] = (<u>5/19</u>) = (59 x 1) = (`-<u>59</u>) = "AGE of `-DEATH for CHEF FLOYD CARDOZ (`-<u>59</u>)"!!!~'

<u>MAY</u> 19[th] = (<u>5/19</u>) = (5 x 19) = (`-<u>95</u>) = RECIPROCAL (MIRROR) = (`-<u>59</u>) = "AGE of `-DEATH for CHEF FLOYD CARDOZ (`-<u>59</u>)"!!!~'

`-<u>DIED</u> (`-<u>54</u>) <u>DAYS</u> before `-HIS `-NEXT `-BIRTHDAY!!!~'
ADDING `-BIRTHDAY # `-NUMBER (`-<u>85</u>) & DEATH/DAY #

`-NUMBER (`-**69**) = (`-**154**) = (54 x 1) = (`-**54**) = **"THE AMOUNT of `-DAYS `-HE had `-DIED IN-BETWEEN /|\ `-DAYS of `-BIRTH & `-DEATH"!!!~'**

FRAGMENTED `-BIRTHDAY # `-NUMBER = (5 + 1 + 9 + 1 + 9 + 4 + 2) = (`-**31**) = "THE AMOUNT of `-DAYS `-HE had `-DIED IN-BETWEEN /|\ `-DAYS of `-BIRTH & `-DEATH /|\ GOING the `-OTHER `-DIRECTION (`-**311**) = (31 x 1) = (`-**31**)"!!!~'

`-**1942** = (42 (-) 19) = (`-**23**) = **-a PROPHETIC # `-NUMBER!!!~'**

BIRTHDAY # `-NUMBER = (5 + 19 + 19 + 42) = **85** = RECIPROCAL (MIRROR) = (`-**58**)!!!~'

DEATH/DAY # `-NUMBER = (3 + 26 + 20 + 20) = **69** = **"AGE of `-DEATH for AMERICAN ACTOR MARK BLUM (`-69)"!!!~'**

(85 (-) 69) = (`-**16**)!!!~'

(85 + 69) = (`-**154**) = (54 x 1) = (`-**54**) = **"SEE `-ABOVE"!!!~'**

(154 + 16) = (`-**170**)!!!~'

HE DIED (`-**54**) DAYS BEFORE HIS NEXT BIRTHDAY!!!~'

(365 (-) 54) = (`-**311**) = **"SEE `-ABOVE"!!!~'**

HE DIED AT THE `-AGE of (`-**77**) = (`-**11** x `-**7**)!!!~'

MAY 19 = (5 x 19) = (`-**95**) = RECIPROCAL (MIRROR) = (`-**59**) = **"AGE of `-DEATH for CHEF FLOYD CARDOZ (`-59)"!!!~'**

MARCH 26 = (3 x 26) = (`-**78**)!!!~'

(95 + 78) = (`-**173**) = `-DAYS AMERICAN HUMAN RIGHTS ACTIVIST JOSEPH LOWERY `-DIED from `-HIS `-BIRTHDAY!!!~'

(95 (-) 78) = (`-**17**)!!!~'

(173 + 17) = (`-**190**) = (19 + 0) = (`-**19**) = RECIPROCAL (MIRROR) = (`-**91**) = `-BIRTHDAY # `-NUMBER of `-CHEF FLOYD CARDOZ (`-**91**)!!!~'

FRAGMENTED BIRTHDAY # `-NUMBER** = MAY 19, 1942 = (5 + 1 + 9 + 1 + 9 + 4 + 2) = (`-31**) = **"SEE `-ABOVE"**!!!~'

FRAGMENTED DEATH/DAY # `-NUMBER** = MARCH 26, 2020 = (3 + 2 + 6 + 2 + 0 + 2 + 0) = (`-15**)!!!~'

(**31** (-) **15**) = (`-**16**)!!!~'

(31 + 15) = (`-**46**) = (`-**23** x `-**2**)!!!~'

(46 + 16) = (`-**62**) = RECIPROCAL (MIRROR) = (`-**26**)!!!~'

MANU DIBANGO & TERRENCE MCNALLY `-BOTH** = `-EQUALED** = (`-**26**)!!!~'

`-**BIRTHDAY**; and, `-**DEATH/DAY**!!!~':

(**519** + **326**) = (`-**845**)!!!~'

(**519** (-) **326**) = (`-**193**) = `-DAYS AMERICAN HUMAN RIGHTS ACTIVIST JOSEPH LOWERY `-**DIED** from `-HIS `-BIRTHDAY!!!~'

(845 (-) 193) = (`-**652**) = (65 x 2) = (`-**130**) = (13 + 0) = (`-**13**) = **"A VERY PIVOTAL # `-NUMBER"**!!!~'

(845 + 193) = (`-**1038**) = (38 + 10) = (`-**48**) = (4 x 8) = (`-**32**) = -a
PROPHETIC # `-NUMBER!!!~'

(1038 + 652) = (`-**1690**) = (69 x 1 + 0) = (`-**69**) = "AGE of `-DEATH
of AMERICAN ACTOR MARK BLUM (`-**69**)!!!~'

MAY 19 (**BIRTH**) + MARCH 26 (**DEATH**) = (5 + 19 + 3 + 26)
= (`-**53**)!!!~'

`-DIED in (`-**3**) & was `-BORN in (`-**5**) = (`-**3/5**) = (`-**35**) =
RECIPROCAL (MIRROR) = (`-**53**) = "**DEATH/DAY** &
BIRTHDAY `-**ADDED** `-**UP** `-**TOGETHER**"!!!~'

AMERICAN ACTOR MARK BLUM (`-**69**) (BIRTH: **MAY** 1**4**,
1**95**0) (DEATH: MARCH 26, 2020)!!!~'

`-**BIRTHDAY** = (**5**/1**4**) = (54 x 1) = (`-**54**) = "**WIFE JANET
ZARISH** was `-**BORN** in (`-**54**)"!!!~'

JANET ZARISH was `-**BORN** on (**4**/**21**/19**54**); and, WAS (`-**65**)
YEARS of `-AGE at the `-**TIME of MARK BLUM'S** `-**DEATH!!!~'**
(**4**/**21**) = (4 x 21) = (`-**84**) = (8 x 4) = (`-**32**) = -a **PROPHETIC #**
`-**NUMBER!!!~'**

MARK BLUM `-**DIED** at the `-**AGE** of (`-**69**) = (6 x 9) = (`-**54**)!!!~'

BIRTHDAY # `-NUMBER = (5 + 14 + 19 + 50) = **88** = "**AGE
of `-DEATH of EVELYN GIBSON LOWERY (`-88**)"!!!~' (*SEE
`-ABOVE & BELOW*)!!!~'

DEATH/DAY # `-NUMBER = (3 + 26 + 20 + 20) = **69** = "**AGE of
`-DEATH (`-69**)"!!!~'

(88 (-) 69) = (`-**19**)!!!~'

(88 + 69) = (`-**157**) = (57 + 1) = (`-**58**) = RECIPROCAL (MIRROR) = (`-**85**) = "SEE `-ABOVE for FREDERICK "CURLY" NEAL"!!!~'

(157 + 19) = (`-**176**) = (76 + 1) = (`-**77**) = "AGE of `-DEATH for FREDERICK "CURLY" NEAL /|\ AMERICAN BASKETBALL PLAYER (`-**77**)"!!!~'

HE DIED (`-**49**) DAYS BEFORE HIS NEXT BIRTHDAY!!!~'

(`-**49**) = (7 x 7) = (`-**77**) = "AGE of `-DEATH for AMERICAN BASKETBALL PLAYER "*THE HARLEM GLOBETROTTERS*" FREDERICK "CURLY" NEAL (`-**77**)!!!~'

(`-BIRTHDAY = 51**4** /|\ `-BIRTHDAY = 51**9**) = (`-**49**)!!!~'

(365 (-) 49) = (`-**316**) = (31 x 6) = (`-**186**) = (86 x 1) = (`-**86**) = "The `-MARK"!!!~'

HE DIED AT THE `-AGE of (`-**69**) = (`-**6** x `-**9**) = (`-**54**) = "**READ & ANALYZE** from `-**ABOVE**"!!!~'

MAY 14 = (5 x 14) = (`-**70**) = `-DEATH/DAY # `-NUMBER for AMERICAN HUMAN RIGHTS ACTIVIST JOSEPH LOWERY (`-**70**)!!!~'

MARCH 26 = (3 x 26) = (`-**78**)!!!~'

(78 + 70) = (` -**148**) = (48 x 1) = (`-**48**) = (4 x 8) = (`-**32**) = -a PROPHETIC # `-NUMBER!!!~'

(78 (-) 70) = (`-**8**)!!!~'

$(148 + 8) = (`\text{-}\underline{156}) = (56 \times 1) = (`\text{-}\underline{56})$ = `-BIRTHDAY # `-NUMBER for **AMERICAN HUMAN RIGHTS ACTIVIST JOSEPH LOWERY (`-56)!!!~'**

**FRAGMENTED BIRTHDAY # `-NUMBER** = MAY 14, 1950 = $(5 + 1 + 4 + 1 + 9 + 5 + 0) = (`\text{-}\underline{25})$ = `-**BIRTH/YEAR** of **EVELYN GIBSON LOWERY** = RECIPROCAL (MIRROR) = $(`\text{-}\underline{52})$!!!~'

**FRAGMENTED DEATH/DAY # `-NUMBER** = MARCH 26, 2020 = $(3 + 2 + 6 + 2 + 0 + 2 + 0) = (`\text{-}\underline{15})$!!!~'

$(\underline{25} (\text{-}) \underline{15}) = (`\text{-}\underline{10})$!!!~'

$(25 + 15) = (`\text{-}\underline{40})$!!!~'

$(40 + 10) = (`\text{-}\underline{50}) = (5 + 0) = (`\text{-}\underline{5})$ = **"The `-HAND of `-GOD"**!!!~'

`-BIRTHDAY; and, `-DEATH/DAY!!!~':

$(\underline{514} + \underline{326}) = (`\text{-}\underline{840})$!!!~'

$(\underline{514} (\text{-}) \underline{326}) = (`\text{-}\underline{188}) = (88 \times 1) = (`\text{-}\underline{88})$ = `-BIRTHDAY # `-NUMBER & **"AGE of `-DEATH of EVELYN GIBSON LOWERY (`-88)"**!!!~' (*SEE `-ABOVE & BELOW*)!!!~'

$(840 (\text{-}) 188) = (`\text{-}\underline{652})$!!!~'

$(840 + 188) = (`\text{-}\underline{1028})$!!!~'

$(1028 + 652) = (`\text{-}\underline{1680}) = (68 \times 1 + 0) =$ **"The `-MARK"**!!!~'

MAY 14 (**BIRTH**) + MARCH 26 (**DEATH**) = $(5 + \underline{14} + \underline{3} + 26) = (`\text{-}\underline{48})$ = RECIPROCAL (MIRROR) = $(`\text{-}\underline{84})$!!!~'

'-DIED in ('-**3**) & was '-BORN in ('-**5**) = ('-**3/5**) = (3 x 5) = ('-**15**) = **FRAGMENTED DEATH/DAY #** '-**NUMBER** = MARCH 26, 2020 = (3 + 2 + 6 + 2 + 0 + 2 + 0) = ('-**15**)!!!~'

AMERICAN HUMAN RIGHTS ACTIVIST JOSEPH LOWERY ('-**98**) (BIRTH: OCTOBER 6, 1921) (DEATH: MARCH 27, 2020)!!!~'

'-**AGE of** '-**DEATH** = ('-**98**) = (9 x 8) = ('-**72**) = RECIPROCAL (MIRROR) = ('-**27**) = **2**(**7's**) = ('-**77**) = "**AGE of** '-**DEATH for AMERICAN BASKETBALL PLAYER** *"THE HARLEM GLOBETROTTERS"* **FREDERICK "CURLY" NEAL** ('-**77**)!!!~'

'-**1921** = (19 + 21) = ('-**40**) = '-**DIED** in ('-**20/20**) = (20 + 20) = ('-**40**)!!!~'

BIRTHDAY # '-NUMBER = (10 + 6 + 19 + 21) = **56** = RECIPROCAL (MIRROR) = ('-**65**)!!!~'

DEATH/DAY # '-NUMBER = (3 + 27 + 20 + 20) = **70**

(70 (-) 56) = ('-**14**)!!!~'

(70 + 56) = ('-**126**) = (26 x 1) = ('-**26**) = "**SEE** '-**ABOVE** & '-**BELOW**"!!!~'

(126 + 14) = ('-**140**)!!!~'

HE DIED ('-**173**) DAYS AFTER HIS LAST BIRTHDAY!!!~'

(366 (-) 173) = ('-**193**) = "**SEE** '-**ABOVE**"!!!~'

HE DIED AT THE '-**AGE of** ('-**98**) = ('-**49** x '-**2**)!!!~'

OCTOBER 6 = (10 x 6) = (`-**60**) = RECIPROCAL (MIRROR) = (`-**06**)!!!~'

MARCH 27 = (3 x 27) = (`-**81**)!!!~'

(81 + 60) = (`-**141**)!!!~'

(81 (-) 60) = (`-**21**)!!!~'

(141 + 21) = (`-**162**) = (62 x 1) = (`-**62**) = RECIPROCAL (MIRROR) = (`-**26**) = "SEE `-**WIFE** `-**BELOW**"!!!~'

FRAGMENTED BIRTHDAY # `-NUMBER = OCTOBER 6, 1921 = (1 + 0 + 6 + 1 + 9 + 2 + 1) = (`-**20**)!!!~'

FRAGMENTED DEATH/DAY # `-NUMBER = MARCH 27, 2020 = (3 + 2 + 7 + 2 + 0 + 2 + 0) = (`-**16**)!!!~'

(**20** (-) **16**) = (`-**4**)!!!~'

(20 + 16) = (`-**36**)!!!~'

(36 (-) 4) = (`-**32**) = -a PROPHETIC # `-NUMBER!!!~'

`-**BIRTHDAY**; and, `-**DEATH/DAY**!!!~':

(**327** + **106**) = (`-**433**)!!!~'

(**327** (-) **106**) = (`-**221**)!!!~'

`-**ABOVE** = (`-**4321**) = "**PROPHETIC**-**LINEAR**-**PROGRESSION**-**PLP**"!!!~'

(433 (-) 221) = (`-**212**) = (21 x 2) = (`-**42**) = "The `-**MARK**"!!!~'

(433 + 221) = (`-**654**) = (65 x 4) = (`-**260**) = (26 + 0) = (`-**26**) = "SEE `-**ABOVE** & `-**BELOW**"!!!~'

(654 (-) 212) = (`-**442**) = (42 x 4) = (`-**168**) = (68 + 1) = (`-**69**) = "AGE of `-DEATH of AMERICAN ACTOR MARK BLUM (`-**69**)!!!~'

(654 (-) 212) = (`-**442**) = (44 x 2) = (`-**88**) = "AGE of `-DEATH of `-WIFE EVELYN GIBSON LOWERY (`-**88**)"!!!~'

OCTOBER 6 (**BIRTH**) + MARCH 27 (**DEATH**) = (10 + 6 + 3 + 27) = (`-**46**) = (`-**23** x `-**2**)!!!~'

`-DIED in (`-**3**) & was `-BORN in (`-**10**) = (`-**3/10**) = (`-**31** + 0) = (`-**31**) = RECIPROCAL (MIRROR) = (`-**13**) = "A VERY PIVOTAL # `-NUMBER"!!!~'

`-HIS `-WIFE EVELYN GIBSON LOWERY was `-ALSO a `-CIVIL `-RIGHTS `-ACTIVIST and `-LEADER!!!~' SHE `-**DIED** at the `-**AGE** of (`-**88**) in (`-**2013**)!!!~' THEY were `-MARRIED in (`-**1950**) = "THE `-**YEAR** AMERICAN ACTOR MARK BLUM was `-**BORN** (`-**1950**)!!!~'

EVELYN GIBSON LOWERY `-BIRTHDAY # `-NUMBER = FEBRUARY 16, 1925 = (2 + 16 + 19 + 25) = (`-**62**) = RECIPROCAL (MIRROR) = (`-**26**) = "HER `-**DAY** of `-**DEATH**"!!!~'

`-**BIRTHDAY** = (**2/16**) = (26 x 1) = (`-**26**) = "HER `-**DAY** of `-**DEATH**"!!!~'

`-**BIRTHDAY** = (**2/16**) = (2 x 16) = (`-**32**) = -a PROPHETIC # `-**NUMBER**!!!~'

EVELYN GIBSON LOWERY `-DEATH/DAY # `-NUMBER = SEPTEMBER **26**, 20**13** = (9 + 26 + 20 + 13) = (`-**68**) = RECIPROCAL (MIRROR) = (`-**86**) = "The `-**MARK**"!!!~'

SHE `-DIED (`-**143**) DAYS BEFORE `-HER `-NEXT `-BIRTHDAY!!!~' (365 (-) **143**) = (`-**222**) = "The `-**OTHER** `-**DIRECTION**"!!!~' (`-**143**) = (14 x 3) = (`-**42**) = "The `-**MARK**"!!!~'

EVELYN GIBSON LOWERY `-DEATH/DAY = (**9**/2**6**) = (92 + 6) = (`-**98**) = "HER `-HUSBAND'S `-**AGE** of `-**DEATH** for AMERICAN HUMAN RIGHTS ACTIVIST JOSEPH LOWERY (`-**98**)"!!!~'

FORMER UNITED STATES REPRESENTATIVE TOM COBURN (`-**72**) (BIRTH: **MARCH 14**, 19**48**) (DEATH: **MARCH 28**, 2020)!!!~'

AMERICAN HUMAN RIGHTS ACTIVIST JOSEPH LOWERY `-**AGE** of `-**DEATH** = (`-**98**) = (9 x 8) = (`-**72**) = RECIPROCAL (MIRROR) = (`-**27**) = **2**(**7's**) = (`-**77**) = "**AGE** of `-**DEATH** for **AMERICAN BASKETBALL PLAYER** *"THE HARLEM GLOBETROTTERS"* **FREDERICK** "CURLY" **NEAL** (`-**77**)!!!~'

`-**BIRTH/YEAR** = `-**1948** = (19 + 48) = (`-**67**) = (6 x 7) = (`-**42**) = `-**BIRTHDAY** = (3 x 14) = (`-**42**)!!!~' (42 + 42) = (`-**84**)!!!~'

`-**DAUGHTER** SARAH COBURN was (`-**42**) at the `-**TIME** of `-HER `-**FATHER'S DEATH**!!!~' HER BIRTHDAY # `-NUMBER = **AUGUST 4**, 19**77** = (**8** + **4** + 19 + **77**) = (`-**108**)!!!~' (`-**1977**) = (77 (-) 19) = (`-**58**) = RECIPROCAL (MIRROR) = (`-**85**) = "**READ** `-**ABOVE**"!!!~'

('-**48**) = RECIPROCAL (MIRROR) = ('-**84**)!!!~'

HER '-FATHER was '-**BORN** in ('-**48**); while, SHE was '-**BORN** on ('-**84**)!!!~'

BIRTHDAY # '-NUMBER = (3 + 14 + 19 + 48) = **84** = RECIPROCAL (MIRROR) = ('-**48**) = "SEE '-ABOVE" just as '-CLEAR as '-DAY"!!!~'

DEATH/DAY # '-NUMBER = (3 + 28 + 20 + 20) = **71** = RECIPROCAL (MIRROR) = ('-**17**) = FRAGMENTED DEATH/ DAY # '-NUMBER ('-**17**)!!!~'

(84 (-) 71) = ('-**13**) = "A VERY PIVOTAL # '-NUMBER"!!!~'

(84 + 71) = ('-**155**) = (55 x 1) = ('-**55**) = (**23** + **32**)!!!~'

(155 (-) 13) = ('-**142**) = (42 x 1) = ('-**42**) = "SEE '-**ABOVE**"!!!~'

(155 + 13) = ('-**168**) = (68 x 1) = ('-**68**) = "The '-**MARK**"!!!~'

HE DIED ('-**14**) DAYS AFTER HIS LAST BIRTHDAY!!!~'

(365 (-) 14) = ('-**351**) = (51 x 3) = ('-**153**) = '-**RECIPROCAL** to ('-**351**)!!!~'

HE DIED AT THE '-AGE of ('-**72**) = ('-**9** x '-**8**) = "SEE '-**ABOVE**"!!!~'

'-BIRTHDAY = MARCH 14 = (3 x 14) = ('-**42**) = "SEE '-**ABOVE**"!!!~'

'-DEATH/DAY = MARCH 28 = (3 x 28) = ('-**84**) = "ACTUAL '-**DEATH/DAY** '-EQUALS '-**BIRTHDAY** # '-**NUMBER** ('-**84**)"!!!~'

(84 + 42) = (`-**126**) = (26 x 1) = (`-**26**) = "**REVIEW from `-PREVIOUS**"!!!~'

(84 (-) 42) = (`-**42**) = "**SEE `-ABOVE**"!!!~'

(126 + 42) = (`-**168**) = (68 x 1) = (`-**68**) = "**The `-MARK**"!!!~'

FRAGMENTED BIRTHDAY # `-NUMBER** = MARCH 14, 1948 = (3 + 1 + 4 + 1 + 9 + 4 + 8) = (`-30**)!!!~'

FRAGMENTED DEATH/DAY # `-NUMBER** = MARCH 28, 2020 = (3 + 2 + 8 + 2 + 0 + 2 + 0) = (`-17**) = RECIPROCAL (MIRROR) = (`-**71**) = `-DEATH/DAY # `-NUMBER (`-**71**)!!!~'

(**30** (-) **17**) = (`-**13**) = "**A VERY PIVOTAL # `-NUMBER**"!!!~'

(30 + 17) = (`-**47**) = RECIPROCAL (MIRROR) = (`-**74**) = ("**JULY 4th**")!!!~'

(47 (-) 13) = (`-**34**) = "**The `-PRESIDENTIAL # `-NUMBERS**"!!!~'

`-**BIRTHDAY; and, `-DEATH/DAY!!!~'**:

(**328** + **314**) = (`-**642**)!!!~'

(**328** (-) **314**) = (`-**14**)!!!~'

(642 (-) 14) = (`-**628**) = (28 x 6) = (`-**168**) = (68 x 1) = (`-**68**) = "**The `-MARK**"!!!~'

(642 + 14) = (`-**656**) = "**RECIPROCAL-SEQUENCING-NUMEROLOGY-RSN**"!!!~'

(656 (-) 628) = (`-**28**) = **2**(**8's**) = (`-**88**) = "**AGE of `-DEATH for EVELYN GIBSON LOWERY (`-88**)**"!!!~'

(656 + 628) = (`-**1284**) = (84 (-) 12) = (`-**72**) = "**AGE of** `-**DEATH for FORMER UNITED STATES REPRESENTATIVE TOM COBURN** (`-**72**)!!!~'

MARCH 14 (**BIRTH**) + MARCH 28 (**DEATH**) = (3 + 14 + 3 + 28) = (`-**48**) = **WAS** `-**BORN in** (`-**48**) **for FORMER UNITED STATES REPRESENTATIVE TOM COBURN**!!!~' HIS `-**BIRTHDAY** & **DEATH/DAY** `-ADDED `-UP `-TOGETHER `-**EQUALS** `-HIS `-**YEAR of** `-BIRTH (`-**48**) = RECIPROCAL (MIRROR) = (`-**84**) = `-**EQUALS** = "HIS `-**BIRTHDAY** # `-**NUMBER** (`-**84**)!!!~'

`-**DIED in** (`-**3**) & was `-**BORN in** (`-**3**) = (`-**3/3**) = (3 x 3) = (`-**9**) = `-HIS `-**DAUGHTER'S** `-**BIRTHDAY** # `-**NUMBER** = (`-**108**) = (8 + 1 + 0) = (`-**9**)!!!~'

`-**NEXT** `-**LAYER**-!!!~'

AMERICAN ACTOR JOHN CALLAHAN (`-**66**) (BIRTH: **DECEMBER 23**, 19**53**) (DEATH: MARCH 28, 2020)!!!~'

FORMER `-WIFE ACTRESS EVA LARUE was (`-**53**) at the `-TIME of `-HER FORMER HUSBAND JOHN CALLAHAN'S `-DEATH = JOHN CALLAHAN was `-BORN in (`-**53**)!!!~' SHE was `-BORN in (`-**66**); WHICH, `-**EQUALS** ACTOR JOHN CALLAHAN'S `-AGE of `-DEATH (`-**66**)!!!~' HER `-BIRTHDAY = (**12/27/1966**)!!!~' **THEY are** `-**RECIPROCALS**-" of `-EACH `-OTHER!!!~' THEIR DAUGHTER KAYA MCKENNA CALLAHAN was `-**BORN** on (**DECEMBER 6**, 2001)!!!~'

JOHN CALLAHAN `-BIRTH/YEAR = (`-19**53**) = (19 + 53) = (`-**72**) = **"FAMILY `-KEY `-FACTOR of `-DEATH"!!!~'**

EVA LARUE `-BIRTH/YEAR = (`-19**66**) = (19 + 66) = (`-**85**) = **"FAMILY `-KEY `-FACTOR of `-DEATH"!!!~'**

`-BIRTHDAY # `-NUMBER = (12 + 23 + 19 + 53) = (`-**107**) = (17 + 0) = (`-**17**)!!!~'

`-DEATH/DAY # `-NUMBER = (3 + 28 + 20 + 20) = (`-**71**)

(`-**17**) = RECIPROCAL (MIRROR) = (`-**71**)

(`-**17**) = **FRAGMENTED DEATH/DAY # `-NUMBER!!!~'**

FRAGMENTED BIRTHDAY # `-NUMBER** = (1 + 2 + 2 + 3 + 1 + 9 + 5 + 3) = (`-26**)!!!~'

FRAGMENTED DEATH/DAY # `-NUMBER** = (3 + 2 + 8 + 2 + 0 + 2 + 0) = (`-17**) = RECIPROCAL (MIRROR) = (`-**71**) = `-DEATH/DAY # `-NUMBER (`-**71**)!!!~'

(26 + 17) = (`-**43**)!!!~'

EVA LARUE FRAGMENTED BIRTHDAY # `-NUMBER = (1 + 2 + 2 + 7 + 1 + 9 + 6 + 6) = (`-**34**)!!!~'

(`-**34**) = RECIPROCAL (MIRROR) = (`-**43**)!!!~'

KAYA MCKENNA CALLAHAN FRAGMENTED BIRTHDAY # `-NUMBER = (1 + 2 + 0 + 6 + 2 + 0 + 0 + 1) = (`-**12**) = **"ALL in the `-FAMILY were `-BORN in the `-MONTH of (`-12) = `-DECEMBER"** = (3 x 12) = (`-**36**) = (6 x 6) = (`-**66**) = **"AGE of `-DEATH for AMERICAN ACTOR JOHN CALLAHAN (`-66)!!!~'**

EVA LARUE `-BIRTHDAY # `-NUMBER = (12 + 27 + 19 + 66) = (`-**124**)!!!~'

KAYA MCKENNA CALLAHAN `-BIRTHDAY # `-NUMBER = (**12** + **06** + 20 + 01) = (`-**39**)!!!~'

MOTHER EVA LARUE `-BIRTHDAY = (**12/27**) = (12 + 27) = (`-**39**)!!!~'

(124 (-) 39) = (`-**85**) = "**FAMILY `-KEY `-FACTOR of `-DEATH**"!!!~'

KAYA MCKENNA CALLAHAN `-BIRTHDAY = (**12/6**) = (12 + 6) = (`-**18**) = "**HER `-AGE at the `-TIME of `-HER `-FATHER'S `-DEATH (`-18)**!!!~'

KAYA MCKENNA CALLAHAN `-**BIRTHDAY** = (12 x 6) = (`-**72**) = "**FAMILY `-KEY `-FACTOR of `-DEATH**"!!!~'

`-BIRTHDAY # `-NUMBER = (12 + 23 + 19 + 53) = (`-**107**) = (17 + 0) = (`-**17**)!!!~'

(`-**17**) = RECIPROCAL (MIRROR) = (`-**71**)

`-DEATH/DAY # `-NUMBER = (3 + 28 + 20 + 20) = (`-**71**)

(`-**17**) = **FRAGMENTED DEATH/DAY # `-NUMBER!!!~'**

(107 (-) 71) = (`-**36**) = (**6 x 6**) = (`-**66**) = "**AGE of `-DEATH**"!!!~'

(107 + 71) = (`-**178**) = (78 (-) 1) = (`-**77**) = "**SEE `-ABOVE**"!!!~'

(178 (-) 36) = (`-**142**) = (42 x 1) = (`-**42**) = "**SEE `-ABOVE**"!!!~'

(178 + 36) = (`-**214**) = (21 x 4) = (`-**84**) = `-**HIS `-DEATH/DAY = (3 x 28)** = (`-**84**)!!!~'

HE DIED (`-**96**) DAYS AFTER HIS LAST BIRTHDAY!!!~'

(`-**96**) = (9 x 6) = (`-**54**) = "SEE `-ABOVE"!!!~'

(366 (-) 96) = (`-**270**) = (27 + 0) = (`-**27**) = **2**(**7's**) = (`-**77**)!!!~'

(366 (-) 96) = (`-**270**) = (27 + 0) = (`-**27**) = `-FORMER `-WIFE EVA LARUE'S `-**DAY** of `-**BIRTH** (`-**27**th)!!!~'

HE DIED AT THE `-AGE of (`-**66**) = (`-**33** x `-**2**) = "SEE `-**ABOVE**"!!!~'

`-BIRTHDAY = DECEMBER 23 = (12 x 23) = (`-**276**) = (76 x 2) = (`-**152**) = (52 + 1) = (`-**53**) = "WAS `-**BORN** in (`-**53**)"!!!~'

`-DEATH/DAY = MARCH 28 = (3 x 28) = (`-**84**) = "SEE `-**ABOVE**"!!!~'

(276 + 84) = (`-**360**) = (36 + 0) = (`-**36**) = (**6 x 6**) = (`-**66**) = "AGE of `-DEATH"!!!~'

(276 (-) 84) = (`-**192**) = (19 x 2) = (`-**38**) = **3**(**8's**) = (8 x 8 x 8) = (`-**512**) = (51 + 2) = (`-**53**) = "WAS `-**BORN** in (`-**53**)"!!!~'

(360 + 192) = (`-**552**) = (52 x 5) = (`-**260**) = (26 + 0) = (`-**26**) = "SEE `-**ABOVE**"!!!~'

(360 (-) 192) = (`-**168**) = (68 x 1) = (`-**68**) = "The `-**MARK**"!!!~'

FRAGMENTED BIRTHDAY # `-NUMBER** = DECEMBER 23, 1953 = (1 + 2 + 2 + 3 + 1 + 9 + 5 + 3) = (`-26**) = "SEE `-**ABOVE**"!!!~'

FRAGMENTED DEATH/DAY # `-NUMBER** = MARCH 28, 2020 = (3 + 2 + 8 + 2 + 0 + 2 + 0) = (`-17**) = RECIPROCAL (MIRROR) = (`-**71**) = `-DEATH/DAY # `-NUMBER (`-**71**)!!!~'

(**26** (-) **17**) = (`-**9**)!!!~'

(26 + 17) = (`-**43**) = "SEE `-<u>ABOVE</u>"!!!~'

(43 (-) 9) = (`-**34**) = "The `-<u>PRESIDENTIAL</u> # `-<u>NUMBERS</u>"!!!~'

`-<u>BIRTHDAY</u>; and, `-<u>DEATH/DAY</u>!!!~':

(**1223** + **328**) = (`-**1551**) = (`-**15**) = RECIPROCAL (MIRROR) = (`-**51**)!!!~'

(**1223** (-) **328**) = (`-**895**)!!!~'

(1551 (-) 895) = (`-**656**) = "RECIPROCAL-<u>S</u>EQUENCING-<u>N</u>UMEROLOGY-<u>RSN</u>"!!!~'

DECEMBER 23 (**<u>BIRTH</u>**) + MARCH 28 (**<u>DEATH</u>**) = (12 + 23 + 3 + 28) = (`-**66**) = "AGE of `-DEATH for AMERICAN ACTOR JOHN CALLAHAN (`-**66**)"!!!~' HIS `-<u>BIRTHDAY</u> & `-<u>DEATH/DAY</u> `-ADDED `-UP `-TOGETHER = `-<u>EQUALS </u>= "HIS `-<u>AGE</u> of `-<u>DEATH</u> (`-**66**)!!!~' (66 + 66) = (`-**132**) = (32 x 1) = (`-**32**) = -a PROPHETIC # `-NUMBER!!!~'

`-DIED in (`-**3**) & was `-BORN in (`-**12**) = (`-**3/12**) = (3 x 12) = (`-**36**) = (6 x 6) = (`-**66**) = "AGE of `-DEATH for AMERICAN ACTOR JOHN CALLAHAN (`-**66**)!!!~'

`-<u>NEXT</u> `-<u>LAYER</u>-!!!~'

AMERICAN BUSINESSMAN (NFL) BILL BIDWILL (`-**88**) (BIRTH: JULY **31**, 19**31**) (DEATH: **OCTOBER 2**, 2019)!!!~'

(31 + 31) = (`-**62**) = "**WIFE'S** `-**BIRTHDAY** # `-**NUMBER** (`-**62**)"!!!~'

`-**BIRTHDAY** = (`-**31**); and, was `-**BORN** in `-**BIRTH/YEAR** of (`-**31**)!!!~'

HIS `-BIRTHDAY # `-NUMBER = (7 + 31 + 19 + 31) = (`-**88**) = "HIS `-VERY OWN `-AGE of `-DEATH (`-**88**) for AMERICAN BUSINESSMAN (NFL) BILL BIDWILL (`-**88**)!!!~'

HIS `-**BIRTHDAY** = (**7/31**) = (7 + 31) = (`-**38**) = "**HIS** `-**WIFE'S** `-**BIRTHDAY** (**3/8**) = **MARCH 8**ᵗʰ!!!~'

`-**DIED** in (`-**2019**) = (2 x 19 + 0) = (`-**38**) = "**HIS** `-**WIFE'S** `-**BIRTHDAY** (**3/8**) = **MARCH 8**ᵗʰ!!!~'

`-HE `-**DIED** (`-**63**) DAYS after `-HIS `-LAST `-BIRTHDAY!!!~'
(365 (-) **63**) = (`-**302**) = (32 + 0) = (`-**32**) = "**HIS** `-**WIFE was** `-**BORN** in (`-**32**)!!!~'

(`-**63**) = RECIPROCAL (MIRROR) = (`-**36**)!!!~'

`-HIS `-**WIFE'S DEATH/DAY** = (**8/17**) = (8 x 17) = (`-**136**) = (36 x 1) = (`-**36**) = RECIPROCAL (MIRROR) = (`-**63**) = "**THE AMOUNT of** `-**DAYS** `-**HE (BILL BIDWILL) had** `-**DIED from** `-**HIS LAST** `-**BIRTHDAY**"!!!~'

(`-**REPEAT**) = `-BIRTHDAY # `-NUMBER = (7 + 31 + 19 + 31) = (`-**88**) = "**HIS** `-**OWN** `-**AGE of** `-**DEATH** `-**ENCAPSULATED in** `-**HIS VERY OWN** `-**BIRTHDAY** # `-**NUMBER of** (`-**88**)!!!~'

`-**DEATH/DAY** # `-**NUMBER** = (10 + 02 + 20 + 19) = (`-**51**) = **SAME** `-**DEATH/DAY** # `-**NUMBER as AMERICAN BUSINESSMAN (NFL) LAMAR HUNT** (`-**51**)!!!~' (51 + 51) = (`-**102**) = `-**DEATH/**

DAY of AMERICAN BUSINESSMAN (NFL) BILL BIDWILL (**10/2**) = "**OCTOBER** (2ⁿᵈ)"!!!~'

(88 (-) 51) = (`-**37**)!!!~'

(88 + 51) = (`-**139**) = (39 (-) 1) = (`-**38**) = "HIS `-WIFE'S `-BIRTHDAY (MARCH 8ᵗʰ)"!!!~'

(139 (-) 37) = (`-**102**) = `-**DEATH/DAY** of AMERICAN BUSINESSMAN (NFL) BILL BIDWILL (**10/2**) = "**OCTOBER** (2ⁿᵈ)"!!!~'

(139 + 37) = (`-**176**) = (76 x 1) = (`-**76**) = (7 x 6) = (`-**42**) = "The `-**MARK**"!!!~'

HE DIED (`-**63**) DAYS AFTER HIS LAST BIRTHDAY!!!~'

(365 (-) **63**) = (`-**302**) = (32 + 0) = (`-**32**) = "WIFE was `-BORN in (`-**32**)!!!~'

HE DIED AT THE `-AGE of (`-**88**) = (`-**11** x `-**8**) = "SEE `-**ABOVE**"!!!~'

`-**BIRTHDAY** = JULY 31 = (7 x 31) = (`-**217**) = (17 x 2) = (`-**34**)!!!~'

`-**DEATH/DAY** = OCTOBER 02 = (10 x 2) = (`-**20**)!!!~'

(217 + 20) = (`-**237**) = (37 x 2) = (`-**74**) = "AGE of `-DEATH for AMERICAN BUSINESSMAN (NFL) LAMAR HUNT (`-**74**)"!!!~'

(217 (-) 20) = (`-**197**) = (19 x 7) = (`-**133**) = "AMERICAN BUSINESSMAN (NFL) LAMAR HUNT had `-DIED (`-**133**) DAYS after `-HIS `-LAST `-BIRTHDAY"!!!~'

(237 + 197) = (`-**434**) = "**RECIPROCAL-SEQUENCING-NUMEROLOGY-RSN**"!!!~'

(237 (-) 197) = (`-**40**) = `-**ADD** `-FRAGMENTED `-**BIRTHDAY #** `-**NUMBER** & FRAGMENTED `-**DEATH/DAY #** `-**NUMBERS ALL** `-**TOGETHER**!!!~'

FRAGMENTED BIRTHDAY # `-**NUMBER** = JULY 31, 1931 = (7 + 3 + 1 + 1 + 9 + 3 + 1) = (`-**25**)!!!~'

FRAGMENTED DEATH/DAY # `-**NUMBER** = OCTOBER 02, 2019 = (1 + 0 + 0 + 2 + 2 + 0 + 1 + 9) = (`-**15**)!!!~'

(**25** (-) **15**) = (`-**10**)!!!~'

(25 + 15) = (`-**40**) = "**SEE** `-**ABOVE**"!!!~'

(40 + 10) = (`-**50**) = (5 + 0) = (`-**5**) = "The `-**HAND** of `-**GOD**"!!!~'
`-**BIRTHDAY;** and, `-**DEATH/DAY**!!!~':

(**731** + **102**) = (`-**833**)!!!~'

(**731** (-) **102**) = (`-**629**)!!!~'

(833 (-) 629) = (`-**204**) / `-2 = (`-**102**) = "**DEATH/DAY (10/2)**" = "**OCTOBER (2nd)**"!!!~'

JULY 31 (**BIRTH**) + OCTOBER 02 (**DEATH**) = (7 + 31 + 10 + 02) = (`-**50**) = "**SEE** `-**ABOVE**" = (5 + 0) = (`-**5**) = "The `-**HAND** of `-**GOD**"!!!~'

`-DIED in (`-10) & was `-BORN in (`-7) = (`-10/7) = "FLIP the (`-7) OVER to a (`-2); and, `-YOU `-HAVE `-HIS `-DEATH/DAY = (10/2) = "OCTOBER (2nd)"!!!~'

`-AGE of `-DEATH = (`-84) NANCY BIDWILL (BILL BIDWILL'S WIFE) was `-MARRIED from (1960 to 2016) for (`-56) YEARS!!!~'

`-DIED in (`-2016) = (2 x 16 + 0) = (`-32) = "SHE was `-BORN in (`-32)"!!!~'

(BORN: **MARCH 8**, 19**32**) (DEATH: **AUGUST 17, 2016**)!!!~'

AGE of `-DEATH = `-EQUALS = (`-84) = (8 x 4) = (`-32) = "WAS `-BORN in (`-32)!!!~'

`-BIRTHDAY # `-NUMBER = (3 + 8 + 19 + 32) = (`-62) = RECIPROCAL (MIRROR) = (`-26)!!!~'

`-DEATH/DAY # `-NUMBER = (8 + 17 + 20 + 16) = (`-61) = RECIPROCAL (MIRROR) = (`-16) = "SHE HAD `-DIED in the `-CALENDAR `-YEAR of (`-16)!!!~' (16 + 16) = (`-32) = "SHE was `-BORN in (`-32)!!!~'

`-SHE `-HAD `-DIED (`-162) DAYS after `-HER `-LAST `-BIRTHDAY = (`-162) = (62 x 1) = (`-62) = "HER VERY OWN `-BIRTHDAY # `-NUMBER of (`-62)!!!~' (365 (-) 162) = (`-203) = (23 + 0) = (`-23) = RECIPROCAL (MIRROR) = (`-32) = "SHE was `-BORN in the `-CALENDAR `-YEAR of (`-32)"!!!~'

`-BIRTHDAY # `-NUMBER = (3 + 8 + 19 + 32) = (`-62)!!!~'

(`-26) = RECIPROCAL (MIRROR) = (`-62)

`-DEATH/DAY # `-NUMBER = (8 + 17 + 20 + 16) = (`-**61**) =
`-**BIRTHDAY # `-NUMBER of AMERICAN BUSINESSMAN
(NFL) LAMAR HUNT (`-61)!!!~'**

(62 (-) 61) = (`-**1**)!!!~'

(62 + 61) = (`-**123**) = (23 x 1) = (`-**23**) = RECIPROCAL (MIRROR)
= (`-**32**) = **"WAS `-<u>BORN</u> in (`-32)!!!~'**

(123 (-) 1) = (`-**122**) = (22 + 1) = (`-**23**) = **"SEE `-<u>ABOVE</u>"!!!~'**

(123 + 1) = (`-**124**) = (24 (-) 1) = (`-**23**) = **"SEE `-<u>ABOVE</u>"!!!~'**

SHE DIED (`-**162**) DAYS AFTER HER LAST BIRTHDAY!!!~'

(`-**162**) = (62 x 1) = (`-**62**) = **"SEE `-<u>ABOVE</u>"!!!~'**

(365 (-) 162) = (`-**203**) = (23 + 0) = (`-**23**) = = **"SEE `-<u>ABOVE</u>"!!!~'**

SHE DIED AT THE `-AGE of (`-**84**) = (`-**42** x `-**2**) = **"SEE
`-<u>ABOVE</u>"!!!~'**

`-**BIRTHDAY = MARCH 8 = (3 x 8) = (`-24)!!!~'**

`-**DEATH/DAY = AUGUST 17 = (8 x 17) = (`-136) = (36 x 1) = (`-
36) = RECIPROCAL (MIRROR) = (`-63) = "SEE `-<u>ABOVE</u>"!!!~'**

(136 + 24) = (`-**160**) = (16 + 0) = (`-**16**) = **"<u>DIED</u> in `-CALENDAR
`-YEAR of (`-20<u>16</u>)"!!!~'**

(136 (-) 24) = (`-**112**) / `-2 = (`-**56**) = **"<u>THEY</u> were `-<u>MARRIED</u>
for (`-56) YEARS (`-BILL & `-NANCY)"!!!~'**

(160 + 112) = (`-**272**) = **"<u>RECIPROCAL-SEQUENCING-
NUMEROLOGY-RSN</u>"!!!~'**

(160 (-) 112) = (`-**48**) = RECIPROCAL (MIRROR) = (`-**84**) = "AGE of `-DEATH for MRS. NANCY BIDWILL (`-**84**)"!!!~'

FRAGMENTED BIRTHDAY # `-NUMBER** = MARCH 8, 1932 = (3 + 8 + 1 + 9 + 3 + 2) = (`-26**) = "SEE `-**ABOVE**"!!!~'

FRAGMENTED DEATH/DAY # `-NUMBER** = AUGUST 17, 2016 = (8 + 1 + 7 + 2 + 0 + 1 + 6) = (`-25**)!!!~'

(**26** (-) **25**) = (`-**1**)!!!~'

(26 + 25) = (`-**51**) = "SEE `-**BELOW**" = `-DEATH/DAY # `-NUMBER for AMERICAN BUSINESSMAN (NFL) LAMAR HUNT (`-**51**)!!!~'

(51 (-) 1) = (`-**50**) = (5 + 0) = (`-**5**) = "The `-**HAND** of `-**GOD**"!!!~'

`-**BIRTHDAY; and, `-DEATH/DAY**!!!~':

(**817** + **38**) = (`-**855**)!!!~'

(**817** (-) **38**) = (`-**779**)!!!~'

(855 (-) 779) = (`-**76**) = (7 x 6) = (`-**42**) = "The `-**MARK**"!!!~'

MARCH 8 (**BIRTH**) + AUGUST 17 (**DEATH**) = (3 + 8 + 8 + 17) = (`-**36**) = RECIPROCAL (MIRROR) = (`-**63**) = "DAYS that `-HER HUSBAND `-PASSED `-AWAY from `-HIS `-BIRTHDAY (`-**63**)"!!!~'

`-**DIED** in (`-**8**) & was `-**BORN** in (`-**3**) = (`-**8/3**) = RECIPROCAL (MIRROR) = (`-**3/8**) = `-HER `-VERY `-OWN `-**BIRTHDAY** (**3/8**) = "**MARCH** (8th)"!!!~'

AMERICAN BUSINESSMAN (NFL) LAMAR HUNT (`-74`) (BIRTH: AUGUST 2, 19**32**) (DEATH: **DECEMBER** 13, 2006)!!!~`

`-**DIED** on a (`-**13**th) within (`-2006) = (26 + 0 + 0) = (`-**26**)!!!~` (`-1**3** x **2**) = (`-**26**) = "**WAS `-BORN in (`-32**)"!!!~`

`-HIS `-**BIRTH/YEAR** = (`-**1932**) = (19 + 32) = (`-**51**) = "**HIS VERY OWN DEATH/DAY # `-NUMBER (`-51**)"!!!~`

WAS `-**MARRIED** to `-**SPOUSE** NORMA HUNT in (`-19**64**)!!!~` (`-**64**) = (8 x 8) = (`-**88**) = "**SEE `-ABOVE**"!!!~`

`-**BIRTHDAY # `-NUMBER** = (8 + 2 + 19 + 32) = (`-**61**) = RECIPROCAL (MIRROR) = (`-**16**)!!!~` (61 + 16) = (`-**77**) = "**SEE `-ABOVE**"!!!~`

`-**DEATH/DAY # `-NUMBER** = (12 + 13 + 20 + 06) = (`-**51**) = RECIPROCAL (MIRROR) = (`-**15**) = (51 + 15) = (`-**66**) = "**SEE `-ABOVE**"!!!~`

`-HE `-HAD `-**DIED** (`-**133**) DAYS after `-HIS `-LAST `-BIRTHDAY!!!~` (365 (-) **133**) = (`-**232**) DAYS **GOING the `-OTHER `-WAY** = "WAS `-**BORN** in (`-**32**); and, had `-DIED on (12/1**3**) = (**23** x 1 x 1) = (`-**23**) = `-**RECIPROCALS** "-(**MIRROR**)-" = "**SEE `-ABOVE**"!!!~`

`-**BIRTHDAY # `-NUMBER** = (8 + 2 + 19 + 32) = (`-**61**) = `-**DEATH/DAY # `-NUMBER of NANCY BIDWILL** (`-**61**) (**BILL BIDWILL'S WIFE**) (**NFL**)!!!~`

(`-**61**) = RECIPROCAL (MIRROR) = (`-**16**)

`-**DEATH/DAY # `-NUMBER** = (12 + 13 + 20 + 06) = (`-**51**) = **SAME `-DEATH/DAY # `-NUMBER as AMERICAN BUSINESSMAN** (**NFL**) **BILL BIDWILL** (`-**51**)!!!~` (51 + 51) = (`-**102**) = `-**DEATH/**

DAY of AMERICAN BUSINESSMAN (NFL) BILL BIDWILL (10/2) = "**OCTOBER (2nd)**"!!!~'

(61 (-) 51) = ('-**10**)!!!~'

(61 + 51) = ('-**112**) = "**SEE '-ABOVE**"!!!~'

(112 (-) 10) = ('-**102**) = '-**DEATH/DAY of AMERICAN BUSINESSMAN (NFL) BILL BIDWILL (10/2)** = "**OCTOBER (2nd)**"!!!~'

(112 + 10) = ('-**122**) = (22 + 1) = ('-**23**) = RECIPROCAL (MIRROR) = ('-**32**) = "**HE was '-BORN in ('-32)**"!!!~'

HE DIED ('-**133**) DAYS AFTER HIS LAST BIRTHDAY!!!~'

('-**133**) = (33 (-) 1) = ('-**32**) = "**HE was '-BORN in ('-32)**"!!!~'

(365 (-) 133) = ('-**232**) = (ALL-IN-ONE-#-NUMBER) '-**BIRTH/ YEAR** & '-**DEATH/DAY** '-ALL '-**INCLUDED** = "YOU can '-**REVIEW from '-ABOVE**"!!!~'

HE DIED AT THE '-**AGE** of ('-**74**) = ('-**37** x '-**2**)!!!~'

'-**BIRTHDAY** = AUGUST 2 = (8 x 2) = ('-**16**)!!!~'

'-**DEATH/DAY** = DECEMBER 13 = (12 x 13) = ('-**156**) = (56 x 1) = ('-**56**) = "**SEE '-ABOVE**"!!!~'

(156 + 16) = ('-**172**)!!!~'

(156 (-) 16) = ('-**140**)!!!~'

(172 + 140) = ('-**312**) = (32 x 1) = ('-**32**) = "**WAS '-BORN in ('-32)**"!!!~'

118

(172 (-) 140) = (`-32) = "WAS `-BORN in (`-32)"!!!~'

FRAGMENTED BIRTHDAY # `-NUMBER = AUGUST 2, 1932
= (8 + 2 + 1 + 9 + 3 + 2) = (`-25)!!!~'

FRAGMENTED DEATH/DAY # `-NUMBER = DECEMBER
13, 2006 = (1 + 2 + 1 + 3 + 2 + 0 + 0 + 6) = (`-15)!!!~'

(25 (-) 15) = (`-10)!!!~'

(25 + 15) = (`-40)!!!~'

(40 + 10) = (`-50) = (5 + 0) = (`-5) = "The `-HAND of `-GOD"!!!~'

`-ALL `-THREE are THE `-HAND of `-GOD!!!~' GO `-BACK;
and, `-REVIEW!!!~'

`-BIRTHDAY; and, `-DEATH/DAY!!!~':

(1213 + 82) = (`-1295)!!!~'

(1213 (-) 82) = (`-1131)!!!~'

(1295 (-) 1131) = (`-164) = (16 x 4) = (`-64) = (`-2 x `-32) = "DAYS
`-AWAY from `-BIRTHDAY in `-DEATH (`-232)"!!!~'

AUGUST 2 (**BIRTH**) + DECEMBER 13 (**DEATH**) = (8 + 2 + 12
+ 13) = (`-35) = (3 x 5) = (`-15) = FRAGMENTED DEATH/DAY
# `-NUMBER = DECEMBER 13, 2006 = (1 + 2 + 1 + 3 + 2 + 0 +
0 + 6) = (`-15)!!!~'

`-DIED in (`-12) & was `-BORN in (`-8) = (`-12/8) = (12 x 8) =
(`-96) = (`-32 x `-3) = "REVIEW from `-ABOVE"!!!~'

`-NEXT `-LAYER-!!!~'

AMERICAN SINGER JAN HOWARD (`-**91**) (BIRTH: **MARCH 13**, **1929**) (DEATH: **MARCH 28**, 2020)!!!~'

`-**BIRTHDAY** = MARCH 13 = (**3**/**13**) = (3 x 3) 1 = (`-**91**) = "**AGE of `-DEATH** (`-**91**)"!!!~'

`-**BIRTHDAY** = (**3**/**13**) = (3 x 13) = (`-**39**)!!!~'

`-**DEATH/DAY** = (**3**/**28**) = (3 x 28) = (`-**84**)!!!~'

`-**BIRTH/YEAR** = `-**1929** = (19 + 29) = (`-**48**) = RECIPROCAL (MIRROR) = (`-**84**)!!!~'

MARCH **28, 2020** = (28 + 20 + 20) = (`-**68**) = "The `-**MARK**"!!!~'

`-BIRTHDAY # `-NUMBER = (3 + 13 + 19 + 29) = (`-**64**)!!!~'

`-**DEATH/DAY** # `-NUMBER = (3 + 28 + 20 + 20) = (`-**71**) = RECIPROCAL (MIRROR) = (`-**17**) = **FRAGMENTED `-DEATH/DAY** # `-NUMBER (`-**17**)!!!~'

(71 (-) 64) = (`-**7**)!!!~'

(71 + 64) = (`-**135**) = (35 x 1) = (`-**35**) = RECIPROCAL (MIRROR) = (`-**53**)!!!~'

(135 (-) 7) = (`-**128**) = (28 x 1) = (`-**28**) = **FRAGMENTED BIRTHDAY** # `-NUMBER (`-**28**)!!!~'

$(135 + 7) = (`-\underline{142}) = (42 \times 1) = (`-\underline{42}) =$ **"The `-MARK"!!!~`**

SHE `-DIED (`-**15**) DAYS AFTER `-HER `-LAST `-BIRTHDAY!!!~`

$(365 (-) \underline{15}) = (`-\underline{350}) = (35 + 0) = (`-\underline{35}) =$ RECIPROCAL (MIRROR) $= (`-\underline{53}) =$ **"SEE `-BELOW"!!!~`**

SHE DIED AT THE `-AGE of (`-**91**) = **"SEE `-BELOW"!!!~`**

`-BIRTHDAY = MARCH 13 = $(3 \times 13) = (`-\underline{39}) =$ **"NOTE (`-39) within `-THIS `-LAYER"!!!~`**

`-DEATH/DAY = MARCH 28 = $(3 \times 28) = (`-\underline{84})$!!!~`

$(84 + 39) = (`-\underline{123}) = (23 \times 1) = (`-\underline{23}) =$ **-a PROPHETIC # `-NUMBER!!!~`**

$(84 (-) 39) = (`-\underline{45})$!!!~`

$(123 + 45) = (`-\underline{168}) = (68 \times 1) = (`-\underline{68}) =$ **"The `-MARK"!!!~`**

$(123 (-) 45) = (`-\underline{78}) / `-2 = (`-\underline{39})$!!!~`

FRAGMENTED BIRTHDAY # `-NUMBER** = MARCH 13, 1929 = $(3 + 1 + 3 + 1 + 9 + 2 + 9) = (`-\underline{28}) =$ `-**DIED** on a (`-28**th) of the `-**MONTH**!!!~`

**FRAGMENTED DEATH/DAY # `-NUMBER** = MARCH 28, 2020 = $(3 + 2 + 8 + 2 + 0 + 2 + 0) = (`-\underline{17})$!!!~`

$(\underline{28} (-) \underline{17}) = (`-\underline{11})$!!!~`

$(28 + 17) = (`-\underline{45})$!!!~`

$(45 + 11) = (`-\underline{56}) =$ **"SEE `-ABOVE & `-BELOW"!!!~`**

`-**BIRTHDAY**; and, `-**DEATH/DAY**!!!~':

(**328** + **313**) = (`-**641**)!!!~'

(**328** (-) **313**) = (`-**15**)!!!~'

(641 (-) 15) = (`-**626**) = "**R**ECIPROCAL-**S**EQUENCING-**N**UMEROLOGY-**RSN**"!!!~'

(641 + 15) = (`-**656**) = "**R**ECIPROCAL-**S**EQUENCING-**N**UMEROLOGY-**RSN**"!!!~'

MARCH 13 (**BIRTH**) + MARCH 28 (**DEATH**) = (3 + 13 + 3 + 28) = (`-**47**)!!!~'

`-**DIED** in (`-**3**) & was `-**BORN** in (`-**3**) = (`-**3/3**) = `-**BIRTHDAY** (`-**313**)!!!~'

AMERICAN ACTOR DAVID SCHRAMM (`-**73**) (BIRTH: **AUGUST 14**, 1946) (DEATH: **MARCH 28**, 2020)!!!~'

`-**BIRTHDAY** = AUGUST 14 = (**8/1/4**) = (8 (-) 1) /|\ (1 (-) 4) = (`-**73**) = "**AGE** of `-**DEATH** (`-**73**)"!!!~'

`-**BIRTHDAY** = (**8/14**) = (84 x 1) = (`-**84**)!!!~'

`-**DEATH/DAY** = (**3/28**) = (3 x 28) = (`-**84**)!!!~'

(84 + 84) = (`-**168**) = (68 x 1) = (`-**68**) = "The `-**MARK**"!!!~'

`-**1946** = (19 + 46) = (`-**65**) = RECIPROCAL (MIRROR) = (`-**56**)!!!~'

`-BIRTHDAY # `-NUMBER = (8 + 14 + 19 + 46) = (`-**87**)!!!~'

`-DEATH/DAY # `-NUMBER = (3 + 28 + 20 + 20) = (`-**71**) = RECIPROCAL (MIRROR) = (`-**17**) = **FRAGMENTED** `-**DEATH/DAY # `-NUMBER** (`-**17**)!!!~'

(87 + 71) = (`-**158**) = (58 x 1) = (`-**58**) = **"AMERICAN SINGER JOE DIFFIE was `-BORN in** (`-**58**)"!!!~'

(87 (-) 71) = (`-**16**)!!!~'

(158 + 16) = (`-**174**) = (17 x 4) = (`-**68**) = **"The `-MARK"**!!!~'

(158 (-) 16) = (`-**142**) = (42 x 1) = (`-**42**) = **"The `-MARK"**!!!~'

`-HE `-DIED (`-**139**) DAYS BEFORE `-HIS `-NEXT `-BIRTHDAY!!!~' (`-**39**) = **"SEE `-ABOVE & `-BELOW"**!!!~'

(365 (-) **139**) = (`-**226**) = (22 x 6) = (`-**132**) = (32 x 1) = (`-**32**) = **-a PROPHETIC # `-NUMBER!!!~'**

HE DIED AT THE `-AGE of (`-**73**)!!!~'

`-**BIRTHDAY = AUGUST 14** = (8 x 14) = (`-**112**)!!!~'

`-**DEATH/DAY = MARCH 28** = (3 x 28) = (`-**84**) = `-**EQUALS** = `-**BIRTHDAY** (`-**84**)!!!~'

(112 + 84) = (`-**196**)!!!~'

(112 (-) 84) = (`-**28**)!!!~'

(196 + 28) = (`-**224**) = (2 x 24) = (`-**48**) = RECIPROCAL (MIRROR) = (`-**84**)!!!~'

(196 (-) 28) = (`-**168**) = (68 x 1) = (`-**68**) = "The `-**MARK**"!!!~'

FRAGMENTED BIRTHDAY # `-NUMBER** = AUGUST 14, 1946 = (8 + 1 + 4 + 1 + 9 + 4 + 6) = (`-33**)!!!~'

FRAGMENTED DEATH/DAY # `-NUMBER** = MARCH 28, 2020 = (3 + 2 + 8 + 2 + 0 + 2 + 0) = (`-17**)!!!~'

(**33** (-) **17**) = (`-**16**)!!!~'

(33 + 17) = (`-**50**) = (5 + 0) = (`-**5**) = "The `-**HAND** of `-**GOD**"!!!~'

(50 + 16) = (`-**66**)!!!~'

`-**BIRTHDAY; and, `-DEATH/DAY**!!!~':

(**814** + **328**) = (`-**1142**) = (11 + 42) = (`-**53**)!!!~'

(**814** (-) **328**) = (`-**486**)!!!~'

(1142 (-) 486) = (`-**656**) = "**R**ECIPROCAL-**S**EQUENCING-**N**UMEROLOGY-**RSN**"!!!~'

AUGUST 14 (**BIRTH**) + MARCH 28 (**DEATH**) = (8 + 14 + 3 + 28) = (`-**53**) = "SEE `-**ABOVE**"!!!~'

`-**DIED** in (`-**3**) & was `-**BORN** in (`-**8**) = (`-**3/8**) = "DAY of `-**DEATH** (**3/28**)!!!~'

AMERICAN SINGER JOE DIFFIE (`-**61**) (BIRTH: DECEMBER **28**, 19**58**) (DEATH: MARCH 29, 2020)!!!~'

`-**BIRTHDAY** = **DECEMBER 28** = (**12/28**)!!!~' (`-**12**) = RECIPROCAL (MIRROR) = (`-**21**)!!!~' (`-**28**) = RECIPROCAL = (`-**82**)!!!~' (82 (-) 21) = (`-**61**) = **"AGE of `-DEATH** (`-**61**)"!!!~'

`-**DEATH/DAY** = (**3/29**) = (3 x 29) = (`-**87**) = (8 x 7) = (`-**56**)!!!~'

(28 + 58) = (`-**86**) = **"The `-MARK"**!!!~'

`-**1958** = (58 (-19) = (`-**39**) = **"SEE `-ABOVE & `-BELOW**"!!!~'

`-**BIRTH/YEAR** = `-**1958** = (19 + 58) = (`-**77**) = **2**(**7's**) = (`-**27**) = RECIPROCAL (MIRROR) = (`-**72**) = `-**DEATH/DAY #** `-**NUMBER**!!!~'

`-**BIRTHDAY** = (**12/28**) + `-**DEATH/DAY** = (**3/29**) = (12 + 28 + 3 + 29) = (`-**72**) = **"HIS VERY OWN `-DEATH/DAY # `-NUMBER** (`-**72**)"!!!~'

`-BIRTHDAY # `-NUMBER = (12 + 28 + 19 + 58) = (`-**117**)!!!~'

`-DEATH/DAY # `-NUMBER = (3 + 29 + 20 + 20) = (`-**72**)!!!~'

(117 (-) 72) = (`-**45**)!!!~'

(117 + 72) = (`-**189**) = (18 x 9) = (`-**162**) = (62 (-) 1) = (`-**61**) = **"AGE of `-DEATH for AMERICAN SINGER JOE DIFFIE"**!!!~'

(189 (-) 45) = (`-**144**) = `-**DEATH/DAY #** `-**NUMBER** (`-**72**) `-**ADDED `-TWICE**!!!~'

(189 + 45) = (`-**234**) = **"PROPHETIC-LINEAR-PROGRESSION-PLP"**!!!~'

HE `-DIED (`-**92**) DAYS after `-HIS `-LAST `-BIRTHDAY!!!~'

(366 (-) **92**) = (`-**274**) = (74 x 2) = (`-**148**) = (48 x 1) = (`-**48**) = RECIPROCAL (MIRROR) = (`-**84**)!!!~'

(366 (-) 92) = (`-**274**) = (27 x 4) = (`-**108**) = (18 + 0) = (`-**18**) = RECIPROCAL (MIRROR) = (`-**81**) = AMERICAN VOCALIST ALAN MERRILL (`-**81**)!!!~'

HE DIED AT THE `-AGE of (`-**61**)!!!~'

`-BIRTHDAY = **DECEMBER 28** = (12 x 28) = (`-**336**)!!!~'

`-**DEATH/DAY** = **MARCH 29** = (3 x 29) = (`-**87**)!!!~'

(336 + 87) = (`-**423**)!!!~'

(336 (-) 87) = (`-**249**)!!!~'

(423 + 249) = (`-**672**) = (67 x 2) = (`-**134**) = (34 x 1) = (`-**34**) = **"The `-PRESIDENTIAL # `-NUMBERS"**!!!~'

(423 (-) 249) = (`-**174**) = (17 x 4) = (`-**68**) = **"The `-MARK"**!!!~'

FRAGMENTED BIRTHDAY # `-NUMBER** = DECEMBER 28, 1958 = (1 + 2 + 2 + 8 + 1 + 9 + 5 + 8) = (`-36**)!!!~'

FRAGMENTED DEATH/DAY # `-NUMBER** = MARCH 29, 2020 = (3 + 2 + 9 + 2 + 0 + 2 + 0) = (`-18**)!!!~'

(**36** (-) **18**) = (`-**18**)!!!~'

(36 + 18) = (`-**54**) = RECIPROCAL (MIRROR) = (`-**45**)!!!~'

(54 + 18) = (`-**72**) = **HIS `-DEATH/DAY # `-NUMBER** (`-**72**)!!!~'

`-**BIRTHDAY; and, `-DEATH/DAY**!!!~':

(<u>1228</u> + <u>329</u>) = (`-<u>1557</u>) = (15 + 57) = (`-<u>72</u>) = HIS `-DEATH/DAY # `-NUMBER (`-<u>72</u>)!!!~'

(<u>1228</u> (-) <u>329</u>) = (`-<u>899</u>) = (99 (-) 8) = (`-<u>91</u>) = "AGE of `-DEATH for AMERICAN SINGER JAN HOWARD (`-<u>91</u>)!!!~'

(1557 + 899) = (`-<u>2456</u>) = (56 (-) 24) = (`-<u>32</u>) = -a PROPHETIC # `-NUMBER!!!~'

DECEMBER 28 (<u>BIRTH</u>) + MARCH 29 (<u>DEATH</u>) = (12 + 28 + 3 + 29) = (`-<u>72</u>) = "HIS VERY OWN `-DEATH/DAY # `-NUMBER (`-<u>72</u>)"!!!~'

`-DIED in (`-<u>3</u>) & was `-BORN in (`-<u>12</u>) = (`-<u>3/12</u>) = (32 x 1) = (`-<u>32</u>) = -a PROPHETIC # `-NUMBER!!!~'

POLISH COMPOSER KRZYSZTOF PENDERECKI (`-<u>86</u>) (BIRTH: NOVEMBER <u>23</u>, 19<u>33</u>) (DEATH: MARCH 29, 2020)!!!~'

`-<u>BIRTHDAY</u> = NOVEMBER 23 = (<u>11/23</u>) = (11 + 23) = (`-<u>34</u>) x `-<u>2</u> = (`-<u>68</u>) = RECIPROCAL (MIRROR) = (`-<u>86</u>) = "<u>AGE</u> of `-<u>DEATH</u> (`-<u>86</u>)"!!!~'

`-<u>BORN</u> on a (`-<u>23</u>rd); and, `-<u>DIED</u> on a (`-<u>32</u>) = `-<u>DEATH/DAY</u> = (3 + 29) = (`-<u>32</u>)!!!~'

`-<u>DEATH/DAY</u> = (<u>3/29</u>) = (3 x 29) = (`-<u>87</u>) = (8 x 7) = (`-<u>56</u>) = RECIPROCAL (MIRROR) = (`-<u>65</u>)!!!~'

WAS `-<u>MARRIED</u> to ELZBIETA PENDERECKA in (`-19<u>65</u>)!!!~'

`-BIRTHDAY # `-NUMBER = (11 + 23 + 19 + 33) = (`-**86**) = `-**AGAIN, ANOTHER `-INDIVIDUAL has `-IT to where their `-BIRTHDAY # `-NUMBER = `-EQUALS = "THEIR `-ACTUAL `-AGE of `-DEATH (`-86)"!!!~'**

`-DEATH/DAY # `-NUMBER = (3 + 29 + 20 + 20) = (`-**72**)!!!~'

(86 (-) 72) = (`-**14**)!!!~'

(86 + 72) = (`-**158**) = (58 x 1) = (`-**58**) = "AMERICAN SINGER JOE `-DIFFIE was `-BORN in (`-**58**)"!!!~'

(158 (-) 14) = (`-**144**) = `-DEATH/DAY # `-NUMBER (`-**72**) `-ADDED `-TWICE!!!~'

(158 + 14) = (`-**172**) = (72 x 1) = (`-**72**) = `-HIS VERY `-OWN `-DEATH/DAY # `-NUMBER (`-**72**)!!!~'

HE `-DIED (`-**127**) DAYS after `-HIS `-LAST `-BIRTHDAY!!!~'
(12 x 7) = (`-**84**) = "SEE `-ABOVE"!!!~'

(366 (-) 127) = (`-**239**) = (39 x 2) = (`-**78**)!!!~'

(366 (-) 127) = (`-**239**) = (23 x 9) = (`-**207**) = (27 + 0) = (`-**27**)!!!~'

HE DIED AT THE `-AGE of (`-**86**) = (`-**8** x `-**6**) = (`-**48**) = RECIPROCAL (MIRROR) = (`-**84**) = "SEE `-ABOVE"!!!~'

`-BIRTHDAY = NOVEMBER 23 = (11 x 23) = (`-**253**)!!!~'

`-DEATH/DAY = MARCH 29 = (3 x 29) = (`-**87**)!!!~'

(253 + 87) = (`-**340**)!!!~'

(253 (-) 87) = (`-**166**)!!!~'

$(340 + 166) = (`-506) = (56 + 0) = (`-56) = $ **"SEE the `-PATTERNS `-ABOVE"!!!~'**

$(340 (-) 166) = (`-174) = (17 \times 4) = (`-68) = $ **"The `-MARK"!!!~'**

FRAGMENTED BIRTHDAY # `-NUMBER** = NOVEMBER 23, 1933 = $(1 + 1 + 2 + 3 + 1 + 9 + 3 + 3) = (`-23) = $ **-a PROPHETIC # `-NUMBER & was `-BORN on a (`-23rd)!!!~'

**FRAGMENTED DEATH/DAY # `-NUMBER** = MARCH 29, 2020 = $(3 + 2 + 9 + 2 + 0 + 2 + 0) = (`-18)$!!!~'

$(23 (-) 18) = (`-5)$!!!~'

$(23 + 18) = (`-41)$!!!~'

$(41 + 5) = (`-46) = (`-23 \times `-2)$!!!~'

`-BIRTHDAY; and, `-DEATH/DAY!!!~':

$(1123 + 329) = (`-1452) = (14 + 52) = (`-66) = $ **`-ADD `-UP `-BIRTHDAY & `-DEATH/DAY `-TOGETHER!!!~'**

$(1123 (-) 329) = (`-794)$!!!~'

$(1452 + 794) = (`-2246) = (22 + 46) = (`-68) = $ **"The `-MARK"!!!~'**

NOVEMBER 23 (**BIRTH**) + MARCH 29 (**DEATH**) = $(11 + 23 + 3 + 29) = (`-66)$!!!~'

$(66 + 66) = (`-132) = (32 \times 1) = (`-32) = $ **-a PROPHETIC # `-NUMBER!!!~'**

`-DIED in (`-**3**) & was `-BORN in (`-**11**) = (`-**3/11**) = (3 x 11) = (`-**33**) = "WAS `-<u>BORN</u> in (`-**33**)"!!!~'

JAPANESE COMEDIAN KEN SHIMURA (`-**70**) (BIRTH: FEBRUARY 20, 1950) (DEATH: MARCH 29, 2020)!!!~'

`-**DAY** of `-**BIRTH** = (`-**20**th) = FLIP the (`-**2**) OVER to a (`-7) = (**70**) = "**AGE** of `-**DEATH** (`-**70**)"!!!~'

`-**BIRTHDAY** = <u>FEBRUARY 20</u> = (**2/20**) = **2**(**20**'s) = (**20/20**) = `-**DIED** `-**WITHIN** `-**CALENDAR** `-**YEAR OF** (`-**2020**)!!!~'

`-**DEATH/DAY** = (**3/29**) = (3 x 29) = (`-**87**) = (8 x 7) = (`-**56**)!!!~'

`-**1950** = (19 + 50) = (`-**69**) = "**AGE** of `-**DEATH** for AMERICAN VOCALIST ALAN MERRILL (`-**69**)"!!!~'

`-BIRTHDAY # `-NUMBER = (2 + 20 + 19 + 50) = (`-**91**) = "**AGE** of `-**DEATH** for AMERICAN SINGER JAN HOWARD (`-**91**) & SAME `-**BIRTHDAY** # `-**NUMBER as** AMERICAN VOCALIST ALAN MERRILL (`-**91**)"!!!~'

`-DEATH/DAY # `-NUMBER = (3 + 29 + 20 + 20) = (`-**72**) = **SAME** `-**DEATH/DAY** # `-**NUMBER as** AMERICAN VOCALIST ALAN MERRILL (`-**72**)"!!!~'

(91 (-) 72) = (`-**19**) = RECIPROCAL (MIRROR) = (`-**91**)!!!~'

(91 + 72) = (`-**163**) = (16 x 3) = (`-**48**) = RECIPROCAL (MIRROR) = (`-**84**)!!!~'

(163 (-) 19) = (`-**144**) = `-**DEATH/DAY** # `-**NUMBER** (`-**72**) `-**ADDED** `-**TWICE**!!!~'

130

(163 + 19) = (`-**182**) = (82 x 1) = (`-**82**) = RECIPROCAL (MIRROR) = (`-**28**) = `-FRAGMENTED BIRTHDAY # `-NUMBER of AMERICAN VOCALIST ALAN MERRILL = FEBRUARY 19, 1951 = (2 + 1 + 9 + 1 + 9 + 5 + 1) = (`-**28**)!!!~'

`-HE `-DIED (`-**38**) DAYS AFTER `-HIS `-LAST `-BIRTHDAY!!!~'

(366 (-) **38**) = (`-**328**) = "DAY of `-DEATH for AMERICAN SINGER JAN HOWARD "MARCH (28th)"!!!~'

HE DIED AT THE `-AGE of (`-**70**)!!!~'

`-BIRTHDAY = FEBRUARY 20 = (2 x 20) = (`-**40**)!!!~'

`-DEATH/DAY = MARCH 29 = (3 x 29) = (`-**87**)!!!~'

(87 + 40) = (`-**127**) = "SEE `-ABOVE" = "POLISH COMPOSER KRZYSZTOF PENDERECKI `-DIED this `-MANY `-DAYS after `-HIS `-BIRTHDAY"!!!~'

(87 (-) 40) = (`-**47**)!!!~'

(127 + 47) = (`-**174**) = (17 x 4) = (`-**68**) = "The `-MARK"!!!~'

(127 (-) 47) = (`-**80**)!!!~' (80 + 47) = (`-**127**)!!!~'

FRAGMENTED BIRTHDAY # `-NUMBER = FEBRUARY 20, 1950 = (2 + 2 + 0 + 1 + 9 + 5 + 0) = (`-**19**)!!!~'

FRAGMENTED DEATH/DAY # `-NUMBER = MARCH 29, 2020 = (3 + 2 + 9 + 2 + 0 + 2 + 0) = (`-**18**)!!!~'

(**19** (-) **18**) = (`-**1**)!!!~'

(19 + 18) = (`-**37**) = RECIPROCAL (MIRROR) = (`-**73**) = "**AGE** of `-**DEATH** for **AMERICAN ACTOR DAVID SCHRAMM** (`-**73**)"!!!~'

(37 + 1) = (`-**38**) = "**JAPANESE COMEDIAN KEN SHIMURA** `-**DIED** this `-**MANY** `-**DAYS** after `-**HIS** `-**BIRTHDAY**"!!!~'

`-**BIRTHDAY**; and, `-**DEATH/DAY**!!!~':

(**329** + **220**) = (`-**549**)!!!~'

(**329** (-) **220**) = (`-**109**)!!!~'

(549 (-) 109) = (`-**440**) / `-2 = (`-**220**) = "**BIRTHDAY** (**2/20**)" = "**FEBRUARY** (**20**th)"!!!~'

FEBRUARY 20 (**BIRTH**) + MARCH 29 (**DEATH**) = (2 + 20 + 3 + 29) = (`-**54**) = (5 x 4) = (`-**20**) = "**WAS** `-**BORN** on a (`-**20**th)"!!!~'

`-**DIED** in (`-**3**) & was `-**BORN** in (`-**2**) = (`-**3/2**) = (`-**32**) = -a **PROPHETIC** # `-**NUMBER**!!!~'

AMERICAN VOCALIST ALAN MERRILL (`-**69**) (BIRTH: **FEBRUARY 19, 1951**) (DEATH: **MARCH 29**, 2020)!!!~'

`-**BIRTHDAY** = FEBRUARY 19 = (**2/19**) = FLIP the (`-**2**) OVER to a (`-7) = (**7/19**) = ((7 (-) 1) 9) = (`-**69**) = "**AGE** of `-**DEATH** (`-**69**)"!!!~'

`-**BIRTHDAY** = **FEBRUARY 19** = (**2/19**) = (2 x 19) = (`-**38**) = "**JAPANESE COMEDIAN KEN SHIMURA** `-**DIED** this `-**MANY** `-**DAYS** from `-**HIS** `-**BIRTHDAY**"!!!~'

`-**DEATH/DAY** = (**3**/**29**) = (3 x 29) = (`-**87**) = (8 x 7) = (`-**56**)!!!~'

`-**1951** = (19 + 51) = (`-**70**) = "AGE of `-DEATH for JAPANESE COMEDIAN KEN SHIMURA (`-**70**)"!!!~'

`-BIRTHDAY # `-NUMBER = (2 + 19 + 19 + 51) = (`-**91**) = "AGE of `-DEATH for AMERICAN SINGER JAN HOWARD (`-**91**) & SAME `-BIRTHDAY # `-NUMBER as JAPANESE COMEDIAN KEN SHIMURA (`-**91**)"!!!~'

"-DEATH/DAY # `-NUMBER = (3 + 29 + 20 + 20) = (`-**72**)!!!~' SAME `-DEATH/DAY # `-NUMBER as JAPANESE COMEDIAN KEN SHIMURA (`-**72**)"!!!~'

(91 (-) 72) = (`-**19**) = RECIPROCAL (MIRROR) = (`-**91**) = RECIPROCAL (MIRROR) = (`-**19**) = "WAS `-**BORN** on a (`-**19**ᵗʰ)"!!!~'

(91 + 72) = (`-**163**) = (16 x 3) = (`-**48**) = RECIPROCAL (MIRROR) = (`-**84**)!!!~'

(163 (-) 19) = (`-**144**) = `-**DEATH/DAY** # `-**NUMBER** (`-**72**) `-**ADDED** `-**TWICE**!!!~'

(163 + 19) = (`-**182**) = (82 x 1) = (`-**82**) = RECIPROCAL (MIRROR) = (`-**28**) = `-HIS VERY OWN `-FRAGMENTED BIRTHDAY # `-**NUMBER** = FEBRUARY 19, 1951 = (2 + 1 + 9 + 1 + 9 + 5 + 1) = (`-**28**)!!!~'

`-HE `-DIED (`-**39**) DAYS AFTER `-HIS `-LAST `-BIRTHDAY!!!~' (`-**39**) = "SEE `-**ABOVE**"!!!~'

(366 (-) **39**) = (`-**327**) = (27 x 3) = (`-**81**) = `-**RECIPROCAL**- `= AMERICAN SINGER JOE DIFFIE = "SEE `-**ABOVE**"!!!~'

HE DIED AT THE `-AGE of (`-**69**) = (`-**6** x `-**9**) = (`-**54**) = RECIPROCAL (MIRROR) = (`-**45**)!!!~'

`-BIRTHDAY = FEBRUARY 19 = (2 x 19) = (`-**38**) = "SEE `-**ABOVE**" = "JAPANESE COMEDIAN KEN SHIMURA `-**DIED** this `-**MANY** `-**DAYS** after `-**HIS** last `-**BIRTHDAY**"!!!~'

`-DEATH/DAY = MARCH 29 = (3 x 29) = (`-**87**)!!!~'

(87 + 38) = (`-**125**)!!!~'

(87 (-) 38) = (`-**49**)!!!~'

(125 + 49) = (`-**174**) = (17 x 4) = (`-**68**) = "The `-**MARK**"!!!~'

(125 (-) 49) = (`-**76**) = (7 x 6) = (`-**42**) = "The `-**MARK**"!!!~'

FRAGMENTED BIRTHDAY # `-NUMBER = FEBRUARY 19, 1951 = (2 + 1 + 9 + 1 + 9 + 5 + 1) = (`-**28**)!!!~'

FRAGMENTED DEATH/DAY # `-NUMBER = MARCH 29, 2020 = (3 + 2 + 9 + 2 + 0 + 2 + 0) = (`-**18**)!!!~'

(**28** (-) **18**) = (`-**10**)!!!~'

(28 + 18) = (`-**46**) = (`-**23** x `-**2**)!!!~'

(46 + 10) = (`-**56**) = `-**DEATH/DAY** = (**3/29**) = (3 x 29) = (`-**87**) = (8 x 7) = (`-**56**)!!!~'

`-**BIRTHDAY**; and, `-**DEATH/DAY**!!!~':

(329 + **219**) = (`-**548**)!!!~'

(**329** (-) **219**) = (`-**110**)!!!~'

(548 (-) 110) = (`-**438**) / `-2 = (`-**219**) = "BIRTHDAY (**2/19**)" = "**FEBRUARY (19**th**)**"!!!~'

FEBRUARY 19 (**BIRTH**) + MARCH 29 (**DEATH**) = (2 + 19 + 3 + 29) = (`-**53**) = AMERICAN SINGER JAN HOWARD (`-**RECIPROCAL**- `'-CALCULATION of `-DEATH from `-BIRTHDAY)!!!~'

`-DIED in (`-**3**) & was `-BORN in (`-**2**) = (`-**3/2**) = (`-**32**) = -a PROPHETIC # `-NUMBER!!!~'

AMERICAN WRITER TOMIE DEPAOLA (`-**85**) (BIRTH: SEPTEMBER 15, 1934) (DEATH: MARCH **30**, **2**020)!!!~'

`-**BIRTHDAY** = `-SEPTEMBER 15 = (**9/15**) = ((9 (-) 1) 5) = (`-**85**) = "**AGE** of `-**DEATH** (`-**85**)"!!!~'

`-**AGE** of `-**DEATH** (`-**85**) = RECIPROCAL (MIRROR) = (`-**58**) = "AMERICAN SINGER JOE DIFFIE was `-**BORN** in (`-**58**)"!!!~'

MARCH 30, 2020 = (**330**/**2020**) = (**33**/**22**/000) = (`-**32**) = -a PROPHETIC # `-NUMBER!!!~'

`-**FRAGMENTED** `-**BIRTHDAY** # `-**NUMBER** = (9 + 1 + 5 + 1 + 9 + 3 + 4) = (`-**32**) = -a PROPHETIC # `-NUMBER!!!~'

`-**1934** = (19 + 34) = (`-**53**)!!!~'

`-**BIRTHDAY** = (**9/15**) = (9 x 15) = (`-**135**) = (35 x 1) = (`-**35**) = RECIPROCAL (MIRROR) = (`-**53**)!!!~'

(9 + 15 + 19) = (`-**43**) = RECIPROCAL (MIRROR) = (`-**34**) = `-**BIRTH/YEAR**!!!~'

'-BIRTHDAY # '-NUMBER = (9 + 15 + 19 + 34) = ('-**77**) = (**43** + **34**) = ('-**77**)!!!~'

'-DEATH/DAY # '-NUMBER = (3 + 30 + 20 + 20) = ('-**73**) = "**AGE** of '-**DEATH** for AMERICAN ACTOR DAVID SCHRAMM ('-**73**)"!!!~'

(77 + 73) = ('-**150**) = (15 + 0) = ('-**15**) = (**5** x **3**)!!!~'

(77 (-) 73) = ('-**4**)!!!~'

(150 (-) 4) = ('-**146**) = (46 x 1) = ('-**46**) = ('-**23** x '-**2**)!!!~'

(150 + 4) = ('-**154**) = (54 x 1) = ('-**54**) = RECIPROCAL (MIRROR) = ('-**45**) = "NOTE '-HOW MANY '-TIMES this (**45/54**) is '-LISTED within THIS '-LAYER"!!!~'

HE '-**DIED** ('-**169**) DAYS before '-HIS '-NEXT '-BIRTHDAY!!!~' ('-**69**) = ('-**3** x '-**23**)!!!~'

(365 (-) **169**) = ('-**196**)!!!~' ('-**69**) = RECIPROCAL (MIRROR) = ('-**96**)!!!~' ('-**96**) = ('-**32** x **3**)!!!~'

HE DIED AT THE '-AGE of ('-**85**)!!!~'

'-BIRTHDAY = SEPTEMBER 15 = (9 x 15) = ('-**135**) = "SEE '-**ABOVE**"!!!~'

'-DEATH/DAY = MARCH 30 = (3 x 30) = ('-**90**)!!!~'

(135 + 90) = ('-**225**)!!!~'

(135 (-) 90) = ('-**45**)!!!~'

(225 + 45) = ('-**270**) = (27 + 0) = ('-**27**) = "SEE '-**ABOVE**"!!!~'

(225 (-) 45) = (`-**180**) = (18 + 0) = (`-**18**) = "SEE `-**ABOVE**"!!!~`

(27 + 18) = (`-**45**) = "NOTE `-HOW MANY `-TIMES this (**45/54**) is `-LISTED within THIS `-LAYER"!!!~`

FRAGMENTED BIRTHDAY # `-NUMBER = SEPTEMBER 15, 1934 = (9 + 1 + 5 + 1 + 9 + 3 + 4) = (`-**32**) = -a PROPHETIC # `-NUMBER!!!~`

FRAGMENTED DEATH/DAY # `-NUMBER = MARCH 30, 2020 = (3 + 3 + 0 + 2 + 0 + 2 + 0) = (`-**10**)!!!~`

(**32** (-) **10**) = (`-**22**)!!!~`

(32 + 10) = (`-**42**) = "The `-**MARK**"!!!~`

(42 + 22) = (`-**64**) = (`-**2** x `-**32**)!!!~`

`-**BIRTHDAY**; and, `-**DEATH/DAY**!!!~`:

(915 + 330) = (`-**1245**) = (12 + 45) = (`-**57**) = (5 x 7) = (`-**35**) = RECIPROCAL (MIRROR) = (`-**53**)!!!~`

(**915** (-) **330**) = (`-**585**) = "RECIPROCAL-**S**EQUENCING-**N**UMEROLOGY-**RSN**"!!!~`

(1245 (-) 585) = (`-**660**) / `-2 = (`-**330**) = "DEATH/DAY (**3/30**)" = "**MARCH** (**30**th)"!!!~`

SEPTEMBER 15 (**BIRTH**) + MARCH 30 (**DEATH**) = (9 + 15 + 3 + 30) = (`-**57**) = `-**DEATH/DAY** & `-**BIRTHDAY** `-ADDED `-UP `-TOGETHER!!!~`

`-DIED in (`-**3**) & was `-BORN in (`-**9**) = (`-**3/9**) = RECIPROCAL (MIRROR) = (`-**9/3**)!!!~' (93 + 39) = (`-**132**) = (32 x 1) = (`-**32**) = -a PROPHETIC # `-NUMBER!!!~'

`-**NEXT** `-**LAYER**-!!!~'

AMERICAN SINGER-SONGWRITER BILL WITHERS (`-**81**) (BIRTH: **JULY 4, 1938**) (DEATH: **MARCH** 3**0**, 20**2**0)!!!~'

MARCH 30, 2020 = (**33**0/20**2**0) = (**33/22**) = (`-**32**) = -a PROPHETIC # `-NUMBER!!!~'

`-**BORN** on `-JULY 4[th] = (**7/4**) = "INDEPENDENCE `-DAY"!!!~'

`-**BIRTHDAY #** `-**NUMBER** = (`-**68**) = "THE `-**MARK**"!!!~'

FRAGMENTED **BIRTHDAY #** `-**NUMBER** = JULY 4, 1938 = (7 + 4 + 1 + 9 + 3 + 8) = (`-**32**) = "The `-**SAME** as for AMERICAN WRITER TOMIE DEPAOLA" = -a PROPHETIC # `-NUMBER!!!~'

`-BIRTHDAY # `-NUMBER = (7 + 4 + 19 + 38) = (`-**68**)

`-DEATH/DAY # `-NUMBER = (3 + 30 + 20 + 20) = (`-**73**) = "**AGE** of `-**DEATH** for AMERICAN ACTOR DAVID SCHRAMM (`-**73**)"!!!~'

(73 + 68) = (`-**141**) = "**RECIPROCAL-SEQUENCING-NUMEROLOGY-RSN**"!!!~'

(73 (-) 68) = (`-**5**)!!!~'

(141 (-) 5) = (`-**136**) = (36 x 1) = (`-**36**)!!!~'

(141 + 5) = (`-**146**) = (46 x 1) = (`-**46**) = (`-**23** x `-**2**)!!!~'

(136 + 146) = (`-**282**) = **"RECIPROCAL-SEQUENCING-NUMEROLOGY-RSN"**!!!~'

(36 + 46) = (`-**82**) = `-**DIED** in `-HIS (`-**82**nd) `-**YEAR** of `-**EXISTENCE**!!!~'

HE `-**DIED** (`-**96**) **DAYS** before `-**HIS** `-**NEXT** `-**BIRTHDAY**!!!~'
(`-**96**) = (`-**32** x `-**3**)!!!~'

(365 (-) **96**) = (`-**269**) = (69 x 2) = (`-**138**) = (38 x 1) = (`-**38**) = "Was `-**BORN** in (`-**38**)"!!!~' (`-**69**) = RECIPROCAL (MIRROR) = (`-**96**)!!!~' (`-**69**) = (`-**3** x **23**)!!!~'

HE DIED AT THE `-**AGE** of (`-**81**)!!!~'

`-**BIRTHDAY** = **JULY 4** = (7 x 4) = (`-**28**)!!!~'

`-**DEATH/DAY** = **MARCH 30** = (3 x 30) = (`-**90**)!!!~'

(90 + 28) = (`-**118**)!!!~'

(90 (-) 28) = (`-**62**)!!!~'

(118 + 62) = (`-**180**) = (18 + 0) = (`-**18**)!!!~'

(118 (-) 62) = (`-**56**) = RECIPROCAL (MIRROR) = (`-**65**)!!!~'

Was `-**MARRIED** to `-**MARCIA JOHNSON** for some (`-**44**) **YEARS**!!!~' (100 (-) **44**) = (`-**56**)!!!~'

FRAGMENTED BIRTHDAY # `-NUMBER** = JULY 4, 1938 = (7 + 4 + 1 + 9 + 3 + 8) = (`-32**) = -a **PROPHETIC # `-NUMBER!!!~'**

FRAGMENTED DEATH/DAY # `-NUMBER** = MARCH 30, 2020 = (3 + 3 + 0 + 2 + 0 + 2 + 0) = (`-10**)!!!~'

(**32** (-) **10**) = (`-**22**)!!!~'

(32 + 10) = (`-**42**) = "The `-**MARK**"!!!~'

(42 + 22) = (`-**64**) = (`-**2** x `-**32**)!!!~'

`-BIRTHDAY; and, `-DEATH/DAY!!!~':

(330 + **74**) = (`-**404**)!!!~'

(**330** (-) **74**) = (`-**256**)!!!~'

(404 + 256) = (`-**660**) / `-2 = (`-**330**) = "**DEATH/DAY (3/30)**" = "**MARCH (30**[th])"!!!~'

(404 (-) 256) = (`-**148**) / `-2 = (`-**74**) = "**BIRTHDAY (7/4)**" = "**JULY (4**[th])"!!!~'

JULY 4 (**BIRTH**) + MARCH 30 (**DEATH**) = (7 + 4 + 3 + 30) = (`-**44**) = **`-DEATH/DAY & `-BIRTHDAY `-ADDED `-UP `-TOGETHER!!!~'**

`-DIED in** (`-3**) **& was `-BORN in** (`-**7**) = (`-**3/7**) = RECIPROCAL (MIRROR) = (`-**7/3**) = **`-BORN the `-VERY `-NEXT `-DAY of** (`-**7/4**) = (JULY 4[th]) = "**INDEPENDENCE `-DAY**"!!!~'

BRITISH DIALECT COACH ANDREW JACK "STAR WARS" (`-**76**) (BIRTH: JANUARY **28**, 1944) (DEATH: **MARCH 31**, 2020)!!!~'

`-**BIRTH/YEAR** = (`-**1944**) = (19 + 44) = (`-**63**) = `-**DIED** this `-**MANY** `-**DAYS** after `-**HIS** `-**LAST** `-**BIRTHDAY**!!!~'

`-**BORN** on a (`-**28**th); and, `-**DIED** with (`-**28**) = (**31** (-) **3**) = "**DAY** of `-**DEATH** & **MONTH** (**MARCH 31**st)"!!!~'

WAS `-**MARRIED** to **WIFE PAULA JACK** from (2000 to **2**018)!!!~' SHE ALSO was a DIALECT COACH!!!~'

`-BIRTHDAY # `-NUMBER = (1 + 28 + 19 + 44) = (`-**92**)!!!~'

`-DEATH/DAY # `-NUMBER = (3 + 31 + 20 + 20) = (`-**74**) = `-**BIRTHDAY of AMERICAN SINGER-SONGWRITER BILL WITHERS** (`-**7/4**)"!!!~'

(92 + 74) = (`-**166**) = (66 + 1) = (`-**67**) = RECIPROCAL (MIRROR) = (`-**76**) = "**AGE of** `-**DEATH for BRITISH DIALECT COACH ANDREW JACK "STAR WARS"** (`-**76**)"!!!~'

(92 (-) 74) = (`-**18**)!!!~'

(166 (-) 18) = (`-**148**) = (48 x 1) = (`-**48**) = RECIPROCAL (MIRROR) = (`-**84**)!!!~'

(166 + 18) = (`-**184**) = (84 x 1) = (`-**84**) = RECIPROCAL (MIRROR) = (`-**48**)!!!~'

(84 + 48) = (`-**132**) = (32 x 1) = (`-**32**) = -a **PROPHETIC #** `-**NUMBER**!!!~'

HE `-**DIED** (`-**63**) DAYS after `-**HIS** `-**LAST** `-**BIRTHDAY**!!!~'

(366 (-) **63**) = ('-**303**) = "**R**ECIPROCAL-**S**EQUENCING-**N**UMEROLOGY-**RSN**"!!!~'

HE DIED AT THE '-AGE of ('-**76**) = (7 x 6) = ('-**42**) = "The '-**MARK**"!!!~'

'-BIRTHDAY = JANUARY 28 = (1 x 28) = ('-**28**)!!!~'

'-DEATH/DAY = MARCH 31 = (3 x 31) = ('-**93**)!!!~'

(93 + 28) = ('-**121**) = "**R**ECIPROCAL-**S**EQUENCING-**N**UMEROLOGY-**RSN**"!!!~'

(93 (-) 28) = ('-**65**) = RECIPROCAL (MIRROR) = ('-**56**)!!!~'

(121 + 65) = ('-**186**) = (86 x 1) = ('-**86**) = "The '-**MARK**"!!!~'

(121 (-) 65) = ('-**56**) = RECIPROCAL (MIRROR) = ('-**65**)!!!~'

(186 + 56) = ('-**242**) = "**R**ECIPROCAL-**S**EQUENCING-**N**UMEROLOGY-**RSN**"!!!~'

FRAGMENTED BIRTHDAY # '-NUMBER = JANUARY 28, 1944 = (1 + 2 + 8 + 1 + 9 + 4 + 4) = ('-**29**)!!!~'

FRAGMENTED DEATH/DAY # '-NUMBER = MARCH 31, 2020 = (3 + 3 + 1 + 2 + 0 + 2 + 0) = ('-**11**)!!!~'

(**29** (-) **11**) = ('-**18**)!!!~'

(29 + 11) = ('-**40**)!!!~'

(40 + 18) = ('-**58**)!!!~'

'-**BIRTHDAY**; and, '-**DEATH/DAY**!!!~':

(331 + 128) = (`-459)!!!-~'

(331 (-) 128) = (`-203) = (23 + 0) = (`-23) = -a PROPHETIC # `-NUMBER!!!-~'

(459 + 203) = (`-662) / `-2 = (`-331) = "DEATH/DAY (3/31)" = "MARCH (31ᵗʰ)"!!!-~'

(459 (-) 203) = (`-256) / `-2 = (`-128) = "BIRTHDAY (1/28)" = "JANUARY (28ᵗʰ)"!!!-~'

JANUARY 28 (BIRTH) + MARCH 31 (DEATH) = (1 + 28 + 3 + 31) = (`-63) = `-DIED this many `-DAYS after `-HIS `-LAST `-BIRTHDAY (`-63)!!!-~'

`-DIED in (`-3) & was `-BORN in (`-1) = (`-3/1) = RECIPROCAL (MIRROR) = (`-1/3) = (`-13) = "A VERY PIVOTAL # `-NUMBER"!!!-~'

`-DIED in (`-3) & was `-BORN in (`-1) = (`-3/1) = (`-31) = `-DAY of `-DEATH (31ˢᵗ)!!!-~'

AMERICAN JAZZ TRUMPETER WALLACE RONEY (`-59) (BIRTH: MAY 25, 1960) (DEATH: MARCH 31, 2020)!!!-~'

`-BIRTHDAY = MAY 25 = (`-525) = "RECIPROCAL-SEQUENCING-NUMEROLOGY-RSN"!!!-~'

`-BORN in (`-60) with `-HIS `-WIFE GERI ALLEN `-DYING at the `-AGE of (`-60)!!!-~'

`-BIRTHDAY # `-NUMBER = (5 + 25 + 19 + 60) = (`-109)!!!-~'

`-DEATH/DAY # `-NUMBER = (3 + 31 + 20 + 20) = (`-**74**) = `-**BIRTHDAY of AMERICAN SINGER-SONGWRITER BILL WITHERS (`-7/4)"!!!~'**

(109 + 74) = (`-**183**) = (83 x 1) = (`-**83**)!!!~'

(109 (-) 74) = (`-**35**)!!!~'

(183 (-) 35) = (`-**148**) = (48 x 1) = (`-**48**) = RECIPROCAL (MIRROR) = (`-**84**)!!!~'

(183 + 35) = (`-**218**) = (21 x 8) = (`-**168**) = (68 x 1) = (`-**68**) = "The `-**MARK**"!!!~'

HE `-**DIED** (`-**55**) **DAYS** before `-**HIS** `-**NEXT** `-**BIRTHDAY!!!~'** (`-**55**) = (`-**23** + `-**32**)!!!~'

(365 (-) **55**) = (`-**310**) = (31 + 0) = (`-**31**) = RECIPROCAL (MIRROR) = (`-**13**) = **"A VERY PIVOTAL # `-NUMBER"!!!~'**

HE DIED AT THE `-AGE of (`-**59**)!!!~'

(**25** + **31**) = (`-**56**) = RECIPROCAL (MIRROR) = (`-**65**)!!!~'

`-**BIRTHDAY** = MAY **25** = (5 x **25**) = (`-**125**)!!!~'

`-**DEATH/DAY** = MARCH **31** = (3 x **31**) = (`-**93**)!!!~'

(125 + 93) = (`-**218**) = (21 x 8) = (`-**168**) = (68 x 1) = (`-**68**) = "The `-**MARK**"!!!~'

(125 (-) 93) = (`-**32**) = -a PROPHETIC # `-NUMBER!!!~'

(218 + 32) = (`-**250**) = (25 + 0) = (`-**25**) = "DAY of `-BIRTH (`-**25**ᵗʰ)"!!!~'

(218 (-) 32) = (`-**186**) = (86 x 1) = (`-**86**) = "The `-**MARK**"!!!~'

(250 (-) 186) = (`-**64**) = (`-**2** x `-**32**)"!!!~'

FRAGMENTED BIRTHDAY # `-NUMBER** = MAY 25, 1960 = (5 + 2 + 5 + 1 + 9 + 6 + 0) = (`-28**)!!!~'

FRAGMENTED DEATH/DAY # `-NUMBER** = MARCH 31, 2020 = (3 + 3 + 1 + 2 + 0 + 2 + 0) = (`-11**)!!!~'

(**28** (-) **11**) = (`-**17**)!!!~'

(28 + 11) = (`-**39**)!!!~'

(39 + 17) = (`-**56**) = RECIPROCAL (MIRROR) = (`-**65**)!!!~'

(39 + 17) = (`-**56**) = "FLIP the (`-**6**) OVER to a (`-**9**)" = (`-**59**) = "**AGE of `-DEATH for AMERICAN JAZZ TRUMPETER WALLACE RONEY (`-59)**"!!!~'

`-BIRTHDAY; and, `-DEATH/DAY!!!~':

(525 + **331**) = (`-**856**)!!!~'

(**525** (-) **331**) = (`-**194**)!!!~'

(856 (-) 194) = (`-**662**) / `-2 = (`-**331**) = "**DEATH/DAY (3/31)**" = "**MARCH (31ˢᵗ)**"!!!~'

(856 + 194) = (`-**1050**) / `-2 = (`-**525**) = "**BIRTHDAY (5/25)**" = "**MAY (25ᵗʰ)**"!!!~'

MAY 25 (**BIRTH**) + MARCH 31 (**DEATH**) = (5 + 25 + 3 + 31) = (`-**64**) = (`-**2** x `-**32**)!!!~'

`-DIED in (`-**3**) & was `-BORN in (`-**5**) = (`-**3/5**) = RECIPROCAL (MIRROR) = (`-**5/3**) = HIS `-**WIFE** was `-**BORN** in (`-**57**) = (5 x 7) = (`-**35**)!!!~'

(35 + 53) = (`-**88**) = "SEE `-**BELOW**"!!!~'

AMERICAN JAZZ PIANIST GERI ALLEN (WIFE of WALLACE RONEY - **PRECEDING**) (`-**60**) (BIRTH: **JUNE** 12, 19**57**) (DEATH: **JUNE 27, 2017**)!!!~'

THEY were `-**MARRIED** in (`-19**95**) = (`-**95**) = RECIPROCAL (MIRROR) = (`-**59**) = "**AGE of `-DEATH for `-HER `-HUSBAND WALLACE RONEY** (`-**59**)!!!~'

`-**DEATH/DAY** = **JUNE 27** = (**6** x **27**) = (`-**162**) = "SWIPE (`-**1**)" = (**612**) = `-**HER VERY OWN** `-**BIRTHDAY**!!!~'

`-**BIRTHDAY** # `-NUMBER = (6 + 12 + 19 + 57) = (`-**94**)!!!~'

`-**DEATH/DAY** # `-NUMBER = (6 + 27 + 20 + 17) = (`-**70**)!!!~'

(94 + 70) = (`-**164**) = (64 x 1) = (`-**64**) = (`-**2** x `-**32**)!!!~'

(94 (-) 70) = (`-**24**)!!!~'

(164 (-) 24) = (`-**140**) = (40 x 1) = (`-**40**)!!!~'

(164 + 24) = (`-**188**) = (88 x 1) = (`-**88**) = (35 + 53) = (`-**88**) = "SEE `-**ABOVE** to `-**HER** `-**HUSBAND** from `-**BIRTH/MONTH** to `-**DEATH/MONTH**"!!!~'

SHE `-**DIED** (`-**15**) DAYS after `-**HER** `-**LAST** `-**BIRTHDAY**!!!~'

146

(365 (-) **15**) = (`-**350**) = (35 + 0) = (`-**35**) = RECIPROCAL (MIRROR) = (`-**53**) = "SEE `-**ABOVE** to `-**HER** `-**HUSBAND** from `-**BIRTH/MONTH** to `-**DEATH/MONTH**"!!!~'

(365 (-) **15**) = (`-**350**) = (35 + 0) = (`-**35**) = (5 x 7) = (`-**57**) = `-**HER VERY OWN** `-**BIRTH/YEAR**!!!~'

SHE DIED AT THE `-AGE of (`-**60**)!!!~'

`-**BIRTHDAY** = **JUNE 12** = (6 x 12) = (`-**72**)!!!~'

`-**DEATH/DAY** = **JUNE 27** = (**6** x **27**) = (`-**162**) = "SWIPE (`-**1**)" = (**612**) = `-**HER VERY OWN** `-**BIRTHDAY**!!!~'

(162 + 72) = (`-**234**) = "**PROPHETIC-LINEAR-PROGRESSION-PLP**"!!!~'

(162 (-) 72 = (`-**90**)!!!~'

(234 + 90) = (`-**324**) = (24 x 3) = (`-**72**) = `-**BIRTHDAY**!!!~'

(234 (-) 90) = (`-**144**) = (14 x 4) = (`-**56**) = RECIPROCAL (MIRROR) = (`-**65**)!!!~'

(324 + 144) = (`-**468**) / `-2 = (`-**234**) = "**PROPHETIC-LINEAR-PROGRESSION-PLP**"!!!~'

FRAGMENTED BIRTHDAY # `-NUMBER** = JUNE 12, 1957 = (6 + 1 + 2 + 1 + 9 + 5 + 7) = (`-31**) = RECIPROCAL (MIRROR) = (`-**13**) = "**A VERY PIVOTAL # `-NUMBER**"!!!~'

FRAGMENTED DEATH/DAY # `-NUMBER** = JUNE 27, 2017 = (6 + 2 + 7 + 2 + 0 + 1 + 7) = (`-25**)!!!~'

(**31** (-) **25**) = (`-**6**)!!!~'

(31 + 25) = (`-**56**) = RECIPROCAL (MIRROR) = (`-**65**)!!!~

(56 (-) 6) = (`-**50**) = (5 + 0) = (`-**5**) = "The `-**HAND** of `-**GOD**"!!!~'

`-**BIRTHDAY**; and, `-**DEATH/DAY**!!!~':

(627 + **612**) = (`-**1239**) = (12 + 39) = (`-**51**)!!!~'

(**627** (-) **612**) = (`-**15**)!!!~'

(`-**15**) = RECIPROCAL (MIRROR) = (`-**51**)!!!~'

(15 + 51) = (`-**66**) = `-**BORN** in (`-**6**) & `-**DIED** in (`-**6**)!!!~'

JUNE 12 (**BIRTH**) + JUNE 27 (**DEATH**) = (6 + 12 + 6 + 27) = (`-**51**) = `-**DEATH/DAY** & `-**BIRTHDAY** `-**ADDED** `-**UP** `-**TOGETHER**!!!~'

`-**DIED** in (`-**6**) & was `-**BORN** in (`-**6**) = (`-**6/6**) = (`-**66**) = "SEE `-**ABOVE**"!!!~'

AMERICAN SINGER & CO-FOUNDER of MUSICAL GROUP "FOUNTAINS of `-WAYNE" ADAM SCHLESINGER (`-**52**) (BIRTH: **OCTOBER 31**, 19**67**) (DEATH: **APRIL 1, 2020**)!!!~' **APRIL 1**st = (`-**41**) = (`-1 + 20 + 20)!!!~'

`-**1967** = (19 + 67) = (`-**86**) = "The `-**MARK**"!!!~'

`-**BIRTHDAY** # `-**NUMBER** = (10 + 31 + 19 + 67) = (`-**127**)!!!~'

`-**DEATH/DAY** # `-**NUMBER** = (4 + 1 + 20 + 20) = (`-**45**)!!!~'

(127 + 45) = (`-**172**) = (72 x 1) = (`-**72**)!!!~'

148

(127 (-) 45) = (`-**82**)!!!~'

(172 (-) 82) = (`-**90**)!!!~'

(172 + 82) = (`-**254**)!!!~'

(254 (-) 90) = (`-**164**) = (64 x 1) = (`-**64**) = (`-**2** x `-**32**)!!!~'

HE `-**DIED** (`-**153**) **DAYS** after `-**HIS** `-**LAST** `-**BIRTHDAY**!!!~'
(`-**153**) = (53 (-) 1) = (`-**52**) = **"AGE of `-DEATH for ADAM
SCHLESINGER"**!!!~' **NON-LEAP-YEAR** = (`-**152**) **DAYS AWAY
from `-BIRTHDAY to `-DEATH/DEATH**!!!~'

(366 (-) **153**) = (`-**213**) = (23 x 1) = (`-**23**) = -a PROPHETIC #
`-NUMBER!!!~'

HE DIED AT THE `-AGE of (`-**52**)!!!~'

`-**BIRTHDAY** = **OCTOBER 31** = (10 x 31) = (`-**310**) = (31 + 0) = (`-
31) = RECIPROCAL (MIRROR) = (`-**13**) = **"A VERY PIVOTAL
`-NUMBER"**!!!~'

`-**DEATH/DAY** = **APRIL 1** = (4 x 1) = (`-**4**)!!!~'

(310 + 4) = (`-**314**)!!!~'

(310 (-) 4) = (`-**306**)!!!~'

(314 + 306) = (`-**620**) = (62 + 0) = (`-**62**)!!!~'

(314 (-) 306) = (`-**8**)!!!~'

(620 + 8) = (`-**628**) = (6 x 28) = (`-**168**) = **"The `-MARK"**!!!~'

FRAGMENTED BIRTHDAY # `-NUMBER** = OCTOBER 31, 1967 = (1 + 0 + 3 + 1 + 1 + 9 + 6 + 7) = (`-28**)!!!~'

FRAGMENTED DEATH/DAY # `-NUMBER** = APRIL 1, 2020 = (4 + 1 + 2 + 0 + 2 + 0) = (`-9**)!!!~'

(**28** (-) **9**) = (`-**19**)!!!~'

(28 + 9) = (`-**37**)!!!~'

(37 + 19) = (`-**56**) = RECIPROCAL (MIRROR) = (`-**65**)!!!~'

`-BIRTHDAY; and, `-DEATH/DAY!!!~':

(1031 + **41**) = (`-**1072**) = (10 + 72) = (`-**82**) = RECIPROCAL (MIRROR) = (`-**28**) = FRAGMENTED `-BIRTHDAY # `-NUMBER (`-**28**)!!!~'

(**1031** (-) **41**) = (`-**990**)!!!~'

(1072 (-) 990) = (`-**82**) / `-2 = (`-**41**) = **"DEATH/DAY (4/1)"** = **"APRIL (1ˢᵗ)"!!!~'**

OCTOBER 31 (**BIRTH**) + APRIL 1 (**DEATH**) = (10 + 31 + 4 + 1) = (`-**46**) = (`-**23** x `-**2**)!!!~'

`-DIED in (`-**4**) & was `-BORN in (`-**10**) = (`-**4/10**) = RECIPROCAL (MIRROR) = (`-**10/4**)!!!~'

(**4/10** + **10/4**) = (14 + 14) = (`-**28**) = `-FRAGMENTED `-BIRTHDAY # `-NUMBER (`-**28**)!!!~'

JAZZ MASTER AND MUSICAL FAMILY PATRIARCH ELLIS MARSALIS JR. (`-85) (BIRTH: NOVEMBER 14, 1934) (DEATH: APRIL 1, 2020)!!!~'

APRIL 1ˢᵗ = (`-41) = (`-1 + 20 + 20)!!!~'

`-DAY of `-BIRTH = (`-14ᵗʰ); AND, `-DEATH/DAY = (`-4/1)!!!~'

(`-41) = RECIPROCAL (MIRROR) = (`-14)!!!~'

(41 + 14) = (`-55) = (`-23 + `-32)!!!~'

`-BIRTHDAY # `-NUMBER = (11 + 14 + 19 + 34) = (`-78)!!!~'

`-DEATH/DAY # `-NUMBER = (4 + 1 + 20 + 20) = (`-45)!!!~'

(78 + 45) = (`-123) = (23 x 1) = (`-23) = -a PROPHETIC # `-NUMBER!!!~'

(78 (-) 45) = (`-33)!!!~'

(123 (-) 33) = (`-90) = `-DEATH/DAY # `-NUMBER (`-45) x `-2 = (`-90)!!!~'

(123 + 33) = (`-156) = (56 x 1) = (`-56) = RECIPROCAL (MIRROR) = (`-65) = "NOTE `-HOW MANY `-TIMES this (65/56) is `-LISTED within THIS `-LAYER"!!!~'

HE `-DIED (`-139) DAYS after `-HIS `-LAST `-BIRTHDAY!!!~' (`-78) = BIRTHDAY # `-NUMBER / `-2 = (`-39)!!!~'

(366 (-) 139) = (`-227) = (22 x 7) = (`-154) = (54 x 1) = (`-54) = RECIPROCAL (MIRROR) = (`-45) = `-HIS VERY OWN `-DEATH/DAY # `-NUMBER (`-45)!!!~'

HE DIED AT THE `-AGE of (`-**85**)!!!~'

`-BIRTHDAY = NOVEMBER 14 = (11 x 14) = (`-**154**) = "SEE `-**ABOVE**"!!!~'

`-DEATH/DAY = APRIL 1 = (4 x 1) = (`-**4**)!!!~'

(154 + 4) = (`-**158**)!!!~'

(154 (-) 4) = (`-**150**)!!!~'

(158 + 150) = (`-**308**) = (38 + 0) = (`-**38**) = NON-LEAP-YEAR = (`-**138**) DAYS from `-**BIRTHDAY** to `-**DEATH/DEATH**!!!~'

(158 (-) 150) = (`-**8**)!!!~'

(308 + 8) = (`-**316**) = (31 x 6) = (`-**186**) = (86 x 1) = (`-**86**) = "The `-**MARK**"!!!~'

FRAGMENTED BIRTHDAY # `-NUMBER = NOVEMBER 14, 1934 = (1 + 1 + 1 + 4 + 1 + 9 + 3 + 4) = (`-**24**)!!!~'

FRAGMENTED DEATH/DAY # `-NUMBER = APRIL 1, 2020 = (4 + 1 + 2 + 0 + 2 + 0) = (`-**9**)!!!~'

(**24** (-) **9**) = (`-**15**)!!!~'

(24 + 9) = (`-**33**)!!!~'

(33 + 15) = (`-**48**) = RECIPROCAL (MIRROR) = (`-**84**)!!!~'

`-**BIRTHDAY**; and, `-**DEATH/DAY**!!!~':

(1114 + **41**) = (`-**1155**) = (11 + 55) = (`-**66**)!!!~'

(1114 (-) 41) = (`-**1073**) = (10 + 73) = (`-**83**) = RECIPROCAL (MIRROR) = (`-**38**) = **"SEE `-ABOVE"!!!~`**

(83 (-) 66) = (`-**17**) x `-**2** = (`-**34**) = **"YEAR of `-BIRTH (34)"!!!~`**

(34 x 2) = (`-**68**) = **"The `-MARK"!!!~`**

NOVEMBER 14 (**BIRTH**) + APRIL 1 (**DEATH**) = (11 + 14 + 4 + 1) = (`-**30**) = `-**DEATH/DAY** & `-**BIRTHDAY** `-**ADDED** `-**UP** `-**TOGETHER!!!~`**

`-**DIED** in (`-**4**) & was `-**BORN** in (`-**11**) = (`-**4/11**) = RECIPROCAL (MIRROR) = (`-**11/4**)!!!~` (4/11 + 11/4) = (15 + 15) = (`-**30**) = `-**DEATH/DAY** & `-**BIRTHDAY** `-**ADDED** `-**UP** `-**TOGETHER!!!~`**

`-**DIED** in (`-**4**) & was `-**BORN** in (`-**11**) = (`-**4/11**) = RECIPROCAL (MIRROR) = (`-**11/4**) = **(ALL-IN-ONE-#-NUMBER)** for `-**BIRTHDAY** = (`-**114**) = **(11/14)!!!~`**

AMERICAN GUITARIST BUCKY PIZZARELLI (`-**94**) (BIRTH: JANUARY 9, **1926**) (DEATH: **APRIL 1**, 2020)!!!~` **APRIL 1ˢᵗ** = (`-**41**) = (`-1 + 20 + 20)!!!~`

`-**BIRTH/YEAR** = (`-**1926**) = (19 + 26) = (`-**45**) = `-**HIS VERY OWN `-DEATH/DAY # `-NUMBER (`-45)!!!~`**

(`-**45**) = RECIPROCAL (MIRROR) = (`-**54**)!!!~`

BUCKY & WIFE RUTH PIZZARELLI were `-**MARRIED** in (`-19**54**)!!!~`

DAUGHTER-IN-LAW AMERICAN ACTOR JESSICA MOLASKEY was `-BORN on the `-SAME `-DAY as `-BUCKY (JANUARY 9th); except, `-RECIPROCAL `-BIRTH/YEAR (`-26) = RECIPROCAL (MIRROR) = (`-62)!!!~' AGE (`-58) at `-TIME of `-BUCKY PIZARELLI'S `-DEATH /|\ BORN JANUARY 9, 1962) = (1 + 9 + 19 + 62) = (`-91) = RECIPROCAL (MIRROR) = (`-19) = `-HER VERY OWN `-BIRTHDAY = (JANUARY 9th)!!!~' SHE is `-MARRIED to JOHN PIZZARELLI SINCE (`-1998)!!!~'

`-BIRTHDAY # `-NUMBER = (1 + 9 + 19 + 26) = (`-55) = (`-23 + `-32)!!!~'

`-DEATH/DAY # `-NUMBER = (4 + 1 + 20 + 20) = (`-45)!!!~'

(55 + 45) = (`-100)!!!~'

(55 (-) 45) = (`-10)!!!~'

(100 (-) 10) = (`-90)!!!~'

(100 + 10) = (`-110)!!!~'

HE `-DIED (`-83) DAYS after `-HIS `-LAST `-BIRTHDAY!!!~'

(366 (-) 83) = (`-283) = (28 x 3) = (`-84) = RECIPROCAL (MIRROR) = (`-48)!!!~'

HE DIED AT THE `-AGE of (`-94)!!!~'

`-BIRTHDAY = JANUARY 9 = (1 x 9) = (`-9)!!!~'

`-DEATH/DAY = APRIL 1 = (4 x 1) = (`-4)!!!~'

`-**BIRTHDAY** & `-**DEATH/DAY** `-**FACTOR** = (`-**94**) = "AGE of `-**DEATH for AMERICAN GUITARIST BUCKY PIZZARELLI** (`-**94**)"!!!~'

(9 + 4) = (`-**13**)!!!~'

(9 (-) 5) = (`-**4**)!!!~'

(13 + 4) = (`-**17**)!!!~'

(13 (-) 4) = (`-**9**)!!!~'

(17 + 9) = (`-**26**) = `-**HIS VERY OWN** `-**BIRTH/YEAR** (`-**26**) = (`-**19**26)!!!~'

FRAGMENTED BIRTHDAY # `-NUMBER** = JANUARY 9, 1926 = (1 + 9 + 1 + 9 + 2 + 6) = (`-28**)!!!~'

FRAGMENTED DEATH/DAY # `-NUMBER** = APRIL 1, 2020 = (4 + 1 + 2 + 0 + 2 + 0) = (`-9**)!!!~'

(**28** (-) **9**) = (`-**19**)!!!~'

(28 + 9) = (`-**37**)!!!~'

(37 + 19) = (`-**56**) = RECIPROCAL (MIRROR) = (`-**65**)!!!~'

`-**BIRTHDAY; and, `-DEATH/DAY!!!~'**:

(**41** + **19**) = (`-**60**)!!!~'

(**41** (-) **19**) = (`-**22**)!!!~'

(60 (-) 22) = (`-**38**) = RECIPROCAL (MIRROR) = (`-**83**) = **AMERICAN GUITARIST BUCKY PIZZARELLI** `-<u>DIED</u> this `-MANY `-DAYS after `-HIS `-LAST `-BIRTHDAY (`-**83**)!!!~'

JANUARY 9 (**<u>BIRTH</u>**) + APRIL 1 (**<u>DEATH</u>**) = (1 + **9** + **4** + 1) = (`-**15**) = `-<u>DEATH/DAY</u> & `-<u>BIRTHDAY</u> `-ADDED `-UP `-<u>TOGETHER</u>!!!~'

`-DIED in (`-**4**) & was `-BORN in (`-**1**) = (`-**4/1**) = <u>EQUALS</u> = `-<u>HIS</u> VERY OWN `-<u>DEATH/DAY</u> (`-**4/1**) = (APRIL 1ˢᵗ)!!!~'

`-<u>NEXT</u> `-<u>LAYER</u>-!!!~'

WITH THE `-<u>**PRESIDENTS**</u>; and, The **#** `-NUMBER (`-**68**) /|\ (`-**168**)!!!~' The `-<u>SAME</u> goes for the `-**FIRST LADIES**!!!~' **FIRST LADY MARTHA WASHINGTON** `-<u>BIRTH/YEAR</u> = (`-**1731**); and, `-<u>DEATH/YEAR</u> = (`-**1802**) = (17 + 31 + 18 + 02) = (`-**68**)!!!~' **#1/PRESIDENT** GEORGE WASHINGTON'S `-<u>DEATH/DAY</u> = (**12/14**) = (12 x 14) = (`-**168**)!!!~' from: (**NEW BOOK** /|\ **REAL MESSAGES of** `-**GOD <u>I</u>, <u>II</u>; & <u>III</u>**-!!!~' /|\)...

4ᵗʰ-U.S. PRESIDENT JAMES MADISON was `-<u>BORN</u> in (`-**1751**) = (17 + 51) = (`-**68**)!!!~' HIS `-<u>DEATH/DAY</u> = <u>EQUALED</u> = (**6/28**) = (6 x 28) = (`-**168**)!!!~'

FIRST LADY BETTY FORD was `-<u>BORN</u> in (`-**1918**); AND, `-<u>DIED</u> in (`-**2011**) = (19 + 18 + 20 + 11) = (`-**68**)!!!~' The `-<u>LIST</u> `-GOES <u>ON</u> and `-<u>ON</u>; GO `-BACK; and, `-<u>REVIEW</u>; `-<u>ALL</u> of `-<u>THEM</u>, (THE FIRST LADIES)!!!~'

ACTOR `-TAB `-HUNTER'S `-BIRTHDAY # `-NUMBER = (7 + 11 + 19 + 31) = (`-**68**) = RECIPROCAL (MIRROR) = (`-**86**) = `-**HIS VERY OWN `-AGE** OF `-**DEATH** (`-**86**)!!!~' from: (**The REAL PROPHET of `-DOOM (KISMET) – INTRODUCTION – PENDULUM FLOW – III)**-'"

`-**NEXT** `-**LAYER**-!!!~'

AMERICAN JOURNALIST PATRICIA BOSWORTH (`-**86**) (BIRTH: **APRIL 24**, 1933) (DEATH: **APRIL 2**, 2020)!!!~' **APRIL 2** = (**4**/**2**) = (`-**42**) = (2 + 20 + 20)!!!~'

`-**BIRTH/YEAR** = (`-**1933**) = (19 + 33) = (`-**52**) = `-**HER (1**[st]**) `-HUSBAND'S `-AGE** of `-**DEATH** (`-**52**)!!!~'

`-**BIRTHDAY** = **APRIL 24**[th] = (**4**/**24**) = (`-**424**) = **"RECIPROCAL-SEQUENCING-NUMEROLOGY-RSN"**!!!~'

`-**DAY** of `-**BIRTH** (`-**24**) /|\ `-**DAY** of `-**DEATH** (`-**2**) = (`-**242**) = **"RECIPROCAL-SEQUENCING-NUMEROLOGY-RSN"**!!!~'

`-**DEATH** = APRIL 2, 2020 /|\ APRIL 2[nd] = (`-**4**/**2**) /|\ (`-**42**) = (2 + 20 + 20)!!!~'

`-BIRTHDAY # `-NUMBER = (4 + 24 + 19 + 33) = (`-**80**)!!!~'

`-DEATH/DAY # `-NUMBER = (4 + 2 + 20 + 20) = (`-**46**)!!!~'

(80 + 46) = (`-**126**)!!!~'

(80 (-) 46) = (`-**34**)!!!~'

(126 (-) 34) = (`-**92**)!!!~'

(126 + 34) = (`-**160**)!!!~'

(160 (-) 92) = (`-**68**) = "The `-**MARK**"!!!~'

SHE `-**DIED** (`-**22**) DAYS before `-HER `-NEXT `-BIRTHDAY!!!~'

(365 (-) **22**) = (`-**343**) = "**RECIPROCAL-SEQUENCING-NUMEROLOGY-RSN**"!!!~'

`-HER `-**AGE** of `-**DEATH** (`-**86**) (-) **MINUS** (-) `-HER (**1**ˢᵗ) `-**HUSBAND'S** `-**AGE** of `-**DEATH** AMERICAN SCREENWRITER MEL ARRIGHI (`-**52**) = (86 (-) 52) = (`-**34**) = "**HE** `-**DIED** in (`-**86**)"!!!~'

(34 + 34) = (`-**68**) = "The `-**MARK**"!!!~'

(43 + 43) = (`-**86**) = "The `-**MARK**"!!!~'

SHE DIED AT THE `-**AGE** of (`-**86**)!!!~'

`-**BIRTHDAY** = APRIL 24 = (4 x 24) = (`-**96**) = (`-**32** x `-**3**)!!!~'

`-**DEATH/DAY** = APRIL 2 = (4 x 2) = (`-**8**)!!!~'

(96 + 8) = (`-**104**)!!!~'

(96 (-) 8) = (`-**88**)!!!~'

(104 + 88) = (`-**192**)!!!~'

(104 (-) 88) = (`-**16**)!!!~'

(192 (-) 16) = (`-**176**) = (76 x 1) = (`-**76**) = RECIPROCAL (MIRROR) = (`-**67**) = `-BIRTHDAY # `-NUMBER of (**1ˢᵗ**) HUSBAND AMERICAN SCREENWRITER MEL ARRIGHI!!!~'

FRAGMENTED BIRTHDAY # `-NUMBER = APRIL 24, 1933 = (4 + 2 + 4 + 1 + 9 + 3 + 3) = (`-**26**)!!!~'

FRAGMENTED DEATH/DAY # `-NUMBER = APRIL 2, 2020 = (4 + 2 + 2 + 0 + 2 + 0) = (`-**10**)!!!~'

(**26** (-) **10**) = (`-**16**)!!!~'

(26 + 10) = (`-**36**)!!!~'

(36 + 16) = (`-**52**) = `-**AGE** of `-**DEATH** of `-**HER** (**1ˢᵗ**) `-**HUSBAND** AMERICAN SCREENWRITER MEL ARRIGHI (`-**52**)!!!~'

`-**BIRTHDAY**; and, `-**DEATH/DAY**!!!~':

(**424** + **42**) = (`-**466**)!!!~'

(**424** (-) **42**) = (`-**382**)!!!~'

(466 (-) 382) = (`-**84**) = RECIPROCAL (MIRROR) = (`-**48**)!!!~'
(42 + 42) = (`-**84**)!!!~'

APRIL 24 (**BIRTH**) + APRIL 2 (**DEATH**) = (**4** + **24** + **4** + **2**) = (`-**34**) = `-**DEATH/DAY** & `-**BIRTHDAY** `-**ADDED** `-**UP** `-**TOGETHER** = "SEE `-**ABOVE**"!!!~'

`-**DIED** in (`-**4**) & was `-**BORN** in (`-**4**) = (`-**4/4**) = **EQUALS** = (`-**44**) = (`-**242**) = 4(2 + 2) = (`-**44**) = `-**BIRTHDAY** & `-**DEATH/ DAY**!!!~'

'-<u>DAYS</u> '-<u>HUSBAND'S</u> '-<u>DIED</u> from '-<u>BIRTHDAY</u> to '-<u>DEATH/DAY</u> = (104 + 19) = ('-<u>123</u>) = (23 x 1) = ('-<u>23</u>) = -a PROPHETIC # '-NUMBER!!!~'

'-<u>DAYS</u> '-<u>HUSBAND'S</u> '-<u>DIED</u> from '-<u>BIRTHDAY</u> to '-<u>DEATH/DAY</u> = (104 + 19) = ('-<u>123</u>) = "<u>P</u>ROPHETIC-<u>L</u>INEAR-<u>P</u>ROGRESSION-<u>PLP</u>"!!!~'

AMERICAN PHOTOGRAPHER TOM PALUMBO ('-<u>87</u>) (PATRICIA BOSWORTH'S (<u>2nd</u>) HUSBAND) (BIRTH: JANUARY 25, 1921) (DEATH: OCTOBER 13, 2008)!!!~' **THEY** were '-<u>MARRIED</u> from (<u>2</u>00<u>2</u>-to-<u>2</u>00<u>8</u>)!!!~'

'-<u>HIS</u> '-<u>WIFE</u> '-<u>DIED</u> ('-<u>22</u>) <u>DAYS</u> '-<u>SHY</u> of '-<u>HER</u> ('-<u>87th</u>) '-<u>BIRTHDAY</u>!!!~' **THEY** were '-<u>MARRIED</u> in ('-<u>2002</u>) = (22 + 0 + 0) = ('-<u>22</u>)!!!~'

'-<u>DEATH/DAY</u> = (<u>10/13</u>) = (10 + 13) = ('-<u>23</u>) = -a PROPHETIC # '-NUMBER!!!~'

'-BIRTHDAY # '-NUMBER = (1 + 25 + 19 + 21) = ('-<u>66</u>) = "WIFE'S (<u>1st</u>) HUSBAND '-HAD '-MARRIED '-<u>HER</u> in ('-<u>66</u>) to AMERICAN SCREENWRITER MEL ARRIGHI!!!~'

'-DEATH/DAY # '-NUMBER = (10 + 13 + 20 + 08) = ('-<u>51</u>)!!!~'

(66 + 51) = ('-<u>117</u>)!!!~'

(66 (-) 51) = ('-<u>15</u>)!!!~'

(117 (-) 15) = ('-<u>102</u>)!!!~'

(117 + 15) = (`-**132**) = (32 x 1) = (`-**32**) = -a **PROPHETIC** # `-**NUMBER!!!**~'

(132 + 102) = (`-**234**) = "**PROPHETIC-LINEAR-PROGRESSION-PLP**"!!!~'

HE `-**DIED** (`-**104**) DAYS before `-**HIS** `-**NEXT** `-**BIRTHDAY!!!**~'

(365 (-) **104**) = (`-**261**) = (61 x 2) = (`-**122**) = (22 + 1) = (`-**23**) = -a **PROPHETIC** # `-**NUMBER!!!**~'

HE DIED AT THE `-AGE of (`-**87**) = (8 x 7) = (`-**56**)!!!~'

`-**BIRTHDAY** = **JANUARY 25** = (1 x 25) = (`-**25**)!!!~'

`-**DEATH/DAY** = **OCTOBER 13** = (10 x 13) = (`-**130**) = (13 + 0) = (`-**13**) = "**A VERY PIVOTAL** # `-**NUMBER**"!!!~'

(130 + 25) = (`-**155**) = (55 x 1) = (`-**55**) = (`-**23** + `-**32**)!!!~'

(130 (-) 25) = (`-**105**)!!!~'

(155 + 105) = (`-**260**)!!!~'

(155 (-) 105) = (`-**50**)!!!~'

(260 + 50) = (`-**310**) = (31 + 0) = (`-**31**) = **RECIPROCAL (MIRROR)** = (`-**13**) = "**A VERY PIVOTAL** # `-**NUMBER**"!!!~'

FRAGMENTED BIRTHDAY # `-**NUMBER** = JANUARY 25, 1921 = (1 + 2 + 5 + 1 + 9 + 2 + 1) = (`-**21**) = `-**HIS VERY OWN** `-**BIRTH/YEAR** = (`-**21**)!!!~'

FRAGMENTED DEATH/DAY # `-**NUMBER** = OCTOBER 13, 2008 = (1 + 0 + 1 + 3 + 2 + 0 + 0 + 8) = (`-**15**)!!!~'

(**21** (-) **15**) = (`-**6**)!!!~'

(21 + 15) = (`-**36**)!!!~'

(36 + 6) = (`-**42**) = "The `-**MARK**"!!!~'

`-**BIRTHDAY**; and, `-**DEATH/DAY**!!!~':

(**1013** + **125**) = (`-**1138**) = (11 + 38) = (`-**49**)!!!~'

(**1013** (-) **125**) = (`-**888**)!!!~'

(1138 (-) 888) = (`-**250**) = (25 + 0) = (`-**25**) = "**DAY** of `-**BIRTH** (`-**25**^(th))"!!!~'

JANUARY 25 (**BIRTH**) + OCTOBER 13 (**DEATH**) = (1 + 25 + 10 + 13) = (`-**49**) = `-**DEATH/DAY** & `-**BIRTHDAY** `-**ADDED** `-**UP** `-**TOGETHER**!!!~'

`-**DIED** in (`-**10**) & was `-**BORN** in (`-**01**) = (`-**10/01**) = (`-**10**) = RECIPROCAL (MIRROR) = (`-**01**)!!!~'

AMERICAN SCREENWRITER MEL ARRIGHI (`-**52**) (PATRICIA BOSWORTH'S (**1**^(st)) HUSBAND) (BIRTH: OCTOBER 5, 1933) (DEATH: SEPTEMBER 16, 19**86**)!!!~'

THEY were `-**MARRIED** from (19**66**-to-19**86**)!!!~'

`-**BIRTH/YEAR** = (`-**1933**) = (19 + 33) = (`-**52**) = `-**HIS VERY OWN** `-**AGE** of `-**DEATH** (`-**52**)!!!~'

(MEL ARRIGHI) `-**DIED** in (`-**86**); AND, `-**HIS** `-**WIFE** (**PATRICIA BOSWORTH**) `-**DIED** at the `-**AGE** of (`-**86**)!!!~'

`-**DEATH/YEAR** = (`-**1986**) = (86 (-) 19) = (`-**67**) = `-**HIS** VERY OWN `-**BIRTHDAY** # `-**NUMBER** (`-**67**)!!!~'

`-BIRTHDAY # `-NUMBER = (10 + 5 + 19 + 33) = (`-**67**)!!!~'

`-DEATH/DAY # `-NUMBER = (9 + 16 + 19 + **86**) = (`-**130**) = (13 + 0) = (`-**13**) = **"A VERY PIVOTAL # `-NUMBER"**!!!~'

(130 + 67) = (`-**197**)!!!~'

(130 (-) 67) = (`-**63**)!!!~'

(197 (-) 63) = (`-**134**)!!!~'

(197 + 63) = (`-**260**)!!!~'

(260 (-) 134) = (`-**126**)!!!~'

HE `-**DIED** (`-**19**) DAYS before `-**HIS** `-**NEXT** `-**BIRTHDAY**!!!~'

(365 (-) **19**) = (`-**346**) = (46 x 3) = (`-**138**) = (38 x 1) = (`-**38**) / `-2 = (`-**19**)!!!~'

HE DIED AT THE `-AGE of (`-**52**)!!!~'

`-**BIRTHDAY** = OCTOBER 5 = (10 x 5) = (`-**50**)!!!~'

`-**DEATH/DAY** = SEPTEMBER 16 = (9 x 16) = (`-**144**)!!!~'

(144 + 50) = (`-**194**)!!!~'

(144 (-) 50) = (`-**94**)!!!~'

(194 + 94) = (`-**288**)!!!~'

(194 (-) 94) = (`-**100**)!!!~'

(288 (-) 100) = (`-**188**) = (**88 x 1**) = (`-**88**)!!!~'

FRAGMENTED BIRTHDAY # `-NUMBER** = OCTOBER 5, 1933 = (1 + 0 + 5 + 1 + 9 + 3 + 3) = (`-22**)!!!~'

FRAGMENTED DEATH/DAY # `-NUMBER** = SEPTEMBER 16, 1986 = (9 + 1 + 6 + 1 + 9 + 8 + 6) = (`-40**)!!!~'

(**40** (-) **22**) = (`-**18**)!!!~'

(40 + 22) = (`-**62**)!!!~'

(62 (-) 18) = (`-**44**)!!!~'

(**88 + 44**) = (`-**132**) = (**32 x 1**) = (`-**32**) = -a **PROPHETIC # `-NUMBER!!!~'**

`-BIRTHDAY; and, `-DEATH/DAY!!!~':

(**916** + **105**) = (`-**1021**) = (**10 + 21**) = (`-**31**) = **RECIPROCAL (MIRROR)** = (`-**13**) = "A VERY PIVOTAL # `-NUMBER"!!!~'

(**916** (-) **105**) = (`-**811**)!!!~'

(1021 (-) 811) = (`-**210**) / `-2 = (`-**105**) = `-**BIRTHDAY** (`-**10/5**) = "(**OCTOBER 5**th)"!!!~'

OCTOBER 5 (**BIRTH**) + SEPTEMBER 16 (**DEATH**) = (10 + 5 + 9 + 16) = (`-**40**) = `-**DEATH/DAY** & `-**BIRTHDAY** `-ADDED `-UP `-**TOGETHER!!!~'**

`-DIED in (`-9) & was `-BORN in (`-10) = (`-9/10) = (9 + 10) = (`-19) = `-DIED (`-19) DAYS from `-BIRTHDAY to `-DEATH/DAY!!!~'

AMERICAN FOOTBALL PLAYER TOM DEMPSEY (`-73) (BIRTH: JANUARY 12, 1947) (DEATH: APRIL 4, 2020)!!!~'

`-DEATH/DAY = APRIL 4 = (4/4) = (`-44) = (4 + 20 + 20)!!!~'

`-BIRTH/YEAR = (`-1947) = (19 + 47) = (`-66) = "SEE `-BELOW & `-ABOVE"!!!~'

(66 (-) 44) = (`-22) = (2 x 11) = (`-211) = RECIPROCAL (MIRROR) = (`-112) = `-BIRTHDAY = "(JANUARY 12ᵗʰ)"!!!~'

(112 + 211) = (`-323) = "RECIPROCAL-SEQUENCING-NUMEROLOGY-RSN"!!!~'

`-BIRTHDAY # `-NUMBER = (1 + 12 + 19 + 47) = (`-79)!!!~'

`-DEATH/DAY # `-NUMBER = (4 + 4 + 20 + 20) = (`-48) = RECIPROCAL (MIRROR) = (`-84)!!!~'

(79 + 48) = (`-127)!!!~'

(79 (-) 48) = (`-31) = RECIPROCAL (MIRROR) = (`-13) = "A VERY PIVOTAL # `-NUMBER"!!!~'

(127 (-) 31) = (`-96) = (`-32 x `-3)!!!~'

(127 + 31) = (`-158)!!!~'

(158 (-) 96) = (`-62) = RECIPROCAL (MIRROR) = (`-26)!!!~'

HE `-**DIED** (`-**83**) **DAYS** after `-**HIS** `-**LAST** `-**BIRTHDAY!!!**~'
SAME `-AS AMERICAN GUITARIST BUCKY PIZZARELLI
(`-**83**) DAYS between `-**BIRTHDAY** & `-**DEATH/DAY!!!**~' 2(**83**)
= (83 + 83) = (`-**166**) = (66 x 1) = (`-**66**)!!!~'

(366 (-) **83**) = (`-**283**) = (28 x 3) = (`-**84**) = RECIPROCAL
(MIRROR) = (`-**48**) = `-**HIS** VERY OWN `-**DEATH/DAY** #
`-**NUMBER** (`-**48**)!!!~'

HE DIED AT THE `-AGE of (`-**73**)!!!~'

`-**BIRTHDAY** = **JANUARY 12** = (1 x 12) = (`-**12**)!!!~'

`-**DEATH/DAY** = **APRIL 4** = (**4** x **4**) = (`-**16**)!!!~'

(16 + 12) = (`-**28**)!!!~'

(16 (-) 12) = (`-**4**)!!!~'

(28 + 4) = (`-**32**) = -a PROPHETIC # `-**NUMBER!!!**~'

(28 (-) 4) = (`-**24**)!!!~'

(32 + 24) = (`-**56**) = RECIPROCAL (MIRROR) = (`-**65**)!!!~'

FRAGMENTED BIRTHDAY # `-NUMBER = JANUARY 12,
1947 = (1 + 1 + 2 + 1 + 9 + 4 + 7) = (`-**25**)!!!~'

FRAGMENTED DEATH/DAY # `-NUMBER = APRIL 4, 2020
= (4 + 4 + 2 + 0 + 2 + 0) = (`-**12**)!!!~'

(**25** (-) **12**) = (`-**13**) = **"A VERY PIVOTAL # `-NUMBER"**!!!~'

(25 + 12) = (`-**37**) = RECIPROCAL (MIRROR) = (`-**73**) = `-**HIS**
VERY OWN `-**AGE** of `-**DEATH** (`-**73**)!!!~'

$(37 + 13) = (`-50) = (5 + 0) = (`-5) =$ **"The `-HAND of `-GOD"**!!!~'

`-BIRTHDAY; and, `-DEATH/DAY!!!~':

$(112 + 44) = (`-156) = (56 x 1) = (`-56) =$ RECIPROCAL (MIRROR) $= (`-65)!!!~'$

$(112 (-) 44) = (`-68) =$ **"The `-MARK"**!!!~'

$(156 (-) 68) = (`-88) / `-2 = (`-44) =$ `-**DEATH/DAY** (`-4/4) = **"(APRIL 4th)"**!!!~'

JANUARY 12 (**BIRTH**) + APRIL 4 (**DEATH**) = $(1 + 12 + 4 + 4) = (`-21) =$ RECIPROCAL (MIRROR) $= (`-12) =$ `-**DAY** of `-**BIRTH**!!!~'

`-**DIED** in (`-4) & was `-**BORN** in (`-1) = (`-4/1) = (41 x 3) = (`-123) = (23 x 1) = (`-23) = -a PROPHETIC # `-**NUMBER**!!!~'

AMERICAN FOOTBALL PLAYER/ACTOR & SINGER TIMOTHY BROWN (`-82) (BIRTH: MAY 24, 1937) (DEATH: **APRIL 4**, 2020)!!!~'

`-**DAY** of `-**BIRTH** = (`-24) = 2(4's) = (`-44) = **"DAY** of `-**DEATH"**!!!~'

`-**DEATH/DAY** = APRIL 4 = (4/4) = (`-44) = (4 + 20 + 20)!!!~'

AMERICAN FOOTBALL PLAYER TOM DEMPSEY `-**DIED** at (`-73) = RECIPROCAL (MIRROR) = (`-37) = AMERICAN FOOTBALL PLAYER/ACTOR & SINGER TIMOTHY BROWN `-was `-**BORN** in (`-37)!!!~'

`-**BIRTH/YEAR** = (`-**1937**) = (19 + 37) = (`-**56**) = RECIPROCAL (MIRROR) = (`-**65**)!!!~'

`-BIRTHDAY # `-NUMBER = (5 + 24 + 19 + 37) = (`-**85**)!!!~'

`-DEATH/DAY # `-NUMBER = (4 + 4 + 20 + 20) = (`-**48**) = RECIPROCAL (MIRROR) = (`-**84**)!!!~'

(85 + 48) = (`-**133**) = (33 (-) 1) = (`-**32**) = -a PROPHETIC # `-NUMBER!!!~'

(85 (-) 48) = (`-**37**) = "**YEAR of `-BIRTH**"!!!~'

(133 (-) 37) = (`-**96**) = (`-**32** x `-**3**)!!!~'

(133 + 37) = (`-**170**)!!!~'

(170 (-) 96) = (`-**74**) = (7 x 4) = (`-**28**) = RECIPROCAL (MIRROR) = (`-**82**) = "**AGE of `-DEATH for AMERICAN FOOTBALL PLAYER/ACTOR & SINGER TIMOTHY BROWN** (`-**82**)!!!~'

(170 + 96) = (`-**266**) = (66 x 2) = (`-**132**) = (32 x 1) = (`-**32**) = -a **PROPHETIC # `-NUMBER!!!~'**

(170 + 96) = (`-**266**) = (26 x 6) = (`-**156**) = (56 x 1) = (`-**56**) = `-**BIRTH/YEAR = (19** + **37**)!!!~'

HE `-**DIED** (`-**50**) DAYS before `-**HIS `-NEXT `-BIRTHDAY!!!~'**

(365 (-) **50**) = (`-**315**) = (15 x 3) = (`-**45**) = RECIPROCAL (MIRROR) = (`-**54**) = `-**MONTH `-BORN & `-MONTH `-DIED!!!~'**

HE DIED AT THE `-AGE of (`-**82**)!!!~'

`-**BIRTHDAY = MAY 24** = (5 x 24) = (`-**120**)!!!~'

`-DEATH/DAY = APRIL 4 = (4 x 4) = (`-16)!!!~'

(120 + 16) = (`-136)!!!~'

(120 (-) 16) = (`-104)!!!~'

(136 + 104) = (`-240)!!!~'

(136 (-) 104) = (`-32) = -a PROPHETIC # `-NUMBER!!!~'

(240 + 32) = (`-272) = "RECIPROCAL-SEQUENCING-NUMEROLOGY-RSN"!!!~'

(240 (-) 32) = (`-208) = (28 + 0) = (`-28) = RECIPROCAL (MIRROR) = (`-82) = "AGE of `-DEATH for AMERICAN FOOTBALL PLAYER/ACTOR & SINGER TIMOTHY BROWN (`-82)!!!~'

FRAGMENTED BIRTHDAY # `-NUMBER = MAY 24, 1937 = (5 + 2 + 4 + 1 + 9 + 3 + 7) = (`-31) = RECIPROCAL (MIRROR) = (`-13) = "A VERY PIVOTAL # `-NUMBER"!!!~'

FRAGMENTED DEATH/DAY # `-NUMBER = APRIL 4, 2020 = (4 + 4 + 2 + 0 + 2 + 0) = (`-12)!!!~'

(31 (-) 12) = (`-19)!!!~'

(31 + 12) = (`-43)!!!~'

(43 (-) 19) = (`-24) = "DAY of `-BIRTH"!!!~'

`-BIRTHDAY; and, `-DEATH/DAY!!!~':

(524 + 44) = (`-568)!!!~'

(<u>524</u> (-) <u>44</u>) = (`-<u>480</u>) = (48 + 0) = (`-<u>48</u>) = `-DEATH/DAY # `-NUMBER!!!~'

(568 + 480) = (`-<u>1048</u>) = (10 + 48) = (`-<u>58</u>) = RECIPROCAL (MIRROR) = (`-<u>85</u>) = `-BIRTHDAY # `-NUMBER!!!~'

MAY 24 (<u>BIRTH</u>) + APRIL 4 (<u>DEATH</u>) = (5 + 24 + 4 + 4) = (`-<u>37</u>) = `-BIRTHDAY & `-DEATH/DAY `-ADDED `-UP `-TOGETHER = `-<u>EQUALS</u> = `-<u>HIS</u> VERY OWN `-<u>YEAR</u> of `-<u>BIRTH</u> (`-<u>37</u>)!!!~'

`-<u>DIED</u> in (`-<u>4</u>) & was `-<u>BORN</u> in (`-<u>5</u>) = (`-<u>4/5</u>) = `-<u>DIED</u> the VERY `-<u>DAY</u> `-<u>PRIOR</u> on (`-<u>4/4</u>)!!!~'

CANADIAN TELEVISION ACTRESS SHIRLEY DOUGLAS (`-<u>86</u>) (BIRTH: **APRIL 2, <u>1934</u>**) (DEATH: **APRIL 5**, 2020)!!!~' **APRIL 5 = (<u>4/5</u>) = (`-<u>45</u>) = (5 + 20 + 20)!!!~'**

`-<u>AGE</u> of `-<u>DEATH</u> = (`-<u>86</u>) = (8 x 6) = (`-<u>48</u>) = RECIPROCAL (MIRROR) = (`-<u>84</u>) = "**CURRENT** `-<u>AGE</u> of `-<u>EX-HUSBAND</u> **DONALD** <u>SUTHERLAND</u> at the `-<u>TIME</u> of `-<u>HER</u> `-<u>DEATH</u> (`-<u>84</u>)!!!~'

`-<u>BIRTH/YEAR</u> = (`-<u>1934</u>) = (19 + 34) = (`-<u>53</u>) = "CURRENT `-<u>AGE</u> (`-<u>53</u>) of `-<u>SON</u> KIEFER SUTHERLAND & `-<u>DAUGHTER</u> RACHEL SUTHERLAND at the `-<u>TIME</u> of `-<u>HER</u> `-<u>DEATH</u>"!!!~'

`-<u>BIRTH/YEAR</u> = (`-<u>1934</u>) = (34 (-) 19) = (`-<u>15</u>) = (4 + 2 + 4 + 5) = SHIRLEY DOUGLAS' `-<u>BIRTHDAY</u> & `-<u>DEATH/DAY</u> `-<u>ADDED</u> `-UP `-<u>TOGETHER</u>!!!~'

FRAGMENTED BIRTHDAY # `-NUMBER** = APRIL 2, 1934 = (4 + 2 + 1 + 9 + 3 + 4) = (`-23**) = -a **PROPHETIC # `-NUMBER!!!~'**

(`-**23**) = RECIPROCAL (MIRROR) = (`-**32**)!!!~'

`-**GRANDDAUGHTER** AMERICAN ACTRESS SARAH SUTHERLAND **was** (`-**32**) YEARS of `-AGE at the `-TIME of `-HER (SHIRLEY DOUGLAS') `-DEATH!!!~'

FRAGMENTED DEATH/DAY # `-NUMBER** = APRIL 5, 2020 = (4 + 5 + 2 + 0 + 2 + 0) = (`-13**) = "A VERY PIVOTAL # `-NUMBER"!!!~'

`-BIRTHDAY # `-NUMBER = (4 + 2 + 19 + 34) = (`-**59**) = "**HEIGHT** of `-**SON** KIEFER SUTHERLAND (5' 9")!!!~'

`-DEATH/DAY # `-NUMBER = (4 + 5 + 20 + 20) = (`-**49**)!!!~'

(59 + 49) = (`-**108**)!!!~'

(59 (-) 49) = (`-**10**)!!!~'

(108 (-) 10) = (`-**98**)!!!~'

(108 + 10) = (`-**118**)!!!~'

(118 + 98) = (`-**216**) = (2 x 16) = (`-**32**) = -a **PROPHETIC # `-NUMBER!!!~'**

SHE `-**DIED** (`-**3**) DAYS after `-HER `-LAST `-BIRTHDAY!!!~'

(365 (-) **3**) = (`-**362**) = (62 x 3) = (`-**186**) = (86 x 1) = (`-**86**) = "The `-**MARK**"!!!~'

SHE DIED AT THE `-AGE of (`-**86**)!!!~'

`-BIRTHDAY = APRIL 2 = (4 x 2) = (`-**8**)!!!~'

`-DEATH/DAY = APRIL 5 = (4 x 5) = (`-**20**)!!!~'

(20 + 8) = (`-**28**)!!!~'

(20 (-) 8) = (`-**12**)!!!~'

(28 + 12) = (`-**40**)!!!~'

(28 (-) 12) = (`-**16**)!!!~'

(40 + 16) = (`-**56**) = RECIPROCAL (MIRROR) = (`-**65**)!!!~'

FRAGMENTED BIRTHDAY # `-**NUMBER** = APRIL 2, 1934 = (4 + 2 + 1 + 9 + 3 + 4) = (`-**23**) = -a **PROPHETIC #** `-**NUMBER!!!~'**

FRAGMENTED DEATH/DAY # `-**NUMBER** = APRIL 5, 2020 = (4 + 5 + 2 + 0 + 2 + 0) = (`-**13**) = **"A VERY PIVOTAL #** `-**NUMBER"!!!~'**

(**23** (-) **13**) = (`-**10**)!!!~'

(23 + 13) = (`-**36**)!!!~'

(36 + 10) = (`-**46**) = (`-**23** x `-**2**)!!!~'

`-**BIRTHDAY; and,** `-**DEATH/DAY!!!~':**

(**45** + **42**) = (`-**87**)!!!~'

(**45** (-) **42**) = (`-**3**)!!!~'

(87 (-) 3) = (`-84) = "CURRENT `-AGE of `-EX-HUSBAND DONALD SUTHERLAND at the `-TIME of `-HER `-DEATH (`-84)!!!~'

APRIL 2 (**BIRTH**) + APRIL 5 (**DEATH**) = (4 + 2 + 4 + 5) = (`-15) = `-DEATH/DAY & `-BIRTHDAY `-ADDED `-UP `-TOGETHER!!!~'

`-DIED in (`-4) & was `-BORN in (`-4) = (`-4/4) = (`-44) = `-BIRTHDAY & `-DEATH/DAY!!!~'

CANADIAN ACTOR DONALD SUTHERLAND'S `-BIRTHDAY # `-NUMBER = (7 + 17 + 19 + 35) = (`-78)!!!~' (7 x 8) = (`-56) = RECIPROCAL (MIRROR) = (`-65)!!!~'

`-BIRTH/YEAR = (`-35) = RECIPROCAL (MIRROR) = (`-53) = "AGE of `-SON KIEFER SUTHERLAND at this `-TIME of `-MOTHER/EX-WIFE'S `-DEATH"!!!~'

DONALD SUTHERLAND `-BIRTHDAY = (7 + 17) = (`-24) = RECIPROCAL (MIRROR) = (`-42) = `-EX-WIFE'S SHIRLEY DOUGLAS `-BIRTHDAY (`-4/`-2) = "(APRIL 2nd)"!!!~' THEY were `-MARRIED from (1966 to 1970)!!!~'

(`-717) = "RECIPROCAL-SEQUENCING-NUMEROLOGY-RSN"!!!~'

CANADIAN ACTOR KIEFER SUTHERLAND'S `-BIRTHDAY # `-NUMBER = (12 + 21 + 19 + 66) = (`-118)!!!~' (11 x 8) = (`-88) = `-DAUGHTER AMERICAN ACTRESS SARAH SUTHERLAND was `-BORN in (`-88)!!!~'

(`-12) = RECIPROCAL (MIRROR) = (`-21)!!!~'

'-**GRANDDAUGHTER** AMERICAN ACTRESS SARAH SUTHERLAND '-BIRTHDAY # '-NUMBER = (2 + 18 + 19 + 88) = ('-**127**) = (12 x 7) = ('-**84**) = "CURRENT '-AGE of '-GRANDFATHER DONALD SUTHERLAND at this '-time ('-**84**)"!!!-'

'-**BIRTH/YEAR** = ('-**1988**) = (19 + 88) = ('-**107**) = (17 + 0) = ('-**17**) = "**DAY** of '-BIRTH for "**GRANDFATHER** ('-**17**ᵗʰ)"!!!-'

'-**BIRTHDAY** = (**2/18**) = (28 x 1) = ('-**28**) = **2**(**8's**) = ('-**88**) = '-**YEAR** of '-BIRTH ('-**88**) for AMERICAN ACTRESS SARAH SUTHERLAND!!!-'

TELEVISION PRODUCER '-**DAUGHTER** RACHEL SUTHERLAND '-**BIRTHDAY** # '-**NUMBER** = (**12** + **21** + 19 + **66**) = ('-**118**)!!!-' (11 x 8) = ('-**88**) = '-**YEAR** that '-**NIECE** AMERICAN ACTRESS SARAH SUTHERLAND was '-**BORN** in ('-**88**)!!!-'

AMERICAN FOOTBALL PLAYER BOBBY CORNELIUS MITCHELL ('-**84**) (BIRTH: **JUNE 6**, **1935**) (DEATH: **APRIL 5**, 2020)!!!-' **APRIL 5** = (**4/5**) = ('-**45**) = (5 + 20 + 20)!!!-'

'-**BIRTH/YEAR** = ('-**1935**) = (19 + 35) = ('-**54**) = RECIPROCAL (MIRROR) = ('-**45**) = '-**HIS** VERY OWN '-**DAY** of '-**DEATH** (**4/5**) = "(**APRIL 5**ᵗʰ)"!!!-'

'-**BIRTHDAY** # '-**NUMBER** = (6 + 6 + 19 + 35) = ('-**66**) = "**HIS** VERY OWN '-**BIRTHDAY** = (**6/6**) = "(**JUNE 6**ᵗʰ)"!!!-'

'-BIRTHDAY # '-NUMBER = (6 + 6 + 19 + 35) = ('-**66**) = "**SEE** '-**ABOVE**"!!!-'

`-DEATH/DAY # `-NUMBER = (4 + 5 + 20 + 20) = (`-**49**) = (`-**7** x `-**7**)!!!~'

(66 + 49) = (`-**115**)!!!~'

(66 (-) 49) = (`-**17**)!!!~'

(115 (-) 17) = (`-**98**)!!!~'

(115 + 17) = (`-**132**) = (32 x 1) = (`-**32**) = -a PROPHETIC # `-NUMBER!!!~'

(132 + 98) = (`-**230**) = (23 + 0) = (`-**23**) = -a PROPHETIC # `-NUMBER!!!~'

(`-**23**) = RECIPROCAL (MIRROR) = (`-**32**)!!!~'

`-HE `-**DIED** (`-**62**) DAYS before `-HIS `-NEXT `-BIRTHDAY!!!~'

(`-**62**) = RECIPROCAL (MIRROR) = (`-**26**) = **2**(**6's**) = (`-**66**) = `-**HIS** VERY OWN `-**BIRTHDAY** = (**6/6**) = "(**JUNE 6**[th])"!!!~'

(365 (-) **62**) = (`-**303**) = (30 x 3) = (`-**90**)!!!~'

HE DIED AT THE `-**AGE** of (`-**84**) = (8 x 4) = (`-**32**) = -a PROPHETIC # `-NUMBER!!!~'

`-BIRTHDAY = JUNE 6 = (6 x 6) = (`-**36**)!!!~'

`-DEATH/DAY = APRIL 5 = (4 x 5) = (`-**20**)!!!~'

(36 + 20) = (`-**56**) = RECIPROCAL (MIRROR) = (`-**65**)!!!~'

(36 (-) 20) = (`-**16**)!!!~'

(56 + 16) = (`-**72**)!!!~'

(56 (-) 16) = (`-**40**)!!!~'

(72 + 40) = (`-**112**) / `-2 = (`-**56**) = RECIPROCAL (MIRROR) = (`-**65**)!!!~'

FRAGMENTED BIRTHDAY # `-NUMBER** = JUNE 6, 1935 = (6 + 6 + 1 + 9 + 3 + 5) = (`-30**)!!!~'

FRAGMENTED DEATH/DAY # `-NUMBER** = APRIL 5, 2020 = (4 + 5 + 2 + 0 + 2 + 0) = (`-13**) = "**A VERY PIVOTAL # `-NUMBER**"!!!~'

(**30** (-) **13**) = (`-**17**)!!!~'

(30 + 13) = (`-**43**)!!!~'

(43 (-) 17) = (`-**26**) = **2**(**6's**) = (`-**66**) = `-**HIS** VERY OWN `-**BIRTHDAY** = (**6/6**) = "(**JUNE 6**th)"!!!~'

`-**BIRTHDAY; and, `-DEATH/DAY**!!!~':

(**66** + **45**) = (`-**111**)!!!~'

(**66** (-) **45**) = (`-**21**)!!!~'

(111 + 21) = (`-**132**) = (32 x 1) = (`-**32**) = -a PROPHETIC # `-**NUMBER**!!!~'

JUNE 6 (**BIRTH**) + APRIL 5 (**DEATH**) = (**6** + **6** + **4** + **5**) = (`-**21**) = `-**DEATH/DAY** & `-**BIRTHDAY** `-ADDED `-UP `-**TOGETHER**!!!~'

`-DIED in (`-4) & was `-BORN in (`-6) = (`-4/6) = (`-46) = (`-23 x `-2)!!!~'

`-DIED in (`-4) & was `-BORN in (`-6) = (`-4/6) = "DAY after `-HIS `-DEATH/DAY"!!!~'

`-NEXT `-LAYER-!!!~'

(`-ALL-in-the-FAMILY-)!!!~'

AMERICAN ENTREPRENEUR EARL G. GRAVES, SR. (`-85) (BIRTH: JANUARY 9, 1935) (APRIL 6, 2020)!!!~' APRIL 6 = (`-46) = (6 + 20 + 20)!!!~'

`-BIRTHDAY # `-NUMBER = (1 + 9 + 19 + 35) = (`-64) = RECIPROCAL (MIRROR) = (`-46) = `-HIS ACTUAL VERY OWN `-DAY of `-DEATH (`-4/`-6) = "(APRIL 6ᵗʰ)"!!!~'

`-DEATH/DAY # `-NUMBER = (4 + 6 + 20 + 20) = (`-50) = (5 + 0) = (`-5) = "The `-HAND of `-GOD"!!!~'

`-AGE of `-DEATH = (`-85) = RECIPROCAL (MIRROR) = (`-58) = "AGE of `-HIS VERY OWN `-SON at the `-TIME of `-HIS `-DEATH"!!!~'

EARL G. GRAVES, JR. `-BIRTHDAY # `-NUMBER = (JANUARY 5, 1962) = (1 + 5 + 19 + 62) = (`-87) = DAYS HIS `-DAD `-DIED from `-DAD'S VERY OWN `-BIRTHDAY!!!~'

IN ('-**REVERSE**) (62 (-) 19 (-) 5 (-) 1) = ('-**37**) = **BARBARA KYDD GRAVES (EARL G. GRAVES, SR.'S WIFE)** was '-**BORN** in ('-**37**)!!!~'

BARBARA KYDD GRAVES (EARL G. GRAVES, SR.'S WIFE) '-DEATH/DAY # '-NUMBER = (**MAY 25, 2012**) = (5 + 25 + 20 + 12) = ('-**62**) = **EARL G. GRAVES, JR.** was '-**BORN** in ('-**62**)!!!~'

BARBARA'S '-**DEATH/DAY** = MAY 25ᵗʰ = ('-**525**) = "**R**ECIPROCAL-**S**EQUENCING-**N**UMEROLOGY-**RSN**"!!!~'

BARBARA'S '-**DEATH/YEAR** = ('-**2012**) = (20 + 12) = ('-**32**) = -a PROPHETIC # '-NUMBER!!!~'

BARBARA KYDD GRAVES (EARL G. GRAVES, SR.'S WIFE) '-**MARRIED** from (**1960-to-2012**) = ('-**52**) = RECIPROCAL (MIRROR) = ('-**25**) = "**DAY** of '-**DEATH** (**25**ᵗʰ) for '-**HER**"!!!~'

'-**HE** '-**DIED** ('-**88**) DAYS after '-**HIS** '-**LAST** '-**BIRTHDAY**!!!~' NON-LEAP-YEAR = ('-**87**)!!!~'

('-**87**) = RECIPROCAL (MIRROR) = ('-**78**)!!!~'

(366 (-) **88**) = ('-**278**) = (78 x 2) = ('-**156**) = (56 x 1) = ('-**56**) = RECIPROCAL (MIRROR) = ('-**65**)!!!~'

('-**88**) = (8 x 8) = ('-**64**) = "**BIRTHDAY** # '-**NUMBER**" = RECIPROCAL (MIRROR) = ('-**46**) = '-**DAY** of '-**DEATH**!!!~'

'-**BIRTHDAY** # '-**NUMBER** = (1 + 9 + 19 + 35) = ('-**64**) = "SEE '-**ABOVE**"!!!~'

'-**DEATH/DAY** # '-**NUMBER** = (4 + 6 + 20 + 20) = ('-**50**) = "SEE '-**ABOVE**"!!!~'

(64 + 50) = (`-**114**)!!!~'

(64 (-) 50) = (`-**14**)!!!~'

(114 (-) 14) = (`-**100**)!!!~'

(114 + 14) = (`-**128**)!!!~'

(128 + 100) = (`-**228**) = (28 x 2) = (`-**56**) = RECIPROCAL (MIRROR) = (`-**65**)!!!~'

`-HE `-**DIED** (`-**88**) DAYS after `-**HIS** `-**LAST** `-**BIRTHDAY**!!!~'

NON-LEAP-YEAR = (`-**87**)!!!~' (`-**87**) = RECIPROCAL (MIRROR) = (`-**78**)!!!~'

(366 (-) **88**) = (`-**278**) = (78 x 2) = (`-**156**) = (56 x 1) = (`-**56**) = RECIPROCAL (MIRROR) = (`-**65**)!!!~' (`-**88**) = (8 x 8) = (`-**64**) = "**BIRTHDAY** # `-**NUMBER**" = RECIPROCAL (MIRROR) = (`-**46**) = `-**DAY** of `-**DEATH**!!!~'

HE DIED AT THE `-**AGE** of (`-**85**)!!!~'

`-**BIRTHDAY** = **JANUARY 9** = (1 x 9) = (`-**9**)!!!~'

`-**DEATH/DAY** = **APRIL 6** = (4 x 6) = (`-**24**)!!!~'

(24 + 9) = (`-**33**)!!!~'

(24 (-) 9) = (`-**15**)!!!~'

(33 + 15) = (`-**48**) = RECIPROCAL (MIRROR) = (`-**84**)!!!~'

(33 (-) 15) = (`-**18**)!!!~'

(48 + 18) = (`-**66**)!!!~'

FRAGMENTED BIRTHDAY # `-NUMBER** = JANUARY 9, 1935 = (1 + 9 + *1* + *9* + 3 + 5) = (`-28**)!!!~'

FRAGMENTED DEATH/DAY # `-NUMBER** = APRIL 6, 2020 = (4 + 6 + 2 + 0 + 2 + 0) = (`-14**)!!!~'

(**28** (-) **14**) = (`-**14**)!!!~'

(28 + 14) = (`-**42**) = "The `-**MARK**"!!!~'

(42 + 14) = (`-**56**) = RECIPROCAL (MIRROR) = (`-**65**)!!!~'

`-BIRTHDAY; and, `-DEATH/DAY!!!~':

(**46** + **19**) = (`-**65**) = RECIPROCAL (MIRROR) = (`-**56**)!!!~'

(**46** (-) **19**) = (`-**27**)!!!~'

(65 (-) 27) = (`-**38**) / `-2 = (`-**19**) = `-**BIRTHDAY** = (**1/9**) = "(**JANUARY 9**ᵗʰ)"!!!~'

JANUARY 9 (**BIRTH**) + APRIL 6 (**DEATH**) = (**1** + **9** + **4** + **6**) = (`-**20**) = `-**DEATH/DAY** & `-**BIRTHDAY** `-**ADDED** `-**UP** `-**TOGETHER!!!~'**

`-DIED** in (`-4**) & was `-**BORN** in (`-**1**) = (`-**4/1**) = (`-**41**) = RECIPROCAL (MIRROR) = (`-**14**)!!!~'

(41 + 14) = (`-**55**) = (`-**23** + `-**32**)!!!~'

`-DIED in (`-4) & was `-BORN in (`-1) = (`-4/1) = (4 + 1) = (`-5) = "The `-HAND of `-GOD"!!!~'

`-NEXT `-LAYER-!!!~'

BOOK TITLE: "GOD is `-the `-MATHEMATICIAN-`"!!!~'

The `-GOD `-EQUATIONS!!!~'

`-NEXT `-LAYER-!!!~'

AMERICAN SINGER/SONGWRITER JOHN PRINE (`-73) (BIRTH: OCTOBER 10, 1946) (DEATH: APRIL 7, 2020)!!!~' APRIL 7 = (`-47) = (7 + 20 + 20)!!!~'

`-BORN in (`-46); AND, `-DIED the `-VERY `-NEXT `-DAY `-AFTERWARD = (`-47)!!!~'

FRAGMENTED `-BIRTHDAY # `-NUMBER = OCTOBER 10, 1946 = (1 + 0 + 1 + 0 + 1 + 9 + 4 + 6) = (`-22)!!!~'

FRAGMENTED `-DEATH/DAY # `-NUMBER = APRIL 7, 2020 = (4 + 7 + 2 + 0 + 2 + 0) = (`-15)!!!~'

FRAGMENTED `-BIRTHDAY # `-NUMBER & `-DEATH/DAY # `-NUMBER `-ADDED `-UP = `-EQUALS = (22 + 15) =

('-37) = RECIPROCAL (MIRROR) = ('-73) = '-HIS VERY OWN '-AGE of '-DEATH for Mr. JOHN PRINE ('-73)!!!~'

('-73) = "ALMOST a '-RECIPROCAL-' of" = ('-47)!!!~'

'-1946 = (19 + 46) = ('-65) = RECIPROCAL (MIRROR) = ('-56)!!!~'

'-BIRTHDAY # '-NUMBER = (10 + 10 + 19 + 46) = ('-85)!!!~'

'-DEATH/DAY # '-NUMBER = (4 + 7 + 20 + 20) = ('-51)!!!~'

(85 + 51) = ('-136)!!!~'

(85 (-) 51) = ('-34)!!!~'

(136 (-) 34) = ('-102)!!!~'

(136 + 34) = ('-170)!!!~'

(170 (-) 102) = ('-68) = "The '-MARK"!!!~'

(170 + 102) = ('-272) = "RECIPROCAL-SEQUENCING-NUMEROLOGY-RSN"!!!~'

'-HE '-DIED ('-180) DAYS after '-HIS '-LAST '-BIRTHDAY!!!~'

(366 (-) 180) = ('-186) = (86 x 1) = ('-86) = "The '-MARK"!!!~'

HE DIED AT THE '-AGE of ('-73)!!!~'

'-BIRTHDAY = OCTOBER 10 = (10 x 10) = ('-100)!!!~'

'-DEATH/DAY = APRIL 7 = (4 x 7) = ('-28)!!!~'

(100 + 28) = (`-**128**)!!!~'

(100 (-) 28) = (`-**72**)!!!~'

(128 + 72) = (`-**200**)!!!~'

(128 (-) 72) = (`-**56**) = RECIPROCAL (MIRROR) = (`-**65**)!!!~'

(200 + 56) = (`-**256**) = (2 x 56) = (`-**112**) / `-2 = (`-**56**) = RECIPROCAL (MIRROR) = (`-**65**)!!!~'

FRAGMENTED BIRTHDAY # `-NUMBER** = OCTOBER 10, 1946 = (1 + 0 + 1 + 0 + 1 + 9 + 4 + 6) = (`-22**)!!!~'

FRAGMENTED DEATH/DAY # `-NUMBER** = APRIL 7, 2020 = (4 + 7 + 2 + 0 + 2 + 0) = (`-15**)!!!~'

(**22** (-) **15**) = (`-**7**)!!!~'

(22 + 15) = (`-**37**) = RECIPROCAL (MIRROR) = (`-**73**) = `-**HIS VERY OWN** `-**AGE** of `-**DEATH** for Mr. **JOHN PRINE** (`-**73**)!!!~'

(37 + 7) = (`-**44**)!!!~' (`-**44**) = `-**DEATH/DAY** & `-**BIRTHDAY** `-**ADDED** `-**UP** `-**TOGETHER** for AMERICAN FILM ACTOR ALLEN GARFIELD!!!~'

`-**BIRTHDAY**; and, `-**DEATH/DAY**!!!~':

(**1010** + **47**) = (`-**1057**) = (10 + 57) = (`-**67**)!!!~'

(**1010** (-) **47**) = (`-**963**)!!!~'

(1057 + 963) = (`-**2020**) = (20/20) = "**YEAR** of `-**DEATH**"!!!~'

OCTOBER 10 (**BIRTH**) + APRIL 7 (**DEATH**) = (**10** + **10** + **4** + **7**) = (`-**31**) = RECIPROCAL (MIRROR) = (`-**13**) = "A VERY PIVOTAL # `-NUMBER"!!!~'

`-**DIED** in (`-**4**) & was `-**BORN** in (`-**10**) = (`-**4/10**) = (4 x 10) = (`-**40**) = (20 + 20) = (**20/20**) = "**YEAR** of `-**DEATH** (`-**20/20**) for AMERICAN SINGER/SONGWRITER JOHN PRINE"!!!~'

AMERICAN FILM ACTOR ALLEN GARFIELD (`-**80**) (BIRTH: NOVEMBER 22, 1939) (DEATH: APRIL 7, 2020)!!!~' **APRIL 7 =** (`-**47**) = (7 + 20 + 20)!!!~'

`-**REMOVE** the `-**ROMAN NUMERAL** for (`-**2**) = (`-**11**) = `-**BIRTHDAY** & `-**BIRTH/YEAR** `-ADDED `-UP = (22 + 19 + 39) = (`-**80**) = `-**HIS** VERY OWN `-**AGE** of `-**DEATH** (`-**80**)!!!~'

(`-**1939**) = (19 + 39) = (`-**58**) = RECIPROCAL (MIRROR) = (`-**85**)!!!~'

`-BIRTHDAY # `-NUMBER = (11 + 22 + 19 + 39) = (`-**91**)!!!~'

`-DEATH/DAY # `-NUMBER = (4 + 7 + 20 + 20) = (`-**51**)!!!~'

(91 + 51) = (`-**142**) = (42 x 1) = "The `-**MARK**"!!!~'

(91 (-) 51) = (`-**40**)!!!~'

(142 (-) 40) = (`-**102**)!!!~'

(142 + 40) = (`-**182**)!!!~'

(182 (-) 102) = (`-**80**) = "**AGE** of `-**DEATH** for AMERICAN FILM ACTOR ALLEN GARFIELD (`-**80**)"!!!~'

`-HE `-**DIED** (`-<u>137</u>) DAYS after `-HIS `-LAST `-BIRTHDAY!!!~'
AMERICAN SINGER/SONGWRITER JOHN PRINE (`-<u>73</u>) =
RECIPROCAL (MIRROR) = (`-<u>37</u>)!!!~'

(366 (-) <u>137</u>) = (`-<u>229</u>) = (29 x 2) = (`-<u>58</u>) = "THE `-<u>YEAR</u> `-<u>HE</u>
was `-<u>BORN</u>" = (19 + 39) = (`-<u>58</u>)!!!~'

HE DIED AT THE `-AGE of (`-<u>80</u>)!!!~'

`-BIRTHDAY = NOVEMBER 22 = (11 x 22) = (`-<u>242</u>) =
"<u>R</u>ECIPROCAL-<u>S</u>EQUENCING-<u>N</u>UMEROLOGY-<u>RSN</u>"!!!~'

`-DEATH/DAY = APRIL 7 = (4 x 7) = (`-<u>28</u>)!!!~'

(242 + 28) = (`-<u>270</u>)!!!~'

(242 (-) 28) = (`-<u>214</u>)!!!~'

(270 + 214) = (`-<u>484</u>) = "<u>R</u>ECIPROCAL-<u>S</u>EQUENCING-
<u>N</u>UMEROLOGY-<u>RSN</u>"!!!~'

(270 (-) 214) = (`-<u>56</u>) = RECIPROCAL (MIRROR) = (`-<u>65</u>)!!!~'

(484 + 56) = (`-<u>540</u>) = (54 + 0) = (`-<u>54</u>) = RECIPROCAL (MIRROR)
= (`-<u>45</u>)!!!~'

FRAGMENTED BIRTHDAY # `-NUMBER = NOVEMBER
22, 1939 = (1 + 1 + 2 + 2 + 1 + 9 + 3 + 9) = (`-<u>28</u>) = RECIPROCAL
(MIRROR) = (`-<u>82</u>)!!!~'

FRAGMENTED DEATH/DAY # `-NUMBER = APRIL 7, 2020
= (4 + 7 + 2 + 0 + 2 + 0) = (`-<u>15</u>)!!!~'

(<u>28</u> (-) <u>15</u>) = (`-<u>13</u>) = "A VERY PIVOTAL # `-NUMBER"!!!~'

(28 + 15) = (`-**43**)!!!~'

(43 + 13) = (`-**56**) = RECIPROCAL (MIRROR) = (`-**65**)!!!~'

`-**BIRTHDAY**; and, `-**DEATH/DAY**!!!~':

(**1122** + **47**) = (`-**1169**) = (11 + 69) = (`-**80**) = "**AGE** of `-**DEATH** for **AMERICAN FILM ACTOR ALLEN GARFIELD** (`-**80**)"!!!~'

(**1122** (-) **47**) = (`-**1075**) = (10 + 75) = (`-85)!!!~'

(1169 + 1075) = (`-**2244**) = (22 + 44) = (`-**66**) / `-2 = (`-**33**) = (**11** + **22**) = (`-**BIRTHDAY**)!!!~'

(80 + 85) = (`-**165**) = (16 x 5) = (`-**80**) = "**AGE** of `-**DEATH** for **AMERICAN FILM ACTOR ALLEN GARFIELD** (`-**80**)"!!!~'

NOVEMBER 22 (**BIRTH**) + APRIL 7 (**DEATH**) = (**11** + **22** + **4** + **7**) = (`-**44**) = `-**DEATH/DAY** & `-**BIRTHDAY** `-**ADDED** `-**UP** `-**TOGETHER**!!!~'

`-**DIED** in (`-**4**) & was `-**BORN** in (`-**11**) = (`-**4/11**) = (4 x 11) = (`-**44**) = "**SEE** `-**RIGHT** `-**ABOVE**"!!!~'

AMERICAN CIVIL SERVANT LINDA TRIPP (`-**70**) (BIRTH: NOVEMBER 24, 19**49**) (DEATH: APRIL 8, 2020)!!!~' **APRIL 8** = (`-**48**) = (8 + 20 + 20)!!!~'

`-**BIRTH/YEAR** = (`-19**49**) = `-**DIED** the `-**DAY** `-**PRIOR** on (`-**4/8**)!!!~'

`-**BIRTH/YEAR** = (`-**1949**) = (19 + 49) = (`-**68**) = "**The** `-**MARK**"!!!~' **PLUS** the **ROMAN NUMERAL** for (`-**2**) = (**11**)

186

= `-**BIRTH/MONTH** = (68 + `-**2**) = (`-**70**) = "**AGE of** `-**DEATH** for AMERICAN CIVIL SERVANT LINDA TRIPP (`-**70**)"!!!~'

`-**BIRTHDAY** = ROMAN `-**NUMERAL for** (`-**2**) = (**11/24**) = (11 + 24) = (`-**35**) x (`-**2**) = (`-**70**) = "**AGE of** `-**DEATH for** AMERICAN CIVIL SERVANT LINDA TRIPP (`-**70**)"!!!~'

`-**BIRTHDAY #** `-**NUMBER** = (11 + 24 + 19 + 49) = (`-**103**)!!!~'

`-**DEATH/DAY #** `-**NUMBER** = (4 + 8 + 20 + 20) = (`-**52**) = (5 + 2) = (`-**7**) = "**JUST** `-**ADD a** `-**ZERO**" = (`-70) = "**AGE of** `-**DEATH** for AMERICAN CIVIL SERVANT LINDA TRIPP (`-**70**)"!!!~'

(103 + 52) = (`-**155**) = (55 x 1) = (`-**55**) = (`-**23** + `-**32**)!!!~'

(103 (-) 52) = (`-**51**)!!!~'

(155 (-) 51) = (`-**104**)!!!~'

(155 + 51) = (`-**206**)!!!~'

(206 + 104) = (`-**310**) = (31 + 0) = (`-**31**) = RECIPROCAL (MIRROR) = (`-**13**) = "**A VERY PIVOTAL #** `-**NUMBER**"!!!~'

`-**SHE** `-**DIED** (`-**136**) DAYS after `-**HER** `-**LAST** `-**BIRTHDAY**!!!~'

(366 (-) **136**) = (`-**230**) = (23 + 0) = (`-**23**) = -a PROPHETIC # `-**NUMBER**!!!~'

SHE DIED AT THE `-**AGE of** (`-**70**)!!!~'

`-**BIRTHDAY** = NOVEMBER 24 = (11 x 24) = (`-**264**)!!!~' (64 / `-**2**) = (`-**32**) = `-**DEATH/DAY**!!!~'

`-DEATH/DAY = APRIL 8 = (4 x 8) = (`-**32**)!!!~' (32 x 2) = (`-**64**) = ((64 / `-2) = (`-32)) = (`-**264**) = `-**BIRTHDAY!!!~'**

(264 + 32) = (`-**296**)!!!~'

(264 (-) 32) = (`-**232**) = "**R**ECIPROCAL-**S**EQUENCING-NUMEROLOGY-**RSN**"!!!~'

(296 + 232) = (`-**528**) = (52 x 8) = (`-**416**) = (46 x 1) = (`-**46**) = (`-**23** x `-**2**)!!!~'

(296 (-) 232) = (`-**64**) = (`-**2** x `-**32**)!!!~'

(528 (-) 64) = (`-**464**) = "**R**ECIPROCAL-**S**EQUENCING-NUMEROLOGY-**RSN**"!!!~'

FRAGMENTED BIRTHDAY # `-NUMBER** = NOVEMBER 24, 1949 = (1 + 1 + 2 + 4 + 1 + 9 + 4 + 9) = (`-31**) = RECIPROCAL (MIRROR) = (`-**13**) = "**A VERY PIVOTAL # `-NUMBER**"!!!~'

FRAGMENTED DEATH/DAY # `-NUMBER** = APRIL 8, 2020 = (4 + 8 + 2 + 0 + 2 + 0) = (`-16**)!!!~'

(**31** (-) **16**) = (`-**15**)!!!~'

(31 + 16) = (`-**47**) = `-**DEATH/DAY** & `-**BIRTHDAY** `-**ADDED** `-**UP** `-**TOGETHER!!!~'**

(47 (-) 15) = (`-**32**) = -a PROPHETIC # `-**NUMBER!!!~'**

`-**BIRTHDAY**; and, `-**DEATH/DAY!!!~'**:

(**1124** + **48**) = (`-**1172**) = (11 + 72) = (`-**83**)!!!~'

(**1124** (-) **48**) = (`-**1076**) = (10 + 76) = (`-**86**) = "The `-**MARK**"!!!~'

(86 + 83) = (`-**169**) = (69 + 1) = (`-**70**) = "**AGE of** `-**DEATH for AMERICAN CIVIL SERVANT LINDA TRIPP** (`-**70**)"!!!~'

NOVEMBER 24 (**BIRTH**) + APRIL 8 (**DEATH**) = (**11** + **24** + **4** + **8**) = (`-**47**) = `-**DEATH/DAY** & `-**BIRTHDAY** `-**ADDED** `-**UP** `-**TOGETHER** & `-**FRAGMENTED** `-**BIRTHDAY** # `-**NUMBER; and,** `-**FRAGMENTED** `-**DEATH/DAY** # `-**NUMBER** `-*ADDED* `-*UP* `-*TOGETHER*!!!~' (47 + 47) = (`-**94**) = **AMERICAN RAPPER CHYNNA ROGERS** = "**SEE** `-**BELOW**"!!!~'

`-**DIED** in (`-**4**) & was `-**BORN** in (`-**11**) = (`-**4/11**) = RECIPROCAL (MIRROR) = (`-**11/4**) = "**SHE** was `-**BORN** (**11/24**); and, would `-**DIE** (**11**-to-**4**)"!!!~'

AMERICAN RAPPER CHYNNA ROGERS (`-**25**) (BIRTH: **AUGUST 19, 1994**) (DEATH: APRIL 8, 2020)!!!~' **APRIL 8** = (`-**48**) = (**8** + **20** + **20**)!!!~'

`-**BIRTH/YEAR** = **AMERICAN CIVIL SERVANT LINDA TRIPP** (`-**49**) = RECIPROCAL (MIRROR) = (`-**94**) = **AMERICAN RAPPER CHYNNA ROGERS**!!!~'

`-**REVERSE** `-**SEQUENCE** on `-**BIRTHDAY** # `-**NUMBER** = (94 (-) 19 (-) 19 (-) 8) = (`-**48**) = `-**HER VERY OWN** `-**DEATH/ DAY** (**4/8**) = "(**APRIL 8**[th])"!!!~'

`-**DEATH/DAY** # `-**NUMBER** = (4 + 8 + 20 + 20) = (`-**52**) = RECIPROCAL (MIRROR) = (`-**25**) = "**AGE of** `-**DEATH for AMERICAN RAPPER CHYNNA ROGERS** (`-**25**)"!!!~'

`-**BIRTHDAY** # `-**NUMBER** = (8 + 19 + 19 + 94) = (`-**140**)!!!~'

`-DEATH/DAY # `-NUMBER = (4 + 8 + 20 + 20) = (`-**52**) = RECIPROCAL (MIRROR) =

(`-**25**) = "**AGE** of `-**DEATH** for AMERICAN RAPPER CHYNNA ROGERS (`-**25**)"!!!~'

(140 + 52) = (`-**192**)!!!~'

(140 (-) 52) = (`-**88**)!!!~'

(192 (-) 88) = (`-**104**)!!!~'

(192 + 88) = (`-**280**)!!!~'

(280 + 104) = (`-**384**) = (38 x 4) = (`-**152**) = (52 x 1) = (`-**52**) = RECIPROCAL (MIRROR) = (`-**25**) = "**AGE** of `-**DEATH** for AMERICAN RAPPER CHYNNA ROGERS (`-**25**)"!!!~'

(280 + 104) = (`-**384**) = (84 x 3) = (`-**252**) = "**R**ECIPROCAL-**S**EQUENCING-**N**UMEROLOGY-**RSN**"!!!~'

`-SHE `-**DIED** (`-**133**) DAYS before `-HER `-NEXT `-BIRTHDAY!!!~'

(366 (-) **133**) = (`-**232**) = "**R**ECIPROCAL-**S**EQUENCING-**N**UMEROLOGY-**RSN**"!!!~'

SHE DIED AT THE `-AGE of (`-**25**)!!!~'

`-BIRTHDAY = AUGUST 19 = (8 x 19) = (`-**152**) = (52 x 1) = (`-**52**) = RECIPROCAL (MIRROR) = (`-**25**) = "**AGE** of `-**DEATH** for AMERICAN RAPPER CHYNNA ROGERS (`-**25**)"!!!~'

`-DEATH/DAY = APRIL 8 = (4 x 8) = (`-**32**) = -a PROPHETIC # `-NUMBER!!!~'

(152 + 32) = (`-**184**) = (84 x 1) = (`-**84**) = RECIPROCAL (MIRROR) = (`-**48**) = `-**HER VERY OWN ACTUAL `-DAY of `-DEATH "(APRIL 8**ᵗʰ**)"!!!~'

(152 (-) 32) = (`-**120**) = "**RECIPROCAL-SEQUENCING-NUMEROLOGY-RSN**"!!!~'

(184 + 120) = (`-**304**)!!!~'

(184 (-) 120) = (`-**64**) = (`-**2** x `-**32**)!!!~'

(304 (-) 64) = (`-**240**) = (24 + 0) = (`-**24**)!!!~'

FRAGMENTED BIRTHDAY # `-NUMBER** = AUGUST 19, 1994 = (8 + 1 + 9 + 1 + 9 + 9 + 4) = (`-41**)!!!~'

FRAGMENTED DEATH/DAY # `-NUMBER** = APRIL 8, 2020 = (4 + 8 + 2 + 0 + 2 + 0) = (`-16**)!!!~'

(**41** (-) **16**) = (`-**25**) = "**AGE of `-DEATH for AMERICAN RAPPER CHYNNA ROGERS (`-25)**"!!!~'

(41 + 16) = (`-**57**)!!!~'

(57 (-) 25) = (`-**32**) = -a PROPHETIC # `-NUMBER!!!~'

`-**BIRTHDAY; and, `-DEATH/DAY**!!!~':

(**819** + **48**) = (`-**867**)!!!~'

(**819** (-) **48**) = (`-**771**)!!!~'

(867 (-) 771) = (`-**96**) / `-**2** = (`-**48**) = `-**DEATH/DAY** = (**4/8**) = "(APRIL 8**ᵗʰ**)"!!!~'

AUGUST 19 (**BIRTH**) + APRIL 8 (**DEATH**) = (**8** + **19** + **4** + **8**) = (`-**39**) = `-**DEATH/DAY** & `-**BIRTHDAY** `-ADDED `-UP `-**TOGETHER**!!!~'

`-**DIED** in (`-**4**) & was `-**BORN** in (`-**8**) = (`-**4/8**) = `-**HER** VERY OWN (CHYNNA ROGERS) `-**DEATH/DAY** (**4/8**) = "(APRIL **8**ᵗʰ)"!!!~'

`-**NEXT** `-**LAYER**-!!!~'

CANADIAN ICE HOCKEY PLAYER TOM WEBSTER (`-**71**) (BIRTH: **OCTOBER 4, 1948**) (DEATH: **APRIL 10, 2020**)!!!~'

`-**BIRTHDAY** = OCTOBER 4ᵗʰ = (**10/4**) = RECIPROCAL (MIRROR) = (**4/10**) = APRIL 10ᵗʰ = `-**DEATH/DAY**!!!~'

`-**BIRTHDAY** = *RECIPROCAL (MIRROR)* = `-**DEATH/ DAY**!!!~'

`-**BIRTH/YEAR** = (`-**1948**) = (19 + 48) = (`-**67**)!!!~'

`-**BIRTH/YEAR** = (`-**1948**) = (48 (-) 19) = (`-**29**) = (100% (-) 29) = (`-**71**) = "AGE of `-**DEATH** for CANADIAN ICE HOCKEY PLAYER TOM WEBSTER (`-**71**)"!!!~'

`-BIRTHDAY # `-NUMBER = (10 + 4 + 19 + 48) = (`-**81**) = "SEE `-**BELOW**"!!!~'

`-DEATH/DAY # `-NUMBER = (4 + 10 + 20 + 20) = (`-**54**)!!!~'

(81 + 54) = (`-**135**)!!!~'

(81 (-) 54) = (`-**27**) = `-FRAGMENTED BIRTHDAY # `-NUMBER!!!~'

(135 (-) 27) = (`-**108**) = (18 + 0) = (`-**18**) = RECIPROCAL (MIRROR) = (`-**81**) = `-BIRTHDAY # `-NUMBER!!!~'

(135 + 27) = (`-**162**)!!!~'

(162 (-) 108) = (`-**54**) = `-DEATH/DAY # `-NUMBER!!!~'

`-HE `-**DIED** (`-**189**) DAYS after `-HIS `-LAST `-BIRTHDAY!!!~'

(366 (-) **189**) = (`-**177**) = (17 x 7) = (`-**119**) (-) (`-71) = (`-**48**) = `-**BIRTH/YEAR**!!!~'

HE DIED AT THE `-AGE of (`-**71**)!!!~'

`-**BIRTHDAY** = OCTOBER 4 = (10 x 4) = (`-**40**)!!!~'

`-**DEATH/DAY** = APRIL 10 = (4 x 10) = (`-**40**)!!!~'

(40 + 40) = (`-**80**)!!!~'

(40 (-) 40) = (`-**0**)!!!~'

(80 + 0) = (`-**80**)!!!~'

(80 (-) 0) = (`-**80**)!!!~'

(80 + 80) = (`-**160**)!!!~'

FRAGMENTED BIRTHDAY # `-NUMBER** = OCTOBER 4, 1948 = (1 + 0 + 4 + 1 + 9 + 4 + 8) = (`-27**)!!!~'

FRAGMENTED DEATH/DAY # `-NUMBER = APRIL 10, 2020
= (4 + 1 + 0 + 2 + 0 + 2 + 0) = (`-9)!!!~'

(27 (-) 9) = (`-18) = RECIPROCAL (MIRROR) = (`-81) =
`-BIRTHDAY # `-NUMBER & `-SEE `-BELOW!!!~'

(27 + 9) = (`-36)!!!~'

(36 + 18) = (`-54) = DEATH/DAY # `-NUMBER!!!~'

`-BIRTHDAY; and, `-DEATH/DAY!!!~':

(410 + 104) = (`-514) = (54 x 1) = (`-54) = DEATH/DAY #
`-NUMBER!!!~'

(410 (-) 104) = (`-306)!!!~'

(514 + 306) = (`-820) = (82 + 0) = (`-82) = "AGE of `-DEATH for
JAPANESE DIRECTOR NOBUHIKO OBAYASHI (`-82)"!!!~'

OCTOBER 4 (**BIRTH**) + APRIL 10 (**DEATH**) = (10 + 4 + 4
+ 10) = (`-28) = RECIPROCAL (MIRROR) = (`-82) = "AGE
of `-DEATH for JAPANESE DIRECTOR NOBUHIKO
OBAYASHI (`-82)"!!!~'

`-DIED in (`-4) & was `-BORN in (`-10) = (`-4/10) = `-HIS VERY
OWN (TOM WEBSTER'S) `-DEATH/DAY (4/10) = "(APRIL
10th)"!!!~'

JAPANESE DIRECTOR NOBUHIKO OBAYASHI (`-82)
(BIRTH: **JANUARY 9, 1949**) (DEATH: **APRIL 10, 2020**)!!!~'

HE `-<u>DIED</u> (`-<u>91</u>) DAYS after `-HIS `-LAST `-BIRTH/ DAY within a (NON-LEAP-YEAR) being `-<u>BORN</u> on the `-<u>RECIPROCAL</u>-'" = (`-<u>1/9</u>)!!!~'

`-<u>BIRTHDAY</u> = JANUARY 9th = (`-<u>19</u>) = RECIPROCAL (MIRROR) = (`-<u>91</u>)!!!~'

(91 (-) 19) = (`-<u>72</u>) = CANADIAN ICE HOCKEY PLAYER TOM WEBSTER `-<u>DIED</u> within `-HIS (`-<u>72nd</u>) `-<u>YEAR</u> of `-<u>EXISTENCE!!!</u>~'

WIFE /|\ FILM PRODUCER KYOKO OBAYASHI was `-<u>BORN</u> in (`-<u>1939</u>); and, was (`-<u>81</u>) at the `-<u>TIME</u> of `-HER `-HUSBAND'S `-<u>DEATH!!!</u>~'

`-<u>BIRTH/YEAR</u> = (`-<u>1949</u>) = (19 + 49) = (`-<u>68</u>) = "The `-<u>MARK</u>"!!!~'

`-<u>BIRTHDAY</u> # `-NUMBER = (1 + 9 + 19 + 49) = (`-<u>78</u>)!!!~'

`-<u>DEATH/DAY</u> # `-NUMBER = (4 + 10 + 20 + 20) = (`-<u>54</u>)!!!~'

(78 + 54) = (`-<u>132</u>) = (32 x 1) = (`-<u>32</u>) = -a PROPHETIC # `-NUMBER!!!~'

(78 (-) 54) = (`-<u>24</u>)!!!~'

(132 (-) 24) = (`-<u>108</u>) = (18 + 0) = (`-<u>18</u>) = RECIPROCAL (MIRROR) = (`-<u>81</u>) = `-AGE of `-WIFE at `-TIME of `-HIS `-DEATH & CANADIAN ICE HOCKEY PLAYER TOM WEBSTER from `-<u>ABOVE</u> = `-BIRTHDAY # `-NUMBER = (`-81)!!!~'

(132 + 24) = (`-<u>156</u>) = (56 x 1) = (`-<u>56</u>) = RECIPROCAL (MIRROR) = (`-<u>65</u>)!!!~'

(156 + 108) = (`-**264**) = (26 x 4) = (`-**104**) = `-BIRTHDAY = "(OCTOBER 4ᵗʰ)" of CANADIAN ICE HOCKEY PLAYER TOM WEBSTER!!!~'

(156 + 108) = (`-**264**) = (64 x 2) = (`-**128**) = (28 x 1) = (`-**28**) = RECIPROCAL (MIRROR) = (`-**82**) = "AGE of `-DEATH for JAPANESE DIRECTOR NOBUHIKO OBAYASHI (`-**82**)"!!!~'

`-HE `-**DIED** (`-**92**) DAYS after `-HIS `-LAST `-BIRTHDAY!!!~' (NON-LEAP-YEAR) = `-HE `-**DIED** (`-**91**) DAYS after `-HIS `-LAST `-**BIRTH/DAY** being `-**BORN** on `-**RECIPROCAL**-'" = (`-**1/9**)!!!~'

(366 (-) **92**) = (`-**274**) = (27 x 4) = (`-**108**) = (18 + 0) = (`-**18**) = RECIPROCAL (MIRROR) = (`-**81**) = `-AGE of `-WIFE at `-TIME of `-HIS `-DEATH!!!~'

HE DIED AT THE `-AGE of (`-**82**)!!!~'

`-BIRTHDAY = JANUARY 9 = (1 x 9) = (`-**9**)!!!~'

`-DEATH/DAY = APRIL 10 = (4 x 10) = (`-**40**)!!!~'

(40 + 9) = (`-**49**) = `-**BORN** in (`-**49**)!!!~'

(40 (-) 9) = (`-**31**) = RECIPROCAL (MIRROR) = (`-**13**) = "A VERY PIVOTAL # `-NUMBER"!!!~'

(49 + 31) = (`-**80**)!!!~'

(49 (-) 31) = (`-**18**) = RECIPROCAL (MIRROR) = (`-**81**) = `-AGE of `-WIFE at `-TIME of `-HIS `-DEATH!!!~'

(80 + 18) = (`-**98**)!!!~'

FRAGMENTED BIRTHDAY # `-NUMBER** = JANUARY 9, 1949 = (1 + 9 + *1* + *9* + 4 + 9) = (`-33**)!!!~'

FRAGMENTED DEATH/DAY # `-NUMBER** = APRIL 10, 2020 = (4 + 1 + 0 + 2 + 0 + 2 + 0) = (`-9**)!!!~'

(**33** (-) **9**) = (`-**24**) = `-**DEATH/DAY** & `-**BIRTHDAY** `-ADDED `-UP `-**TOGETHER**!!!~'

(33 + 9) = (`-**42**) = "The `-**MARK**"!!!~'

(`-**42**) = RECIPROCAL (MIRROR) = (`-**24**)!!!~'

(42 (-) 24) = (`-**18**) = RECIPROCAL (MIRROR) = (`-**81**) = `-**AGE** of `-WIFE at `-TIME of `-HIS `-DEATH & CANADIAN ICE HOCKEY PLAYER TOM WEBSTER from `-**ABOVE** = `-BIRTHDAY # `-NUMBER = (`-81)!!!~'

`-**BIRTHDAY**; and, `-**DEATH/DAY**!!!~':

(**410** + **19**) = (`-**429**)!!!~'

(**410** (-) **19**) = (`-**391**)!!!~'

(429 + 391) = (`-**820**) = (82 + 0) = (`-**82**) = "AGE of `-DEATH for JAPANESE DIRECTOR NOBUHIKO OBAYASHI (`-**82**)"!!!~'

JANUARY 9 (**BIRTH**) + APRIL 10 (**DEATH**) = (**1** + **9** + **4** + **10**) = (`-**24**) = `-**DEATH/DAY** & `-**BIRTHDAY** `-ADDED `-UP `-**TOGETHER**!!!~'

`-**DIED** in (`-**4**) & was `-**BORN** in (`-**1**) = (`-**4/1**) = (`-**41**) x `-**2**) = (`-**82**) = "AGE of `-DEATH for JAPANESE DIRECTOR NOBUHIKO OBAYASHI (`-**82**)"!!!~'

`-**DIED** in (`-**4**) & was `-**BORN** in (`-**1**) = (`-**4/1**) = "JUST `-**ADD** a `-**ZERO**" = (`-**4/10**) = "**DAY** of `-**DEATH**" = "(APRIL 10ᵗʰ)"!!!~'

`-**NEXT** `-**LAYER**-!!!~'

MEMBER OF THE LOUISIANA HOUSE of `-REPRESENTATIVES REGGIE BAGALA (`-**54**) (BIRTH: JULY 8, 19**65**) (DEATH: APRIL 9, 2020)!!!~' **APRIL 9 = (`-49) = (9 + 20 + 20)**!!!~'

`-**BIRTHDAY** = **JULY 8ᵗʰ** = (**7/8**) = (7 x 8) = (`-**56**) = RECIPROCAL (MIRROR) = (`-**65**) = "**YEAR** of `-**BIRTH** (`-**65**)!!!~'

`-**BIRTH/YEAR** = (`-**1965**) = (19 + 65) = (`-**84**) = "**THE PRESIDENTIAL** `-**MARK**"!!!~'

`-**BIRTH/YEAR** = (`-**1965**) = (65 (-) 19) = (`-**46**) = (`-**23** x `-**2**)!!!~'

`-DEATH/DAY # `-NUMBER (`-**53**); AND, `-FRAGMENTED `-BIRTHDAY # `-NUMBER (`-**36**) + `-FRAGMENTED `-DEATH/DAY # `-NUMBER (`-**17**) = (36 + 17) = `-**EACH** `-**ADDED** `-**UP to** (`-**53**)!!!~'

`-BIRTHDAY # `-NUMBER = (7 + 8 + 19 + 65) = (`-**99**)!!!~'

`-DEATH/DAY # `-NUMBER = (4 + 9 + 20 + 20) = (`-**53**)!!!~'

(99 + 53) = (`-**152**) = (52 x 1) = (`-**52**) = RECIPROCAL (MIRROR) = (`-**25**) = "**AGE** of `-**DEATH** for **CANADIAN ICE HOCKEY CENTRE COLBY CAVE** (`-**25**)"!!!~'

(99 (-) 53) = (`-**46**) = (`-**23** x `-**2**)!!!~`

(152 (-) 46) = (`-**106**) = (`-**53** + `-**53**) = "SEE `-**ABOVE** & `-**BELOW**"!!!~`

(152 + 46) = (`-**198**) = (98 + 1) = (`-**99**) = `-**BIRTHDAY** # `-**NUMBER**!!!~`

(198 + 106) = (`-**304**) = (34 + 0) = (`-**34**) = "The `-**PRESIDENTIAL** # `-**NUMBERS**"!!!~`

`-HE `-**DIED** (`-**90**) DAYS before `-HIS `-**NEXT** `-**BIRTHDAY**!!!~`
(`-**90**) / `-2 = (`-**45**) = RECIPROCAL (MIRROR) = (`-**54**) = "AGE of `-**DEATH** for REGGIE BAGALA (`-**54**)!!!~`

(365 (-) **90**) = (`-**275**) = (27 x 5) = (`-**135**)!!!~` (53 + 1) = (`-**54**) = "**HIS** VERY OWN `-**AGE** of `-**DEATH** for REGGIE BAGALA (`-**54**)"!!!~` (`-**35**) = RECIPROCAL (MIRROR) = (`-**53**)!!!~`

HE DIED AT THE `-AGE of (`-**54**)!!!~`

`-**BIRTHDAY** = JULY 8 = (7 x 8) = (`-**56**)!!!~`

`-**DEATH/DAY** = APRIL 9 = (4 x 9) = (`-**36**) = `-**FRAGMENTED** BIRTHDAY # `-**NUMBER** (`-**36**)!!!~`

(56 + 36) = (`-**92**)!!!~`

(56 (-) 36) = (`-**20**)!!!~`

(92 + 20) = (`-**112**) / `-2 = (`-**56**) = RECIPROCAL (MIRROR) = (`-**65**) = `-**BORN** in (`-**1965**)!!!~`

(92 (-) 20) = (`-**72**)!!!~`

$(112 + 72) = (`-\underline{\textbf{184}}) = (84 \times 1) = (`-\underline{\textbf{84}}) = $ RECIPROCAL (MIRROR) $= (`-\underline{\textbf{48}})!!!\sim{}'$

FRAGMENTED BIRTHDAY # `-NUMBER** = JULY 8, 1965 = $(7 + 8 + 1 + 9 + 6 + 5) = (`-\underline{\textbf{36}}) = $ **`-DEATH/DAY `-FACTOR!!!~'

**FRAGMENTED DEATH/DAY # `-NUMBER** = APRIL 9, 2020 $= (4 + 9 + 2 + 0 + 2 + 0) = (`-\underline{\textbf{17}})!!!\sim{}'$

$(\underline{\textbf{36}} (-) \underline{\textbf{17}}) = (`-\underline{\textbf{19}})!!!\sim{}'$

$(36 + 17) = (`-\underline{\textbf{53}}) = $ **`-DEATH/DAY # `-NUMBER!!!~'**

$(53 (-) 19) = (`-\underline{\textbf{34}}) = $ "The **`-PRESIDENTIAL** # **`-NUMBERS**"!!!~'

`-BIRTHDAY; and, `-DEATH/DAY!!!~':

$(\underline{\textbf{78}} + \underline{\textbf{49}}) = (`-\underline{\textbf{127}})!!!\sim{}'$

$(\underline{\textbf{78}} (-) \underline{\textbf{49}}) = (`-\underline{\textbf{29}})!!!\sim{}'$

$(127 + 29) = (`-\underline{\textbf{156}}) = (56 \times 1) = (`-\underline{\textbf{56}}) = $ RECIPROCAL (MIRROR) $= (`-\underline{\textbf{65}}) = $ **"YEAR of `-BIRTH (`-65)"!!!~'**

JULY 8 (**BIRTH**) + APRIL 9 (**DEATH**) = $(\underline{\textbf{7}} + \underline{\textbf{8}} + \underline{\textbf{4}} + \underline{\textbf{9}}) = $ (`-**28**) = **`-DEATH/DAY & `-BIRTHDAY `-ADDED `-UP `-TOGETHER!!!~'**

`-DIED in (`-4) & was `-BORN in (`-7) = (`-**4/7**) = RECIPROCAL (MIRROR) = (`-**7/4**)!!!~' (`-**47**) = RECIPROCAL (MIRROR) = (`-**74**) = (74 (-) 47) = (`-**27**) = RECIPROCAL (MIRROR) = (`-**72**) = (72 (-) 27) = (`-**45**) = RECIPROCAL (MIRROR) = (`-**54**) =

"HIS VERY OWN `-AGE of `-DEATH for REGGIE BAGALA (`-54)"!!!~'

CANADIAN ICE HOCKEY CENTRE **COLBY CAVE** (`-25) (BIRTH: DECEMBER 26, 1994) (DEATH: APRIL 11, 2020)!!!~'

`-**BIRTH/YEAR** = (`-**1994**) = (19 + 94) = (`-**113**) = (13 x 1) = (`-**13**) = **"A VERY PIVOTAL # `-NUMBER"!!!~'**

`-**BIRTH/YEAR** = (`-**1994**) = (94 (-) 19) = (`-**75**) = **"FLIP the (`-7) OVER to a (`-2)"** = (`-**25**) = **"AGE of `-DEATH for CANADIAN ICE HOCKEY CENTRE COLBY CAVE (`-25)"!!!~'**

`-BIRTHDAY # `-NUMBER = (12 + 26 + 19 + 94) = (`-**151**) = (51 + 1) = (`-**52**) = RECIPROCAL (MIRROR) = (`-**25**) = `-**HIS VERY OWN `-AGE of `-DEATH (`-25)!!!~'**

`-DEATH/DAY # `-NUMBER = (4 + 11 + 20 + 20) = (`-**55**) = **2(5's)** = (`-**25**) = **"AGE of `-DEATH for CANADIAN ICE HOCKEY CENTRE COLBY CAVE (`-25)"!!!~'**

`-BIRTHDAY # `-NUMBER = (12 + 26 + 19 + 94) = (`-**151**) = **"SEE `-ABOVE"!!!~'**

`-DEATH/DAY # `-NUMBER = (4 + 11 + 20 + 20) = (`-**55**) = **"SEE `-ABOVE"!!!~'**

(151 + 55) = (`-**206**)!!!~'

(151 (-) 55) = (`-**96**) = (`-**32** x `-**3**)!!!~'

(206 (-) 96) = (`-**110**)!!!~'

(206 + 96) = (`-**302**) = (32 + 0) = (`-**32**) = -a PROPHETIC # `-NUMBER!!!~'

(302 + 110) = (`-**412**) = (42 x 1) = (`-**42**) = "The `-**MARK**"!!!~'

`-HE `-**DIED** (`-**107**) DAYS after `-HIS `-LAST `-BIRTHDAY!!!~' (NON-LEAP-YEAR) = (`-**106**) = (53 + 53) = REGGIE BAGALA; `-also = "SEE `-**ABOVE**"!!!~'

(366 (-) **107**) = (`-**259**) = (25 x 9) = (`-**225**) = **2**(25's) = "HIS VERY OWN AGE of `-DEATH (`-**25**) `-EMPHATICALLY `-STATED"!!!~'

HE DIED AT THE `-AGE of (`-**25**)!!!~'

`-BIRTHDAY = DECEMBER 26 = (12 x 26) = (`-**312**) = (32 x 1) = (`-**32**) = -a PROPHETIC # `-NUMBER!!!~'

`-DEATH/DAY = APRIL 11 = (4 x 11) = (`-**44**)!!!~'

(312 + 44) = (`-**356**)!!!~'

(312 (-) 44) = (`-**268**)!!!~'

(356 + 268) = (`-**624**)!!!~'

(356 (-) 268) = (`-**88**)!!!~'

(624 + 88) = (`-**712**) = (71 x 2) = (`-**142**) = (42 x 1) = (`-**42**) = "The `-**MARK**"!!!~'

FRAGMENTED BIRTHDAY # `-NUMBER = DECEMBER 26, 1994 = (1 + 2 + 2 + 6 + 1 + 9 + 9 + 4) = (`-**34**) = "The `-**PRESIDENTIAL** # `-**NUMBERS**"!!!~'

FRAGMENTED DEATH/DAY # `-NUMBER = APRIL 11, 2020
= (4 + 1 + 1 + 2 + 0 + 2 + 0) = (`-**10**)!!!~'

(**34** (-) **10**) = (`-**24**)!!!~'

(34 + 10) = (`-**44**) = `-DEATH/DAY `-PRODUCT `-FACTOR!!!~'

(44 + 24) = (`-**68**) = "The `-**MARK**"!!!~'

`-BIRTHDAY; and, `-DEATH/DAY!!!~':

(**1226** + **411**) = (`-**1637**) = (16 + 37) = (`-**53**) = "SEE `-**ABOVE** &
`-**BELOW**"!!!~'

(**1226** (-) **411**) = (`-**815**) = (85 x 1) = (`-**85**) = RECIPROCAL
(MIRROR) = (`-**58**)!!!~'

(85 (-) 53) = (`-**32**) = -a PROPHETIC # `-NUMBER!!!~'

DECEMBER 26 (**BIRTH**) + APRIL 11 (**DEATH**) = (**12** + **26** +
4 + **11**) = (`-**53**) = `-**DEATH/DAY** & `-**BIRTHDAY** `-**ADDED**
`-**UP** `-**TOGETHER**!!!~' SEE `-**ABOVE** for the # `-NUMBER
(`-**53**) with REGGIE BAGALA; `-too = `-HIS `-DEATH/DAY #
`-NUMBER & `-OTHER with `-TIME from `-DEATH/DAY to
`-BIRTHDAY!!!~'

`-**DIED** in (`-**4**) & was `-**BORN** in (`-**12**) = (`-**4/12**) = (4 x 12) = (`-
48) = RECIPROCAL (MIRROR) = (`-**84**) = "The `-**MARK**"!!!~'

`-**DIED** in (`-**4**) & was `-**BORN** in (`-**12**) = (`-**4/12**) = (42 x 1) =
(`-**42**) = "The `-**MARK**"!!!~'

`-**DIED** in (`-**4**) & was `-**BORN** in (`-**12**) = (`-**4/12**) =
RECIPROCAL (MIRROR) = (`-**12/4**) = (1 + 24) = (`-**25**) = "AGE

of `-<u>DEATH</u> for **CANADIAN ICE HOCKEY CENTRE COLBY CAVE** (`-<u>25</u>)"!!!~'

`-<u>NEXT</u> `-<u>LAYER</u>-!!!~'

AMERICAN ARTIST MORT DRUCKER (`-<u>91</u>) (BIRTH: MARCH 22, 1<u>929</u>) (DEATH: APRIL 9, 2020)!!!~' **APRIL 9** = (`-<u>49</u>) = (9 + 20 + 20)!!!~'

AMERICAN ARTIST MORT DRUCKER (`-<u>91</u>) & BRITISH RACING DRIVER STIRLING MOSS (`-<u>90</u>) = (91 + 90) = (`-<u>181</u>) = "<u>RECIPROCAL-SEQUENCING-NUMEROLOGY-RSN</u>"!!!~' **BOTH** were `-<u>BORN</u> in (`-<u>29</u>) = (29 + 29) = (`-<u>58</u>) = ONE `-<u>DIED</u> (`-<u>18</u>) **DAYS AWAY from** `-<u>BIRTHDAY</u>; and, the `-*OTHER* `-*ONE* `-<u>DIED</u> (`-<u>158</u>) **DAYS AWAY from** `-<u>BIRTHDAY</u>!!!~'

<u>TAKE</u> the (`-<u>1</u>) from (`-<u>181</u>); and, `-<u>ATTACH</u> `-<u>IT</u> -to the (`-<u>58</u>)!!!~'

`-<u>BIRTH/YEAR</u> = (`-1<u>929</u>) = (`-<u>92</u>) = RECIPROCAL (MIRROR) = (`-<u>29</u>)!!!~' (92 (-) 29) = (`-<u>63</u>) = RECIPROCAL (MIRROR) = (`-<u>36</u>) = <u>3</u>(<u>6</u>'s) = (`-<u>666</u>) = "The `-<u>MARK</u>"!!!~'

`-<u>BIRTH/YEAR</u> = (`-1<u>929</u>) = (19 + 29) = (`-<u>48</u>) = RECIPROCAL (MIRROR) = (`-<u>84</u>)!!!~'

`-<u>BIRTH/YEAR</u> = (`-<u>48</u>) = `-<u>DIED</u> the `-<u>VERY</u> `-<u>NEXT</u> `-<u>DAY</u>; OR, `-<u>DIED</u> right `-<u>AFTER</u> = `-<u>DEATH/DAY</u> = (`-<u>4/9</u>)!!!~'

`-<u>BIRTH/YEAR</u> = (`-1<u>929</u>) = (92 (-) 19) = (`-<u>73</u>) = `-<u>BIRTHDAY</u> # `-<u>NUMBER</u> (`-<u>73</u>)!!!~'

`-BIRTHDAY # `-NUMBER = (3 + 22 + 19 + 29) = (`-**73**)!!!~'

`-DEATH/DAY # `-NUMBER = (4 + 9 + 20 + 20) = (`-**53**)!!!~'

(73 + 53) = (`-**126**)!!!~'

(73 (-) 53) = (`-**20**)!!!~'

(126 (-) 20) = (`-**106**) = (`-**53** + `-**53**) = "SEE `-**ABOVE**"!!!~'

(126 + 20) = (`-**146**) = (46 x 1) = (`-**46**) = (`-**23** x `-**2**)!!!~'

(146 + 106) = (`-**252**) = "**RECIPROCAL-SEQUENCING-NUMEROLOGY-RSN**"!!!~'

`-HE `-**DIED** (`-**18**) DAYS after `-**HIS** `-**LAST** `-**BIRTHDAY**!!!~'

(365 (-) **18**) = (`-**347**) = (47 x 3) = (`-**141**) = "**RECIPROCAL-SEQUENCING-NUMEROLOGY-RSN**"!!!~'

HE DIED AT THE `-**AGE** of (`-**91**)!!!~'

`-**BIRTHDAY** = MARCH 22 = (3 x 22) = (`-**66**)!!!~'

`-**DEATH/DAY** = APRIL 9 = (4 x 9) = (`-**36**)!!!~'

(66 + 36) = (`-**102**)!!!~'

(66 (-) 36) = (`-**30**)!!!~'

(102 + 30) = (`-**132**) = (32 x 1) = (`-**32**) = -a **PROPHETIC** # `-**NUMBER**!!!~'

(102 (-) 30) = (`-**72**)!!!~'

(132 + 72) = (`-**204**) = (24 + 0) = (`-**24**) = RECIPROCAL (MIRROR) = (`-**42**) = "The `-**MARK**"!!!~'

FRAGMENTED BIRTHDAY # `-NUMBER** = MARCH 22, 1929 = (3 + 2 + 2 + 1 + 9 + 2 + 9) = (`-28**)!!!~' (28 + 28) = (`-**56**) = RECIPROCAL (MIRROR) = (`-**65**)!!!~'

FRAGMENTED DEATH/DAY # `-NUMBER** = APRIL 9, 2020 = (4 + 9 + 2 + 0 + 2 + 0) = (`-17**)!!!~'

(**28** (-) **17**) = (`-**11**)!!!~'

(28 + 17) = (`-**45**)!!!~'

(45 (-) 11) = (`-**34**) = "The `-**PRESIDENTIAL** # `-**NUMBERS**"!!!~'

(45 + 11) = (`-**56**) = `-**DEATH/DAY** # `-**NUMBER** of BRITISH RACING DRIVER STIRLING MOSS (`-**56**) = RECIPROCAL (MIRROR) = (`-**65**)!!!~'

`-**BIRTHDAY; and, `-DEATH/DAY**!!!~':

(**322** + **49**) = (`-**371**)!!!~'

(**322** (-) **49**) = (`-**273**)!!!~'

(371 (-) 273) = (`-**98**) / `-2 = (`-**49**) = `-**DEATH/DAY** = "(APRIL **9**th)"!!!~'

MARCH 22 (**BIRTH**) + APRIL 9 (**DEATH**) = (**3** + **22** + **4** + **9**) = (`-**38**) = `-**DEATH/DAY** & `-**BIRTHDAY** `-ADDED `-UP `-**TOGETHER**!!!~' FRAGMENTED `-BIRTHDAY # `-NUMBER of BRITISH RACING DRIVER STIRLING MOSS (`-**38**)!!!~'

`-**DIED** in (`-**4**) & was `-**BORN** in (`-**3**) = (`-**4/3**) = RECIPROCAL (MIRROR) = (`-**3/4**)!!!~' (`-**43**) = RECIPROCAL (MIRROR) = (`-**34**) = (43 + 34) = (`-**77**) = (7 x 7) = (`-**49**) = (**4**/**9**) = `-**DEATH/ DAY** = "(APRIL 9ᵗʰ)"!!!~'

BRITISH RACING DRIVER STIRLING MOSS (`-**90**) (BIRTH: SEPTEMBER 17, 1**929**) (DEATH: APRIL 12, 2020)!!!~'

AMERICAN ARTIST MORT DRUCKER (`-**91**) & BRITISH RACING DRIVER STIRLING MOSS (`-**90**) = (91 + 90) = (`-**181**) = "**RECIPROCAL-SEQUENCING-NUMEROLOGY-RSN**"!!!~' **BOTH** were `-**BORN** in (`-**29**) = (29 + 29) = (`-**58**) = ONE `-**DIED** (`-**18**) DAYS AWAY from `-**BIRTHDAY**; and, the `-*OTHER* `-*ONE* `-**DIED** (`-**158**) DAYS AWAY from `-**BIRTHDAY**!!!~'

TAKE the (`-**1**) from (`-**181**); and, `-**ATTACH** `-**IT** -*to the* (`-**58**)!!!~'

`-**BIRTH/YEAR** = (`-**1929**) = (19 + 29) = (`-**48**) = RECIPROCAL (MIRROR) = (`-**84**)!!!~'

`-**BIRTH/YEAR** = (`-1**929**) = (`-**92**) = RECIPROCAL (MIRROR) = (`-**29**)!!!~' (92 (-) 29) = (`-**63**) = RECIPROCAL (MIRROR) = (`-**36**) = **3**(**6**'s) = (`-**666**) = "The `-**MARK**"!!!~'

`-**DEATH/DAY** = APRIL 12ᵗʰ = (**4**/**12**) = (4 x 12) = (`-**48**) = RECIPROCAL (MIRROR) = (`-**84**)!!!~'

`-**BIRTH/YEAR** & **DEATH/DAY** (`-*ADD* `-*UP*) as `-**EQUALS**-'"!!!~'

`-**DEATH/DAY** = APRIL 12ᵗʰ = (**4**/**12**) = (42 x 1) = (`-**42**) = "The `-**MARK**"!!!~'

'-BIRTHDAY # '-NUMBER = (9 + 17 + 19 + 29) = ('-**74**)!!!~'

'-DEATH/DAY # '-NUMBER = (4 + 12 + 20 + 20) = ('-**56**)!!!~'

(74 + 56) = ('-**130**) = (13 + 0) = ('-**13**) = **"A VERY PIVOTAL # '-NUMBER"**!!!~'

(74 (-) 56) = ('-**18**)!!!~'

(130 (-) 18) = ('-**112**) / '-2 = ('-**56**) = **'-DEATH/DAY # '-NUMBER**!!!~'

(130 + 18) = ('-**148**) = (48 x 1) = ('-**48**) = RECIPROCAL (MIRROR) = ('-**84**)!!!~'

(148 (-) 112) = ('-**36**) = **3**(**6's**) = ('-**666**) = **"The '-MARK"**!!!~'

'-HE '-**DIED** ('-**158**) DAYS before '-HIS '-NEXT '-**BIRTHDAY**!!!~'

(365 (-) **158**) = ('-**207**) = (27 + 0) = ('-**27**)!!!~' **"AGE of '-DEATH"** ('-**90**) (-) ('-**27**) = ('-**63**) = RECIPROCAL (MIRROR) = ('-**36**) = **3**(**6's**) = ('-**666**) = **"The '-MARK"**!!!~'

HE DIED AT THE '-AGE of ('-**90**)!!!~'

'-**BIRTHDAY** = SEPTEMBER 17 = (9 x 17) = ('-**153**) = (53 x 1) = ('-**53**) = **"SEE '-ABOVE"**!!!~'

'-**DEATH/DAY** = APRIL 12 = (4 x 12) = ('-**48**) = RECIPROCAL (MIRROR) = ('-**84**)!!!~'

(153 + 48) = ('-**201**)!!!~'

(153 (-) 48) = ('-**105**)!!!~'

(201 + 105) = (`-**306**)!!!~`

(201 (-) 105) = (`-**96**) = (`-**32** x `-**3**)!!!~`

(306 + 96) = (`-**402**) = (42 + 0) = (`-**42**) = "The `-**MARK**"!!!~`

FRAGMENTED BIRTHDAY # `-NUMBER** = SEPTEMBER 17, 1929 = (9 + 1 + 7 + 1 + 9 + 2 + 9) = (`-38**)!!!~`

FRAGMENTED DEATH/DAY # `-NUMBER** = APRIL 12, 2020 = (4 + 1 + 2 + 2 + 0 + 2 + 0) = (`-11**)!!!~`

(**38** (-) **11**) = (`-**27**)!!!~`

(38 + 11) = (`-**49**) = `-**DEATH/DAY** for AMERICAN ARTIST MORT DRUCKER (**4**/**9**) = "(APRIL 9ᵗʰ)"!!!~`

(49 + 27) = (`-**76**) / `-2 = (`-**38**) = `-FRAGMENTED `-BIRTHDAY # `-NUMBER (`-**38**) &

AMERICAN ARTIST MORT DRUCKER'S `-DEATH/DAY & `-BIRTHDAY `-ADDED `-UP `-TOGETHER (`-38)!!!~`

`-**BIRTHDAY**; and, `-**DEATH/DAY**!!!~`:

(**917** + **412**) = (`-**1329**) = (13 + 29) = (`-**42**) = "The `-**MARK**"!!!~`

(**917** (-) **412**) = (`-**505**) = "RECIPROCAL-**S**EQUENCING-**N**UMEROLOGY-**RSN**"!!!~`

(1329 + 505) = (`-**1834**) / `-2 = (`-**917**) = `-**BIRTHDAY** = "(SEPTEMBER 17ᵗʰ)"!!!~`

SEPTEMBER 17 (**BIRTH**) + APRIL 12 (**DEATH**) = (**9** + **17** + **4** + **12**) = (`-**42**) = `-**DEATH/DAY** & `-**BIRTHDAY** `-ADDED `-UP `-**TOGETHER** = "The `-**MARK**"!!!~'

`-**DIED** in (`-**4**) & was `-**BORN** in (`-**9**) = (`-**4/9**) = (4 x 9) = (`-**36**) = **3**(**6**'s) = (`-**666**) = "The `-**MARK**"!!!~'

`-**NEXT** `-**LAYER**-!!!~'

AMERICAN PROFESSIONAL BASEBALL PLAYER **GLENN BECKERT** (`-**79**) (BIRTH: OCTOBER **12**, 1940) (DEATH: APRIL **12**, 2020)!!!~'

`-**BIRTH/YEAR** = (`-**1940**) / **20**20 = (19 + 40 + 20) = (`-**79**) = "**AGE** of `-**DEATH**"!!!~'

`-WAS `-**BORN** on a (`-**12**th); AND, `-**DIED** on a (`-**12**th)!!!~'

`-**DEATH/DAY** = APRIL 12th = (**4/12**) = (4 x 12) = (`-**48**) = RECIPROCAL (MIRROR) = (`-**84**)!!!~'

`-**DEATH/DAY** = APRIL 12th = (**4/12**) = (42 x 1) = (`-**42**) = "The `-**MARK**"!!!~'

`-BIRTHDAY # `-NUMBER = (10 + 12 + 19 + 40) = (`-**81**)!!!~'

`-DEATH/DAY # `-NUMBER = (4 + 12 + 20 + 20) = (`-**56**)!!!~'

(81 + 56) = (`-**137**)!!!~'

(81 (-) 56) = (`-**25**)!!!~'

(137 (-) 25) = (`-**112**) / `-2 = (`-**56**) = `-DEATH/DAY # `-NUMBER!!!~'

(137 + 25) = (`-**162**)!!!~'

(162 + 112) = (`-**274**) = (74 x 2) = (`-**148**) = (48 x 1) = (`-**48**) = RECIPROCAL (MIRROR) = (`-**84**)!!!~'

`-HE `-**DIED** (`-**183**) DAYS after `-HIS `-LAST `-BIRTHDAY!!!~'

(366 (-) **183**) = "CUT the `-YEAR right in `-HALF (`-**183**)"!!!~'

HE DIED AT THE `-AGE of (`-**79**) = (7 x 9) = (`-**63**) = RECIPROCAL (MIRROR) = (`-**36**) = **3**(**6**'s) = (`-**666**) = "The `-**MARK**"!!!~'

`-BIRTHDAY = OCTOBER 12 = (10 x 12) = (`-**120**)!!!~'

`-DEATH/DAY = APRIL 12 = (4 x 12) = (`-**48**) = RECIPROCAL (MIRROR) = (`-**84**)!!!~'

(120 + 48) = (`-**168**) = "The `-**MARK**"!!!~'

(120 (-) 48) = (`-**72**)!!!~'

(168 + 72) = (`-**240**)!!!~'

(168 (-) 72) = (`-**96**) = (`-**32** x `-**3**)!!!~'

(240 (-) 96) = (`-**144**) = (14 x 4) = (`-**56**) = RECIPROCAL (MIRROR) = (`-**65**)!!!~'

FRAGMENTED BIRTHDAY # `-NUMBER** = OCTOBER 12, 1940 = (1 + 0 + 1 + 2 + 1 + 9 + 4 + 0) = (`-18**)!!!~'

FRAGMENTED DEATH/DAY # `-NUMBER** = APRIL 12, 2020 = $(4 + 1 + 2 + 2 + 0 + 2 + 0)$ = (`-11**)!!!`

($\underline{18}$ (-) $\underline{11}$) = (`-**7**)!!!`

($18 + 11$) = (`-**29**)!!!`

($29 + 7$) = (`-**36**) = **3**(**6**'s) = (`-**666**) = "The `-**MARK**"!!!`

`-**BIRTHDAY**; and, `-**DEATH/DAY**!!!`:

($\underline{1012} + \underline{412}$) = (`-**1424**) = ($14 + 24$) = (`-**38**)!!!`

($\underline{1012}$ (-) $\underline{412}$) = (`-**600**)!!!`

($1424 + 600$) = (`-**2024**) / `-2 = (`-**1012**) = `-**BIRTHDAY** = "(OCTOBER 12th)"!!!`

OCTOBER 12 (**BIRTH**) + APRIL 12 (**DEATH**) = ($\underline{10} + \underline{12} + \underline{4} + \underline{12}$) = (`-**38**) = `-**DEATH/DAY** & `-**BIRTHDAY** `-**ADDED** `-**UP** `-**TOGETHER**!!!`

`-**DIED** in (`-**4**) & was `-**BORN** in (`-**10**) = (`-**4/10**) = ($4 \times 10$) = (`-**40**) = "SEE `-**BELOW**"!!!`

BRITISH COMEDIAN **TIM BROOKE-TAYLOR** (`-**79**) (BIRTH: **JULY 17**, 1940) (DEATH: **APRIL 12**, 2020)!!!`

`-**BIRTH/YEAR** = (`-**1940**) / **20**20 = ($19 + 40 + 20$) = (`-**79**) = "**AGE** of `-**DEATH**"!!!`

`-**BIRTHDAY** = JULY 17$^{\text{th}}$ = ($\underline{7}/\underline{17}$) = (`-**717**) = "**R**ECIPROCAL-**S**EQUENCING-**N**UMEROLOGY-**RSN**"!!!`

WAS `-**MARRIED** to `-HIS `-WIFE CHRISTINE WEADON from (`-19**68**-to-**2020**)!!!~'

`-**DEATH/DAY** = APRIL 12ᵗʰ = (**4**/**12**) = (4 x 12) = (`-**48**) = RECIPROCAL (MIRROR) = (`-**84**)!!!~'

`-**DEATH/DAY** = APRIL 12ᵗʰ = (**4**/**12**) = (42 x 1) = (`-**42**) = "The `-**MARK**"!!!~'

`-BIRTHDAY # `-NUMBER = (7 + 17 + 19 + 40) = (`-**83**) = GLENN BECKERT `-**DIED** (`-**183**) DAYS from `-HIS `-**BIRTHDAY**!!!~'

`-DEATH/DAY # `-NUMBER = (4 + 12 + 20 + 20) = (`-**56**)!!!~'

(83 + 56) = (`-**139**)!!!~'

(83 (-) 56) = (`-**27**)!!!~'

(139 (-) 27) = (`-**112**) / `-2 = (`-**56**) = `-**DEATH/DAY** # `-**NUMBER**!!!~'

(139 + 27) = (`-**166**) = (66 x 1) = (`-**66**) = (6 x 6) = (`-**36**) = 3(**6's**) = (`-**666**) = "The `-**MARK**"!!!~'

(166 + 112) = (`-**278**) = (78 x 2) = (`-**156**) = (56 x 1) = (`-**56**) = RECIPROCAL (MIRROR) = (`-**65**)!!!~'

`-HE `-**DIED** (`-**96**) DAYS before `-HIS `-NEXT `-**BIRTHDAY**!!!~'

(`-**96**) = (`-**32** x `-**3**)!!!~'

(365 (-) **96**) = (`-**269**) = (69 x 2) = (`-**138**) = (38 x 1) = (`-**38**) = "SEE GLENN BECKERT `-**ABOVE**"!!!~'

HE DIED AT THE `-AGE of (`-**79**) = (7 x 9) = (`-**63**) = RECIPROCAL (MIRROR) = (`-**36**) = **3**(**6's**) = (`-**666**) = "The `-**MARK**"!!!~'

`-**BIRTHDAY** = **JULY 17** = (7 x 17) = (`-**119**)!!!~'

`-**DEATH/DAY** = **APRIL 12** = (4 x 12) = (`-**48**) = RECIPROCAL (MIRROR) = (`-**84**)!!!~'

(119 + 48) = (`-**167**)!!!~'

(119 (-) 48) = (`-**71**)!!!~'

(167 + 71) = (`-**238**)!!!~'

(167 (-) 71) = (`-**96**) = (`-**32** x `-**3**)!!!~'

(238 (-) 96) = (`-**142**) = (42 x 1) = (`-**42**) = "The `-**MARK**"!!!~'

FRAGMENTED BIRTHDAY # `-NUMBER** = JULY 17, 1940 = (7 + 1 + 7 + 1 + 9 + 4 + 0) = (`-29**)!!!~'

FRAGMENTED DEATH/DAY # `-NUMBER** = APRIL 12, 2020 = (4 + 1 + 2 + 2 + 0 + 2 + 0) = (`-11**)!!!~'

(**29** (-) **11**) = (`-**18**)!!!~'

(29 + 11) = (`-**40**) = `-**FRAGMENTED `-BIRTHDAY # `-NUMBER & `-FRAGMENTED `-DEATH/DAY # `-NUMBER `-ADDED `-UP `-TOGETHER**!!!~'

(40 + 18) = (`-**58**)!!!~' GLENN BECKERT (`-**79**) (+) TIM BROOKE-TAYLOR (`-**79**) = (`-**158**)!!!~'

`-**BIRTHDAY; and, `-DEATH/DAY**!!!~':

($\underline{717}$ + $\underline{412}$) = (`-$\underline{1129}$) = (11 + 29) = (`-$\underline{40}$) = "SEE `-$\underline{ABOVE}$" & "SEE `-$\underline{BELOW}$"!!!~'

($\underline{717}$ (-) $\underline{412}$) = (`-$\underline{305}$)!!!~'

(1129 + 305) = (`-$\underline{1434}$) / `-2 = (`-$\underline{717}$) = `-$\underline{BIRTHDAY}$ = "(JULY 17$^{\underline{th}}$)"!!!~'

JULY 17 ($\underline{BIRTH}$) + APRIL 12 ($\underline{DEATH}$) = ($\underline{7}$ + $\underline{17}$ + $\underline{4}$ + $\underline{12}$) = (`-$\underline{40}$) = `-$\underline{DEATH/DAY}$ & `-$\underline{BIRTHDAY}$ `-ADDED `-UP `-$\underline{TOGETHER}$ = & = `-FRAGMENTED `-BIRTHDAY # `-NUMBER & `-FRAGMENTED `-DEATH/DAY # `-NUMBER `-ADDED `-UP `-TOGETHER!!!~'

`-$\underline{DIED}$ in (`-$\underline{4}$) & was `-$\underline{BORN}$ in (`-$\underline{7}$) = (`-$\underline{4/7}$) = RECIPROCAL (MIRROR) = (`-$\underline{7/4}$)!!!~' (`-$\underline{74}$) = RECIPROCAL (MIRROR) = (`-$\underline{47}$)!!!~' (74 + 47) = (`-$\underline{121}$) = "$\underline{R}$ECIPROCAL-$\underline{S}$EQUENCING-$\underline{N}$UMEROLOGY-$\underline{RSN}$"!!!~'

`-$\underline{NEXT}$ `-$\underline{LAYER}$-!!!~'

AMERICAN ACTRESS $\underline{MARILYN}$ $\underline{MONROE}$ (`-$\underline{36}$) (BIRTH: $\underline{JUNE\ 1}$, $\underline{1926}$) (DEATH: $\textbf{AUGUST 4, 1962}$)!!!~'

`-$\underline{BIRTHDAY}$ = JUNE 1$^{st}$ = ($\underline{6/1}$) = (`-$\underline{61}$) = "SEE the `-BEGINNING of this `-$\underline{BOOK}$"!!!~'

`-$\underline{BIRTH/YEAR}$ = (`-$\underline{26}$) = RECIPROCAL (MIRROR) = (`-$\underline{62}$) = `-DEATH/YEAR!!!~'

`-**DEATH/DAY** = AUGUST 4ᵗʰ = (**8**/**4**) = (`-**84**) = "**THE PRESIDENTIAL** `-**MARK**"!!!~'

`-**DEATH/DAY** = AUGUST 4ᵗʰ = (**8**/**4**) = (`-**84**) = (8 x 4) = (`-**32**) = -a **PROPHETIC** # `-**NUMBER**!!!~'

`-**FRAGMENTED BIRTHDAY** # `-**NUMBER** (`-**25**) = **RECIPROCAL (MIRROR)** = (`-**52**) = `-**BIRTHDAY** # `-**NUMBER**!!!~'

`-**DEATH/DAY** # `-**NUMBER** = (`-**93**) = "**FLIP the** (`-**9**) **OVER to a** (`-**6**)" = (`-**63**) = RECIPROCAL (MIRROR) = (`-**36**) = "**AGE of** `-**DEATH for AMERICAN ACTRESS MARILYN MONROE** (`-**36**)"!!!~'

`-BIRTHDAY # `-NUMBER = (6 + 1 + 19 + **26**) = (`-**52**)!!!~'

(6 + 1 + 19) = (`-**26**)!!!~' (26 x 2) = (`-**52**)!!!~'

`-DEATH/DAY # `-NUMBER = (8 + 4 + 19 + **62**) = (`-**93**)!!!~'

(8 + 4 + 19) = (`-**31**)!!!~' (31 x 2) = (`-**62**)!!!~'

`-DEATH/DAY # `-NUMBER **in** `-**REVERSE** = (62 (-) 19 (-) 4 (-) 8) = (`-**31**) = RECIPROCAL (MIRROR) = (`-**13**) = "**A VERY PIVOTAL** # `-**NUMBER**"!!!~'

(93 + 52) = (`-**145**)!!!~'

(93 (-) 52) = (`-**41**)!!!~'

(145 (-) 41) = (`-**104**) / `-2 = (`-**52**) = `-**BIRTHDAY** # `-**NUMBER**!!!~'

(145 + 41) = (`-**186**) = (86 x 1) = (`-**86**) = "**The** `-**MARK**"!!!~'

(186 + 104) = (`-**290**) = (29 + 0) = (`-**29**) = "**FLIP the** (`-**9**) **OVER to a** (`-**6**)" = (`-**26**) = "**YEAR of** `-**BIRTH** (`-**26**)"!!!~'

`-SHE `-**DIED** (`-**64**) **DAYS before** `-**HER** `-**NEXT** `-**BIRTHDAY**!!!~' (`-**64**) = (`-**2** x `-**32**)!!!~'

(365 (-) **64**) = (`-**301**) = (31 + 0) = (`-**31**) = RECIPROCAL (MIRROR) = (`-**13**) = "**A VERY PIVOTAL #** `-**NUMBER**"!!!~'

SHE DIED AT THE `-AGE of (`-**36**)!!!~'

`-**BIRTHDAY** = **JUNE 1** = (6 x 1) = (`-**6**)!!!~'

`-**DEATH/DAY** = **AUGUST 4** = (8 x 4) = (`-**32**) = -a **PROPHETIC #** `-**NUMBER**!!!~'

(32 + 6) = (`-**38**)!!!~'

(32 (-) 6) = (`-**26**) = "**WAS** `-**BORN in** (`-**26**)"!!!~'

(38 + 26) = (`-**64**) = `-**DIED this** `-**MANY** `-**DAYS from** `-**BIRTHDAY** (`-**64**)!!!~'

(38 (-) 26) = (`-**12**)!!!~'

(64 (-) 12) = (`-**52**) = `-**BIRTHDAY #** `-**NUMBER**!!!~'

FRAGMENTED BIRTHDAY # `-**NUMBER** = JUNE 1, 1926 = (6 + 1 + 1 + 9 + 2 + 6) = (`-**25**) = RECIPROCAL (MIRROR) = (`-**52**) = `-**HER VERY OWN** `-**BIRTHDAY #** `-**NUMBER** (`-**52**)!!!~'

FRAGMENTED DEATH/DAY # `-**NUMBER** = AUGUST 4, 1962 = (8 + 4 + 1 + 9 + 6 + 2) = (`-**30**)!!!~'

(**30** (-) **25**) = (`-**5**)!!!~'

(30 + 25) = (`-**55**) = **2**(**5's**) = (`-**25**) = RECIPROCAL (MIRROR) = (`-**52**) = `-BIRTHDAY # `-NUMBER!!!~'

(55 (-) 5) = (`-**50**) = (5 + 0) = (`-**5**) = "The `-HAND of `-GOD"!!!~'

`-BIRTHDAY; and, `-DEATH/DAY!!!~'

(**84** + **61**) = (`-**145**) = `-BIRTHDAY # `-NUMBER (`-**52**); and, `-DEATH/DAY # `-NUMBER (`-**93**) `-ADDED `-UP `-TOGETHER!!!~'

(**84** (-) **61**) = (`-**23**) = -a PROPHETIC # `-NUMBER!!!~'

(145 + 23) = (`-**168**) = "The `-MARK"!!!~'

JUNE 1 (**BIRTH**) + AUGUST 4 (**DEATH**) = (**6** + **1** + **8** + **4**) = (`-**19**) = `-DEATH/DAY & `-BIRTHDAY `-ADDED `-UP `-TOGETHER!!!~'

`-DIED in (`-**8**) & was `-BORN in (`-**6**) = (`-**8/6**) = (`-**86**) = "The `-MARK"!!!~'

ACTOR BRUCE LEE (`-**32**) (BIRTH: NOVEMBER 27, 1940) (DEATH: JULY 20, 19**73**)!!!~'

`-BIRTH/YEAR = (`-**1940**) = (19 + 40) = (`-**59**) (-) **32**) = (`-**27**) = "DAY of `-BIRTH (`-27ᵗʰ)"!!!~'

BRUCE LEE = `-AGE of `-DEATH = (`-**32**) = -a PROPHETIC # `-NUMBER!!!~'

`-DAY of `-BIRTH (`-**27**) = RECIPROCAL (MIRROR) = (`-**72**) = "DAY of `-DEATH (`-**7/20**)"!!!~'

`-BIRTHDAY # `-NUMBER = (11 + 27 + 19 + 40) = (`-**97**)!!!~`

`-DEATH/DAY # `-NUMBER = (7 + 20 + 19 + 73) = (`-**119**)!!!~`

`-DEATH/DAY # `-NUMBER in `-**REVERSE** = (73 (-) 19 (-) 20 (-) 7) = (`-**27**) = "**DAY** of `-**BIRTH** (`-27ᵗʰ)"!!!~`

(119 + 97) = (`-**216**) = (2 x 16) = (`-**32**) = "**AGE** of `-**DEATH**" & -a **PROPHETIC # `-NUMBER!!!~`**

(119 (-) 97) = (`-**22**)!!!~`

(216 (-) 22) = (`-**194**) / `-2 = (`-**97**) = `-**BIRTHDAY # `-NUMBER!!!~`**

(216 + 22) = (`-**238**) = (38 x 2) = (`-**76**) = (7 x 6) = (`-**42**) = "The `-**MARK**"!!!~`

(238 + 194) = (`-**432**) = (43 x 2) = (`-**86**) = "The `-**MARK**"!!!~`

`-HE `-**DIED** (`-**130**) DAYS before `-HIS `-NEXT `-**BIRTHDAY!!!~`**

(`-**130**) = (13 + 0) = (`-**13**) = "**A VERY PIVOTAL # `-NUMBER**"!!!~`

(365 (-) **130**) = (`-**235**) = (35 x 2) = (`-**70**)!!!~`

HE DIED AT THE `-AGE of (`-**32**)!!!~`

`-**BIRTHDAY** = NOVEMBER 27 = (11 x 27) = (`-**297**)!!!~`

`-**DEATH/DAY** = JULY 20 = (7 x 20) = (`-**140**)!!!~`

(297 + 140) = (`-**437**)!!!~`

(297 (-) 140) = (`-**157**)!!!~`

(437 + 157) = (`-**594**)!!!~'

(437 (-) 157) = (`-**280**)!!!~'

(594 (-) 280) = (`-**314**) = (34 x 1) = (`-**34**) = "The `-<u>PRESIDENTIAL</u> # `-<u>NUMBERS</u>"!!!~'

FRAGMENTED BIRTHDAY # `-NUMBER** = NOVEMBER 27, 1940 = (1 + 1 + 2 + 7 + 1 + 9 + 4 + 0) = (`-25**)!!!~'

FRAGMENTED DEATH/DAY # `-NUMBER** = JULY 20, 1973 = (7 + 2 + 0 + 1 + 9 + 7 + 3) = (`-29**)!!!~'

(**29** (-) **25**) = (`-**4**)!!!~'

(29 + 25) = (`-**54**)!!!~'

(54 (-) 4) = (`-**50**) = (5 + 0) = (`-**5**) = "The `-<u>HAND</u> of `-<u>GOD</u>"!!!~'

`-<u>BIRTHDAY</u>; and, `-<u>DEATH/DAY</u>!!!~':

(**1127** + **720**) = (`-**1847**) = (18 + 47) = (`-**65**) = RECIPROCAL (MIRROR) = (`-**56**)!!!~'

(**1127** (-) **720**) = (`-**407**)!!!~'

(1847 + 407) = (`-**2254**) = (54 (-) 22) = (`-**32**) = "<u>AGE</u> of `-<u>DEATH</u>" & -a <u>PROPHETIC</u> # `-<u>NUMBER</u>!!!~'

NOVEMBER 27 (**BIRTH**) + JULY 20 (**DEATH**) = (**11** + **27** + **7** + **20**) = (`-**65**) = `-<u>DEATH/DAY</u> & `-<u>BIRTHDAY</u> `-ADDED `-UP `-<u>TOGETHER</u>!!!~'

`-**DIED** in (`-**7**) & was `-**BORN** in (`-**11**) = (`-**7/11**) = (7 x 11) = (`-**77**) = **2**(**7's**) = (`-**27**) = "**DAY** of `-**BIRTH** (`-**27**th)"!!!~'

AMERICAN SINGER ELVIS PRESLEY (`-**42**) (BIRTH: **JANUARY 8**, **1935**) (DEATH: **AUGUST 16**, 1977)!!!~'

`-**BIRTH/YEAR** = (`-**1935**) = (19 + 35) = (`-**54**) = RECIPROCAL (MIRROR) = (`-**45**) = "**DIED** (`-**145**) *DAYS AWAY* from `-**HIS** `-**BIRTHDAY**"!!!~'

`-**DEATH/YEAR** = (`-**1977**) = (19 + 77) = (`-**96**) = (`-**32** X `-**3**)!!!~'

`-**AGE** of `-**DEATH** = (`-**42**) = "The `-**MARK**"!!!~'

`-**BIRTHDAY** = **JANUARY 8**<sup>th</sup> = (**1/8**) = RECIPROCAL (MIRROR) = (**8/1**) = "**PART** of `-**DEATH/DAY** (**81/6**)"!!!~'

`-**DEATH/DAY** = **AUGUST 16**<sup>th</sup> = (**8/16**) = (86 x 1) = (`-**86**) = "The `-**MARK**"!!!~'

`-BIRTHDAY # `-NUMBER = (1 + 8 + 19 + 35) = (`-**63**) = RECIPROCAL (MIRROR) = (`-**36**) = **3**(**6's**) = (`-**666**) = "The `-**MARK**"!!!~'

`-DEATH/DAY # `-NUMBER = (8 + 16 + 19 + 77) = (`-**120**)!!!~'

`-DEATH/DAY # `-NUMBER in `-**REVERSE** = (77 (-) 19 (-) 1**6** (-) **8**) = (`-**34**) = "The `-**PRESIDENTIAL** # `-**NUMBERS**"!!!~'

(120 + 63) = (`-**183**)!!!~'

(120 (-) 63) = (`-**57**)!!!~'

(183 (-) 57) = (`-**126**) / `-2 = (`-**63**) = `-BIRTHDAY # `-NUMBER!!!~'

(183 + 57) = (`-**240**)!!!~'

(240 + 126) = (`-**366**) = (ALL-IN-ONE-#-NUMBER) = (`-**36**/`-**66**) = "The `-**MARK**"!!!~'

`-HE `-**DIED** (`-**145**) DAYS before `-HIS `-NEXT `-BIRTHDAY!!!~'

(365 (-) **145**) = (`-**220**) = (2 x 20) = (`-**40**)!!!~'

HE DIED AT THE `-AGE of (`-**42**)!!!~'

`-BIRTHDAY = JANUARY 8 = (1 x 8) = (`-**8**)!!!~'

`-DEATH/DAY = AUGUST 16 = (8 x 16) = (`-**128**)!!!~'

(128 + 8) = (`-**136**) = (36 x 1) = (`-**36**) = "SEE `-**ABOVE** & `-**BELOW**"!!!~'

(128 (-) 8) = (`-**120**)!!!~'

(136 + 120) = (`-**256**)!!!~'

(136 (-) 120) = (`-**16**)!!!~'

(256 + 16) = (`-**272**) = "RECIPROCAL-**S**EQUENCING-NUMEROLOGY-**RSN**"!!!~'

FRAGMENTED BIRTHDAY # `-NUMBER = JANUARY 8, 1935 = (1 + 8 + 1 + 9 + 3 + 5) = (`-**27**)!!!~'

FRAGMENTED DEATH/DAY # `-NUMBER = AUGUST 16, 1977 = (8 + 1 + 6 + 1 + 9 + 7 + 7) = (`-**39**)!!!~'

(**39** (-) **27**) = (`-**12**)!!!~'

(39 + 27) = (`-**66**) = `-FRAGMENTED `-BIRTHDAY # `-NUMBER & `-FRAGMENTED `-DEATH/DAY # `-NUMBER `-ADDED `-UP `-TOGETHER!!!~'

(66 (-) 12) = (`-**54**) = `-**BIRTH/YEAR** = (`-**1935**) = (19 + 35) = (`-**54**) = RECIPROCAL (MIRROR) = (`-**45**) = "**DIED** (`-**145**) *DAYS AWAY* from `-HIS `-**BIRTHDAY**"!!!~'

`-**BIRTHDAY**; and, `-**DEATH/DAY**!!!~':

(**816** + **18**) = (`-**834**)!!!~'

(**816** (-) **18**) = (`-**798**)!!!~'

(834 (-) 798) = (`-**36**) = **3**(**6**'s) = (`-**666**) = "The `-**MARK**"!!!~'

JANUARY 8 (**BIRTH**) + AUGUST 16 (**DEATH**) = (**1** + **8** + **8** + **16**) = (`-**33**) = `-**DEATH/DAY** & `-**BIRTHDAY** `-**ADDED** `-**UP** `-**TOGETHER**!!!~' (`-**33** x 2) = (`-**66**) = `-FRAGMENTED `-BIRTHDAY # `-NUMBER & `-FRAGMENTED `-DEATH/DAY # `-NUMBER `-ADDED `-UP `-TOGETHER!!!~'

`-**DIED** in (`-**8**) & was `-**BORN** in (`-**1**) = (`-**8/1**) = RECIPROCAL (MIRROR) = (`-**1/8**) = `-**BIRTHDAY** = "(JANUARY 8th)"!!!~'

FORMER FIRST LADY of the UNITED STATES ELEANOR ROOSEVELT (`-**78**) (BIRTH: **OCTOBER 11, 1884**) (DEATH: **NOVEMBER 7, 1962**)!!!~'

(`-**32nd**) PRESIDENT FRANKLIN DELANO ROOSEVELT `-**DIED** (`-**72**) DAYS after `-HIS `-LAST `-BIRTHDAY =

RECIPROCAL (MIRROR) = (`-**27**) = FIRST LADY ELEANOR ROOSEVELT `-**DIED** (`-**27**) DAYS after `-HER `-LAST `-BIRTHDAY!!!~'

FIRST LADY ELEANOR ROOSEVELT'S `-**BIRTHDAY** # `-**NUMBER** = (10 + 11 + 18 + 84) = (`-**123**); while, `-**HER** `-**HUSBAND'S** FRANKLIN DELANO ROOSEVELT'S `-**FRAGMENTED BIRTHDAY** # `-**NUMBER** = JANUARY 30, 1882 = (1 + 3 + 0 + 1 + 8 + 8 + 2) = (`-**23**)!!!~'

(`-**23**) = RECIPROCAL (MIRROR) = (`-**32**)!!!~'

`-**BIRTH/YEAR** = (`-**1884**) = (84 (-) 18) = (`-**66**) = (6 x 6) = (`-**36**) = **3**(**6's**) = (`-**666**) = "The `-**MARK**"!!!~'

`-**DEATH/YEAR** = (`-**1962**) = (19 + 62) = (`-**81**)!!!~'

`-BIRTHDAY # `-NUMBER = (10 + 11 + 18 + 84) = (`-**123**) = (23 x 1) = (`-**23**) = -a PROPHETIC # `-NUMBER!!!~'

`-BIRTHDAY # `-NUMBER in `-**REVERSE** = (84 (-) 18 (-) 11 (-) 10) = (`-**45**) = "The `-**YEAR** that `-HER `-HUSBAND the **32**nd/PRESIDENT FRANKLIN DELANO ROOSEVELT had `-**DIED**"!!!~'

`-DEATH/DAY # `-NUMBER = (11 + 7 + 19 + 62) = (`-**99**) = "**FLIP** the (`-**9's**) OVER to (`-**6's**)" = (`-**66**) = `-SEE `-**ABOVE**!!!~'

`-**DEATH/DAY** # `-NUMBER in `-**REVERSE** = (62 (-) 19 (-) 7 (-) 11) = (`-**25**) = RECIPROCAL (MIRROR) = (`-**52**)!!!~' (52 + 25) = (`-**77**) = "SHE `-**DIED** the VERY `-**NEXT** `-**YEAR** `-**AFTERWARD** at the `-**AGE** of (`-**78**)"!!!~'

(123 + 99) = (`-**222**)!!!~'

(123 (-) 99) = (`-**24**)!!!~'

(222 (-) 24) = (`-**198**) / `-2 = (`-**99**) = `-DEATH/DAY # `-NUMBER!!!~'

(222 + 24) = (`-**246**)!!!~'

(246 (-) 198) = (`-**48**) = (4 x 8) = (`-**32**) = "HER `-HUSBAND was the `-32nd `-PRESIDENT of the `-UNITED `-STATES of `-AMERICA"!!!~'

`-SHE `-**DIED** (`-**27**) DAYS after `-HER `-LAST `-BIRTHDAY!!!~'

(`-**27**) = **2**(**7's**) = (`-**77**) = `-**DAY** of `-**DEATH** = (**11**/**7**) = (11 x 7) = (`-**77**) = **2**(**7's**)!!!~'

(365 (-) **27**) = (`-**338**)!!!~'

SHE DIED AT THE `-AGE of (`-**78**) = (7 x 8) = (`-**56**) = RECIPROCAL (MIRROR) = (`-**65**)!!!~'

`-BIRTHDAY = OCTOBER 11 = (10 x 11) = (`-**110**)!!!~'

`-DEATH/DAY = NOVEMBER 7 = (11 x 7) = (`-**77**) = "SEE *RIGHT* `-ABOVE"!!!~'

(110 + 77) = (`-**187**) = (87 x 1) = (`-**87**) = RECIPROCAL (MIRROR) = (`-**78**) = "HER VERY OWN `-**AGE** of `-**DEATH** (`-**78**)"!!!~'

(110 (-) 77) = (`-**33**)!!!~'

(187 + 33) = (`-**220**)!!!~'

(187 (-) 33) = (`-**154**) = (54 x 1) = (`-**54**) = RECIPROCAL (MIRROR) = (`-**45**) = "THE `-YEAR that `-HER `-HUSBAND had `-DIED"!!!~'

(220 (-) 154) = (`-**66**) = "FLIP the (`-**6's**) OVER to (`-**9's**)" = (`-**99**) = `-DEATH/DAY # `-NUMBER = & = ALSO; `-SEE `-ABOVE!!!~'

FRAGMENTED BIRTHDAY # `-NUMBER = OCTOBER 11, 1884 = (1 + 0 + 1 + 1 + 1 + 8 + 8 + 4) = (`-**24**)!!!~'

FRAGMENTED DEATH/DAY # `-NUMBER = NOVEMBER 7, 1962 = (1 + 1 + 7 + 1 + 9 + 6 + 2) = (`-**27**)!!!~'

(**27** (-) **24**) = (`-**3**)!!!~'

(27 + 24) = (`-**51**)!!!~'

(51 + 3) = (`-**54**) = RECIPROCAL (MIRROR) = (`-**45**) = "The `-YEAR that `-HER `-HUSBAND the 32nd/U.S. PRESIDENT FRANKLIN DELANO ROOSEVELT had `-DIED"!!!~'

`-BIRTHDAY; and, `-DEATH/DAY!!!~':

(**1011** + **117**) = (`-**1128**) = (11 + 28) = (`-**39**) = "FLIP the (`-**9**) OVER to (`-**6**)" = (`-**36**) = **3**(**6's**) = (`-**666**) = "The `-MARK"!!!~'

(**1011** (-) **117**) = (`-**894**)!!!~'

(1128 (-) 894) = (`-**234**) = "PROPHETIC-LINEAR-PROGRESSION-PLP"!!!~'

OCTOBER 11 (**BIRTH**) + NOVEMBER 7 (**DEATH**) = (**10** + **11** + **11** + **7**) = (`-**39**) = `-DEATH/DAY & `-BIRTHDAY `-ADDED `-UP `-TOGETHER = & = "SEE `-ABOVE"!!!~'

`-**DIED** in (`-**11**) & was `-**BORN** in (`-**10**) = (`-**11/10**) = (11 x 10) = (`-**110**) = (110 (-) 78) = "**AGE** of `-**DEATH** (`-**78**)" = (`-**32**) = -a PROPHETIC # `-NUMBER!!!~'

(`-**32ⁿᵈ**) UNITED STATES PRESIDENT FRANKLIN D. ROOSEVELT (`-**63**) (BIRTH: **JANUARY 30, 1882**) (DEATH: **APRIL 12, 1945**)!!!~'

(`-**32ⁿᵈ**) PRESIDENT FRANKLIN DELANO ROOSEVELT `-**DIED** (`-**72**) DAYS after `-HIS `-LAST `-BIRTHDAY = **RECIPROCAL (MIRROR)** = (`-**27**) = FIRST LADY ELEANOR ROOSEVELT `-**DIED** (`-**27**) DAYS after `-HER `-LAST `-BIRTHDAY!!!~'

FIRST LADY ELEANOR ROOSEVELT'S `-**BIRTHDAY** # `-**NUMBER** = (10 + 11 + 18 + 84) = (`-**123**); while, `-**HER** `-**HUSBAND'S** FRANKLIN DELANO ROOSEVELT'S `-**FRAGMENTED BIRTHDAY** # `-**NUMBER** = JANUARY 30, 1882 = (1 + 3 + 0 + 1 + 8 + 8 + 2) = (`-**23**)!!!~'

(`-**23**) = RECIPROCAL (MIRROR) = (`-**32**)!!!~'

`-**BIRTH/YEAR** = (`-**1882**) = (82 (-) 18) = (`-**64**) = (`-**2** x `-**32**)!!!~'

`-**DEATH/YEAR** = (`-**1945**) = (19 + 45) = (`-**64**) = (`-**2** x `-**32**)!!!~'

`-**BIRTHDAY** = JANUARY 30ᵗʰ = (**1/30**) = (1 + 30) = (`-**31**) = RECIPROCAL (MIRROR) = (`-**13**) = "**A VERY PIVOTAL #** `-**NUMBER**"!!!~'

`-BIRTHDAY # `-NUMBER = (1 + 30 + 18 + 82) = (`-**131**) = (13 x 1) = (`-**13**) = "**A VERY PIVOTAL #** `-**NUMBER**"!!!~'

227

`-BIRTHDAY # `-NUMBER in `-<u>REVERSE</u> = (82 (-) 18 (-) 30 (-) 1) = (`-<u>33</u>) x 3 = (`-<u>99</u>) = "WIFE'S `-DEATH/DAY # `-NUMBER (`-<u>99</u>)"!!!~'

`-DEATH/DAY # `-NUMBER = (4 + 12 + 19 + 45) = (`-<u>80</u>)!!!~'

(131 + 80) = (`-<u>211</u>)!!!~'

(131 (-) 80) = (`-<u>51</u>)!!!~'

(211 (-) 51) = (`-<u>160</u>) / `-2 = (`-<u>80</u>) = `-DEATH/DAY # `-NUMBER!!!~'

(211 + 51) = (`-<u>262</u>) = "RECIPROCAL-<u>S</u>EQUENCING-<u>N</u>UMEROLOGY-RSN"!!!~'

(262 + 160) = (`-<u>422</u>) = (42 x 2) = (`-<u>84</u>) = "<u>WIFE</u> was `-<u>BORN</u> in (`-<u>84</u>)"!!!~'

`-HE `-<u>DIED</u> (`-<u>72</u>) DAYS after `-HIS `-LAST `-BIRTHDAY!!!~'

(365 (-) <u>72</u>) = (`-<u>293</u>) = (29 x 3) = (`-<u>87</u>) = RECIPROCAL (MIRROR) = (`-<u>78</u>) = "<u>HIS</u> `-WIFE'S VERY OWN `-<u>AGE</u> of `-<u>DEATH</u> (`-<u>78</u>)"!!!~'

HE DIED AT THE `-AGE of (`-<u>63</u>)!!!~'

`-BIRTHDAY = JANUARY 30 = (1 x 30) = (`-<u>30</u>)!!!~'

`-DEATH/DAY = APRIL 12 = (4 x 12) = (`-<u>48</u>) = RECIPROCAL (MIRROR) = (`-<u>84</u>)!!!~'

(48 + 30) = (`-<u>78</u>) = "THE `-PRODUCT `-FACTOR `-<u>ADDITION</u> of `-HIS VERY OWN `-<u>BIRTHDAY</u> & `-<u>DEATH/DAY</u>" = `-<u>EQUALS</u> = "HIS VERY OWN WIFE'S `-<u>AGE</u> of `-<u>DEATH</u> (`-<u>78</u>)"!!!~'

(48 (-) 30) = (`-**18**)!!!~’

(78 + 18) = (`-**96**) = (`-**32** x `-**3**)!!!~’

(78 (-) 18) = (`-**60**)!!!~’

(96 (-) 60) = (`-**36**) = RECIPROCAL (MIRROR) = (`-**63**) = **“HIS VERY OWN `-AGE of `-DEATH (`-63)”**!!!~’

FRAGMENTED BIRTHDAY # `-NUMBER = JANUARY 30, 1882 = (1 + 3 + 0 + 1 + 8 + 8 + 2) = (`-**23**) = RECIPROCAL (MIRROR) = (`-**32**) = **“WAS the (`-32ⁿᵈ) U.S. *PRESIDENT*”**!!!~’

FRAGMENTED DEATH/DAY # `-NUMBER = APRIL 12, 1945 = (4 + 1 + 2 + 1 + 9 + 4 + 5) = (`-**26**)!!!~’

(**26** (-) **23**) = (`-**3**)!!!~’

(26 + 23) = (`-**49**)!!!~’

(49 (-) 3) = (`-**46**) = (`-**23** x `-**2**)!!!~’

`-BIRTHDAY; and, `-DEATH/DAY!!!~’:

(**412** + **130**) = (`-**542**)!!!~’

(**412** (-) **130**) = (`-**282**) = **“RECIPROCAL-SEQUENCING-NUMEROLOGY-RSN”**!!!~’

(542 (-) 282) = (`-**260**) / `-2 = (`-**130**) = `-**BIRTHDAY** = **“(JANUARY 30ᵗʰ)”**!!!~’

JANUARY 30 (**BIRTH**) + APRIL 12 (**DEATH**) = (**1** + **30** + **4** + **12**) = (`-**47**) = RECIPROCAL (MIRROR) = (`-**74**) = (**7/4**) = **“JULY 4ᵗʰ”** = **INDEPENDENCE `-DAY** = **`-DEATH/DAY & `-BIRTHDAY**

`-ADDED `-UP `-<u>TOGETHER</u> = & = "The `-PRESIDENTIAL `-<u>MARK</u>"!!!~'

`-<u>DIED</u> in (`-<u>4</u>) & was `-<u>BORN</u> in (`-<u>1</u>) = (`-<u>4/1</u>) = RECIPROCAL (MIRROR) = (`-<u>1/4</u>)!!!~' (`-<u>14</u>) = RECIPROCAL (MIRROR) = (`-<u>41</u>)!!!~' (41 + 14) = (`-<u>55</u>) = (`-<u>23</u> + `-<u>32</u>)!!!~'

BOOK TITLE: "<u>GOD</u> is `-the `-<u>MATHEMATICIAN</u>-'"!!!~'

/|\ The `-<u>GOD</u> `-<u>EQUATIONS</u> /|\ !!!~'

FOUNDER & DISCOVERER/ORIGINATOR/AUTHOR: DWAYNE W. ANDERSON!!!~'

Printed in the United States
By Bookmasters